# Toxic Friends/True Friends

ALSO BY FLORENCE ISAACS

*Just a Note to Say . . .*
*Business Notes*

# TOXIC
# *Friends*
# TRUE
# *Friends*

## How Your Friends Can Make or
## Break Your Health, Happiness,
## Family, and Career

# Florence Isaacs

WILLIAM MORROW AND COMPANY, INC.

*New York*

Library of Congress Cataloging-in-Publication Data

Isaacs, Florence.
    Toxic friends, true friends: how your friends can make or break your health, happiness, family, and career / Florence Isaacs.
      p.    cm.
    Includes index.
    ISBN 0-688-15442-5
    1. Friendship.   2. Interpersonal relations.   I. Title.
BF575.F66I83   1999
155.9'25—dc21                                   98-39534
                                                                  CIP

Printed in the United States of America

First Edition

1   2   3   4   5   6   7   8   9   10

BOOK DESIGN BY SUSAN HOOD

www.williammorrow.com

To HARVEY, JONATHAN, AND ANDREW

# Acknowledgments

THIS BOOK COULD not have been completed without the assistance of a number of people. I particularly wish to acknowledge Dr. Rosemary Blieszner, who was never too busy to take my calls, answer my questions, and point me to resources. For his invaluable insights, I thank Dr. William K. Rawlins. I also thank New York organizational psychologist Rhoda F. Green, Ph.D., Rhoda F. Green & Co., Inc.; Arlene Eisenberg, coauthor of *What to Expect the First Year* and *What to Expect When You're Expecting;* Lawrence Balter, Ph.D., author of *Who's in Control? Dr. Balter's Guide to Discipline Without Combat;* Robert M. Milardo, Ph.D., professor of family relations, University of Maine; Joe Bargmann, senior editor of the Condé Nast Internet site, SWOON.

My agent, Linda Konner, who recognized the potential of this book from the beginning, offered crucial support and encouragement. My editor, Toni Sciarra, provided wise editorial guidance.

Many thanks to the superb staff at the Woodstock Library, Woodstock, New York, who were always available, happy to help, and made my research tasks so much easier.

Above all, I thank my husband, Harvey Isaacs, my "at-home editor," whose sharp eye and understanding helped keep me on track throughout this long and complex project.

# Contents

# CONTENTS

# *What You Must Know Before You Read This Book*

THE LUNCHROOM AT Lord & Taylor hums with the din of the noontime crowd. Shoppers and occasionally office workers fill the tables as waitresses in black uniforms and white aprons rush by, toting trays of soups and salads. Despite the decibel level, it's the perfect spot for my friend Martha and me to catch up. Though we live twenty minutes away from each other in New York, our lives are so crammed with work and family that we haven't seen each other face-to-face in two months. It's time to compare notes, and the menu is ideal—varied enough for both my perennial diet and Martha's sweet tooth.

We're talking nonstop. We have a lot of territory to cover and I munch on forkfuls of Waldorf salad in between sentences—when I suddenly feel a chunk of chicken lodged in my throat, unchewed. I calmly swallow, but it does not budge. I take a sip of water. It does not budge. I consider eating a piece of bread to force it down, then fear it will simply settle atop the chicken. I feel myself start to choke and I panic. Pointing at my throat with one hand and gasping, I grab Martha's wrist with the other as beads of perspiration collect on my forehead.

Martha jumps from her seat and tries pounding on my back,

concurrently screaming across the room, "Does anybody know the Heimlich maneuver?" The room grows instantly silent, but nobody moves. I am sure that this is *it*—I am going to die, choking on chicken at Lord & Taylor. The cashier calls downstairs for an emergency medical technician. Martha, who has never used the Heimlich maneuver but is the ex-wife of a doctor, grabs me from behind and tries it. I cough, but nothing moves in my throat. She yells again, "Can't anyone help?" This time, a tall gray-haired man two tables away gets up and says, "Fold her over the back of the chair and push." I fold myself over and by now the man (a doctor, he finally admits) has come over to supervise. The chicken pops out of my mouth.

Martha literally saved my life that day. On other occasions, she has saved it figuratively with her gentle nurturing, wise advice, and unconditional acceptance of me. She is the only person I have ever met who is totally nonjudgmental. I firmly believe that if I told Martha I was an ax murderer she would love me still.

My friend Harriet has saved my sanity. It's to her I go at times of family conflict. She listens, validates my feelings, and always slices through to the heart of the matter with an insight that helps me make sense of it all. Whether I've discussed my husband, my children, or other family issues, I feel I have connected with someone I can trust implicitly. As the years have passed, our friendship has grown and blossomed. It's not without its ups and downs. But it has endured, ripened, deepened. My husband is my best friend. But so are Harriet and Martha. They are my sisters of the soul.

My friend Dodi has saved my professional life. She's been there during work-related crises and disappointments, giving me the gift of calm perspective, always reminding me of my successes and affirming my abilities—piercing through the clouds of self-doubt when I've felt demoralized and rejected. Other friends have led me to passionate new interests or to fun and play that have brought pleasure to my life. My friend Rita, ten years older than I, is my own personal dose of serotonin. She fills a room with laughter and spirit and energy.

I am so fortunate to have friends like these, friends who, like fine art, have stood the test of time and nourished my life—who have molded and changed me. But there are others, too. They may be newer friends or old friends I don't see very often, yet they have touched me in significant ways.

For me, as for so many other women, friends are sources of help, hope, and growth—at home and in the world. They help us to define ourselves, to develop our identities and values. They serve as role models, supports, companions, and unpaid psychotherapists and make a remarkable impact on all the dimensions of our lives. Along with family, friends are sources of our greatest satisfaction and joys.

But there is also another side to friendship that has received little attention. Friendships are *not* always as satisfying as we would like them to be. Some can actually be poisonous, causing grief and hurt. While some of our most profound happiness is found with friends, so is some of our deepest pain.

That has been true in my own life. There are some friends I remember not with joy but with sorrow. One friend brought enormous satisfaction to my life for twelve years. We met at a toddlers playgroup attended by her daughter and my son and found we shared a passion for art. I was a novice writer, Marie a full-time mom, and we started to visit museums and galleries on Wednesday afternoons. Our excursions quickly became a ritual. We'd meet for lunch, then roam the latest shows, eager to look and learn.

We took courses, read art magazines, and had a generally wonderful time educating ourselves—until cracks began to appear in our relationship. Here and there I felt the sting of a caustic comment. One day she left me standing on a street corner, never showing up to meet as agreed. The excuse was—well, there was no real excuse. A short time later, after I mentioned an article I had written, she told me calmly over coffee, "You know, if you ever published a book, I couldn't be your friend anymore. I'd feel too envious." Soon after, she picked a fight—then refused to take my calls. I never saw her again.

Recalling the times we shared, I wonder what has become of

her. I still feel pangs of sadness and a sense of loss. You can't have a friendship all by yourself.

More recently, another even longer friendship has come to a close. Once rich and gratifying, it changed and grew hurtful. It was time to let go.

Many women have talked to me poignantly of their disappointments in friendship. Years later, wounds inflicted by friends still haunt them; sometimes there are still tears and there is always pain.

Why do some friendships go so right, while others go wrong? Why does it take so long to acknowledge that there are problems between friends, and why is it so difficult to deal with them? The answers are as complex as friendship itself, yet the need to understand them has never been greater.

The enormous changes in the lives of women today make the support of friends not just an advantage but, often, a matter of survival. Most of us have joined the workforce and struggle with demands on our time and energy. Divorce, later marriage, and the single life have increased and broadened friendship needs. Along with geographical mobility has come the loss of traditional family and community supports. For many, friends *are* family. We're also living longer, which for women is accompanied by the near certainty of surviving mates or companions—alone.

Friends are a lifeline. Reaping *all* their benefits requires us to understand more about the dynamics of friendship, its imprint on our lives, the pressures that surround it, and the dark side. The pages that follow shed light.*

*Names and identifying details in most personal stories have been changed to protect privacy.

# Toxic Friends/True Friends

# The Realities of Friendship: What's Healthy, What's Not

FRIENDS ENRICH VIRTUALLY every aspect of our life. Research by psychologists and sociologists, clinical observations, and personal experiences confirm that friends advance your career and improve your job performance. Friends support your relationships with others (such as with your spouse and your child) and help you adjust to life changes like divorce and retirement. Friends are companions when you're single and family when you're far from kin. They lift your mood and your self-esteem, enhance your mental and physical health, and even influence how successfully you age. "People who get along best in life and deal with uncertainties and trials and tribulations have friends," says Alan Booth, Ph.D., professor of sociology and human development at Penn State University.

Yet few of us realize the power of friends as healthy forces in our lives. We rarely understand why friendships work in such positive ways—or how problems arise and play out. Because we tend to idealize friendship, we expect it to sail effortlessly through our lives, bringing comfort and caring and fun. When bumps appear, as they do in any close relationship, we're confused and unprepared. We expect friendship to be free of the static that runs through many family relationships.

But friendship is not as simple as that. Tugging at its fabric are needs, emotions, and influences that emerge and interact in different settings and stages of your life. It's important to know your way around them.

Friendship is a journey that involves pleasure, satisfaction—and strain at times. The task is to manage it, avoiding traps along the way. Because friends really *can* make or break key portions of your life, the challenge is to recognize good friendships, strengthen and protect the ones you've got, and reduce the risk of getting hurt.

## DEFINING FRIENDSHIP

So much about friendship remains unspoken. Ambiguities abound, which is one reason why misunderstandings occur and why you need to know what is really meant by the term "friendship." The answer may seem obvious; it is not. Our definitions may vary. It helps to have Paul Wright, Ph.D., a leading expert on friendship, explain, "Friendship is a relationship of voluntary interdependence where two people get together because they want to—and take a personalized interest in (and feel concern for) each other."

Friendship includes certain elements: mutual trust, intimacy, respect, understanding, affection, compatibility, acceptance, and affirmation. There are mutual obligations and responsibilities. These components vary in degree, depending on the level of friendship. Adult men and women typically have anywhere from three to more than seven friends but don't feel the same concern or trust for (or the same sense of obligation toward) all of them. They generally fall into three categories:

## Best Friends

These are your intimate circle. They are people you feel very close to who unconditionally accept you and understand you, in whom you can confide, with whom you can share your secrets, and on whom you can rely. There is mutual empathy, history, and frequent contact. You see and/or talk to each other often. If either of you moved far away, both of you would make an effort to continue the relationship long-distance. There are also obligations to help each other.

Many people don't have one best friend; they have a circle of close friends. For me it's Harriet and Martha.

## Good Friends

These are people to whom you tell intimacies only selectively. The degree of trust is a bit less than for best friends, either because they haven't yet earned it or because they don't show the appropriate judgment or understanding. But you like them, share activities and hobbies with them, enjoy spending time with them. They're people you socialize with, but (unless you work with them) you see and talk to them less frequently than your intimate circle. Most people with normal friendship patterns have at least one good or best friend, according to Jeffrey Young, Ph.D., a psychologist who has studied friendship.

## Casual Friends

These include transitional relationships in which the two of you have less in common than good or best friends. Casual friendships develop because of circumstances in your life and because you share a specific situation. You may be neighbors, colleagues, belong to the same professional organization, or have children in the same school. But if conditions change—you move, change jobs or fields, for example—the friendship will end. Says a forty-eight-year-old travel agent and mother of a five-year-old, "I've developed friendships with women in the community I ordinarily never would have. They're significantly younger than me, but because we have children the same age and issues in common, they've become people I define as my friends. I don't necessarily feel intimate with them, but if there's a PTA meeting, I go with them, and if there are children's birthday parties, we invite each other."

Many casual friendships are based on shared activities, such as bowling, the health club, or volunteer work. Such relationships stimulate us and add variety to our lives. They involve obligations, too. You *are* expected to show up for the bridge game (or to call when you can't make it). But the obligations are generally limited to the shared situation or activity.

As one woman describes their importance, "I've had the same group of golf friends on and off for eighteen years. If not for golf, I wouldn't see them. We don't go out socially. They rejoice for me that my youngest son is getting married, but they're not invited to the wedding. Yet they're vital to me. I have another friend who is available to go to the ballet anytime I want to go. Since my husband isn't interested in ballet, she's crucial to my life. Yes, I could go alone, but it's so much more pleasant to go with her."

## FRIENDS CHANGE

It's a myth that friendship is forever. The reality is that very few friendships last a lifetime. "The inner circle is fairly stable. Not many best friends are added or deleted over time, certainly not once you're in middle age. A best friend who has moved away might become a good friend because you're in touch less often than in the past. Conversely, a good friend can grow into a best friend and move up. But the cast of casual friends constantly fluctuates. It's not that the friends have an argument; the friendships fade and they don't see each other," says Rebecca Adams,

Ph.D., coauthor of *Adult Friendship* and associate professor of sociology, University of North Carolina at Greensboro.

Your friends change when your life and your needs change. When you get divorced or return to school, for example, you tend to look for friends who share your experience. I've actively searched for and added new friends at certain transitions in my life, such as when I got married and when I had a baby. As my sons became teenagers, I moved into full-time freelance writing and longed for the companionship of others facing the same challenges. I looked for and added such friends.

Although we're all attracted to and mesh with different kinds of people and personalities, we tend to choose friends who are like us in gender, education, income level, values, and attitudes. Friends are people who understand you. The more alike you are, the easier it is to maintain a friendship. Different views make the relationship spicier, but you may also have to work harder to keep it going. Women's friendships generally involve more intimacy, nurturing, emotional expressiveness, and sharing of confidences than men's friendships, which tend to revolve around shared activities, such as sports.

## ORIGINS OF FRICTION

When friendship is good, it's a blessing. It's easy to find women who speak passionately about their friends. They often make comments such as "My friends are my family" or "I couldn't survive without my friends." Yet research on older women found they are dissatisfied with about 30 percent of friendships. "Researchers have assumed that if you're friends, you must be getting along or you'd end the friendship. We found that isn't true. People will see a friend even when there's a problematic relationship," says Dr. Adams.

Although we tend to expect friendships to be models of altruism and loyalty, the reality is that people are not perfect. *We* are

5

not perfect. Friendship is stressed by factors that can test the strongest bonds. In other words, friendship is complicated—and sometimes it's hard. Both external and internal tensions can stir trouble between friends, and the impact of those tensions has been underestimated, according to William K. Rawlins, Ph.D., professor of communication at Purdue University, who examines these tensions in his book, *Friendship Matters.*

Tensions originating *outside* the friendship often emerge when friendship must take a backseat to changes in women's lives. We have a limited amount of time and energy, and when we make a major commitment to something else—a career, marriage, raising a family—we have less time for friends. Says Dr. Rawlins, "One of you moves or assumes more responsibilities at work or takes a job while the other remains a full-time mom—and suddenly you're not as available as you used to be. Lack of time for each other is the most significant source of problems between women friends. You might still care deeply about each other, but there are fewer opportunities for contact. Conditions can also occur that make it hard to be there for someone else."

Relationships with other people can cause fallout between friends. A spouse may not like a friend or may treat a friend badly. Your child can develop serious problems (or experience immense success), which suddenly stirs feelings and changes attitudes. Strains like divorce or health problems and life-cycle shifts like retirement can shake long-established friendship patterns, making it difficult to stay in contact.

Tensions also arise *within* friendship, posing these questions:

## How independent can we be?

"We give each other two freedoms: the freedom to be independent from and the freedom to depend on and call on each other. Internal problems often develop when friends try to manage the degree to which they can exercise both," says Dr. Rawlins.

Issues of availability and obligation arise. If you're offered a great job that requires a move to Cincinnati (and it's clearly right for you and your life), a friend who has your best interests at heart will encourage you to take it, even though that means a loss for the friend—you can't have lunch on Tuesdays or browse flea markets together anymore.

With so many demands on our lives, a friend will understand when you say, "I have to be out of town and can't attend your party" or "We wanted to go to your son's graduation, but we can't." Friends must also understand that there are times when you cannot say no.

Interdependence, a hallmark of friendship, means that your activities, plans, and decisions influence those of your friend and hers influence yours. If you're invited to go sailing on the same weekend your friend really needs your computer skills to finish her graduate school thesis, that's a problem.

The question is: Whose freedom gets respected—and whose need to depend on a friend gets respected? We like to be there for friends, but we don't like to cash that check very often. We're careful. Nobody likes to be used in friendship.

## How much unconditional caring is given—and expected?

There's a tension between affection (we care about each other and therefore help each other out) and needing and using each other for aid (such as getting a project done). Of course, we all depend on each other at times. "For men, the tension between sentiment and assistance isn't a big deal because men aren't as emotionally involved and as deeply affectionate with each other as women are. We expect friendship to serve the work. It's 'I'll help you build your patio and you help me with my deck.' But tensions develop for women, especially in the workplace and for full-time moms," says Dr. Rawlins.

Because women manage many tasks, we need each other to carpool or to watch the kids. We'll say, "Help me out with the reception." But friends are not always willing or able to help out. The resulting tensions can cause problems that get expressed as

"I can't believe you won't do this for me" or "How could you ask me to do that for you?"

On the job, does a friend expect you to recommend her for a raise because she needs it rather than because she deserves it? It may be hard at times to separate caring behavior from professional obligations.

## How open can we be?

How much can we express to each other and how much do we protect our own privacy by *not* discussing certain subjects? Tensions arise in women's friendships because women disclose more to each other than men do. In a close friendship you can reveal who you are deep down and air private thoughts and feelings. Willingness to share, especially to share personal information about oneself, is a basic feature of friendship. If someone confides in you and you never reciprocate, it weakens the relationship. People can't feel close without mutual self-disclosure.

But what's off-limits? Do you tell a friend about your marital problems? As you open up, you become more vulnerable.

In some cases, you don't confide because you don't want to jeopardize a friend's opinion of you. If you tell someone you're doing something very dishonest, for example, that places a burden on the listener. Often the response is "I really didn't want to know that about you" or "I wish you hadn't told me that."

Friends also respect each other's privacy and feelings and try not to intrude. How candid can you be about your opinion of what a friend says and does? Do you tell a friend she's put on a lot of weight? "Women say, 'We know when we've gained weight and we don't want to hear it.' Say something negative about a friend's child and you can cause a rift in the relationship," says Dr. Rawlins. Unsolicited advice, no matter how well-intentioned, tends to be experienced as criticism.

We're obligated, too, not to use confidential information to exploit a friend's vulnerability. If a friend confides that she's taking antidepressants, you don't turn the information against her during an argument, saying, "Don't tell me what to do. *You're* the one who needs Prozac."

## How much can we judge and accept each other?

There's a tension between our desire for a friend's good judgment and objectivity and our need for confirmation and unconditional acceptance. These are closely related to issues of openness—and ambiguities quickly surface. If you say, "I'm thinking of quitting my job," you *might* want the friend to agree and respond, "I think you're right. It's killing you." You might not want to hear that your friend *really* thinks you should stay. But we also rely on friends as compasses and want their unbiased views, as in "Do you think this nursery school is right for my child?" The question is, are we *really* asking for an honest opinion? Do we *want* the truth about our boyfriend—or our hairdo?

These are difficult situations and there is no one correct way to answer them. You might criticize a friend because you care about her health or fear her happiness is threatened—or you might decide to hold your tongue because you believe that your honesty may do more harm than good. What do you risk by telling the awful truth sometimes? Will the person wind up angry at you? Is that a risk worth taking if she might benefit? A friend has to make this calculation and weigh it. Some people say, "I won't give an opinion unless I'm asked for it," but it may not be that simple.

Tensions can arise due to fickleness or capriciousness, as well. Women have been dropped by a friend when someone more attractive came along. Such experiences, which seem like throwbacks to junior high school, can be very hurtful and hard to understand, causing deep anger and resentment. It's "You chose her and turned your back on me."

Sexual tensions often appear in friendships with the opposite sex. That's one reason why single women are more likely to have male friends than married women are. I had three or four platonic male friends before I got married. The first was Jeff, who changed my life forever. We met when we both worked in the mailroom of Exquisite Form Brassieres for the summer, tearing invoices along the dotted line. I was sixteen; he was an "older man," an English major headed for the University of Michigan in the fall.

Jeff and I became an instant version of *Pygmalion*. He thought I was not only pretty but also smart and funny—raw material waiting to be molded and polished. Marveling that I'd read virtually none of the great works of literature, Jeff drew up a list of books I was to finish if I wanted to consider myself even en route to being literate. I was a willing pupil.

That summer is the only vivid memory I have of my high school years, a period when I felt largely like an outsider, full of hopes and dreams that nobody else seemed to share. Jeff was the only person in the world (except for my Uncle Joe, who had no children of his own) who thought I was special. I saw myself reflected in his eyes as someone of intelligence and value and potential.

I knew that Jeff had romantic feelings toward me, which he would have expressed had I given him the least bit of encouragement. But he had bad skin, wore black-rimmed glasses with thick lenses, and I was not physically attracted to him. I adored him as the older brother I'd never had. Later I had other platonic friendships in college and until I got married. Then my husband was my male friend.

## OTHER CAUSES OF TROUBLE

Emotional tensions aren't the only factors that create discord between friends. So can certain attitudes and behaviors (both our own and those of our friends). Though we often blame the other person—"I always have to call her" or "She let me down"—sometimes we have caused or at least contributed to the problem. Major troublemakers include:

1. *Unrealistic expectations.*

Satisfaction with a friendship depends on the degree to which expectations are met. But expectations of how a friend should behave vary widely. We may have different priorities and/or expect more than a friend is willing to give. Because we rarely (if ever) verbalize our expectations to each other, it's easy to feel disappointed.

One woman offered to mortgage her house to help a friend launch a business venture. Would you be willing to make such a sacrifice? Would you expect a friend to do it for you? Would you skip a Paris vacation (and absorb the cancellation costs) to attend a friend's engagement party? How far would you travel to see a friend in the hospital? Some people hop a plane without hesitation; others flinch at a drive across town.

Sometimes we set ourselves up for letdowns. If you expect a casual friend to feel the same obligations toward you and to go to the same trouble to support you as a close friend, you're likely to get hurt.

2. *Poor friendship choices.*

In her book *Women Who Run with the Wolves,* Clarissa Pinkola Estés, Ph.D., speaks of "life-sapping choices in mates, work or friendships" as symptoms of women who have lost connection with their deepest selves. Most of us have made a less than stellar choice of friend at one time or another, but some women are repeatedly drawn to people who treat them badly or who make them feel uncomfortable.

Friends also have different strengths and weaknesses; no one friend can fill all your needs. Some people who are valuable for certain situations are poor choices for others. If a friend never has a good word to say about men, she probably isn't the best person with whom to objectively discuss problems with your fiancé. She might be a great help, however, in resolving career issues or elderly-parent crises. Someone self-centered with a great sense of humor might be wonderful company for a light evening of fun, yet a poor choice for a heart-to-heart about the direction of your life.

### 3. *Rushing friendships.*

Many friendships start because one woman reveals a lot of personal information and the other person gives good advice and confides her own experience; it can get very deep very fast. You make an instant connection, find you're on the same wavelength, and it's exciting and exhilarating. You feel you've found a soul mate. But it's dangerous to think you're friends. You don't know the other person yet. It takes time to observe behavior, to see if this is someone you can trust.

Heather Helms-Erikson, M.S., a psychotherapist conducting major research on friendship at Penn State University, believes you often get embedded in difficult friendships during transitions in your life when you're hungry for relationships. You moved or started a new job or just got divorced. "These are times you're particularly at risk for relationships that aren't healthy—when you may jump quickly into a relationship without first considering 'Is this *really* someone I want to get involved with?' " she says.

### 4. *Envy.*

Envy is a feeling of discontent and resentment stirred by desire for the possessions or qualities of someone else. "It has to do with the feeling that the other person has all the stuff and you're empty," says Roberta Satow, Ph.D., a psychoanalyst and professor of sociology at Brooklyn College.

We all have moments when we envy our friends, and it's no wonder. We're swamped by so many messages telling us we're supposed to be thin, successful at work, in marriage, at parenting—and in our spare time entertain and garden like Martha Stewart, too. It's hard *not* to feel inadequate sometimes. A little envy can be a powerful motivator. But left unchecked, envy is poisonous. It can kill a friendship and eat *you* up, too.

It's especially difficult to keep envy at bay when your lives have gone in different directions—one of you has moved up, while the other treads water or slips down. Equality is basic to friendship, and when the scenario is "I've got a husband and a house and vacations—and you've got a divorce, a custody battle, and a job you hate," it can be tough to remain friends. "[The situation] asks us what is the moral fiber of friendship? Can we get beyond this?" says Dr. Rawlins.

Fear of envy does another kind of damage. Humorist Fran Lebowitz has written of the guilt and anxiety women tend to feel when others envy them, while men see envy as evidence of their success. Some of us hesitate to share good news such as "Jane is going to Harvard," or even "I'm pregnant," when we know that although a friend wants to be happy for us, she is not. Fear of envy can stop some women from achieving, afraid that success will mean loss of relationships.

Constance Buxer, Ph.D., a psychoanalyst who specializes in women's relationships at work and play, describes a fantasy she often hears from women beginning or succeeding in a career: "There are variations, but one went like this, 'I'm on a diving board all alone and I fall in the water and nobody has a life preserver for me.' There's a feeling of being isolated. It stops many people from pushing harder."

5. *Competition.*

Men compete with their friends all the time—in sports as well as in everything else. Their biggest problem is that competition gets out of hand. But women still haven't learned to feel comfortable with the thought of winning—with the idea of triumphing over others. Frequently, competitive instincts are denied and directed instead into rivalry over men, children, money, clothes, the living room sofa. Because women find it so hard to acknowledge competitive feelings, according to psychotherapist Lillian B. Rubin, Ph.D., in her book *Just Friends: The Role of Friendship in Our Lives,* these feelings are distorted into petty jealousy, envy, and rivalry that can corrode a friendship and result in mistrust and betrayal.

Yet it's natural to be competitive with friends. "You don't need to feel guilty if you are," says Linda Sapadin, Ph.D., a psychologist at Hofstra University's School of Continuing Education. "We do compare ourselves socially with the people who are our peers. We feel richer, poorer, prettier, uglier, successful, or unsuccessful, not based on general statistics, but on how we are doing compared to those in our social circle."

In her study of the friendships of professional men and women, Dr. Sapadin found that when women talk about being competitive with their friends, they often mean being jealous of them. Jealousy is a hindrance to friendship. It leads to resentment and envy of a friend's success or advantage. "Competition is a healthier response than jealousy because when you are feeling competitive with a friend, it can stir you on to achieve more for yourself. You can say, 'Okay, she's been working out and looks great; maybe I should get myself down to the gym, too.' Or 'She got a wonderful job through networking; perhaps it's also an approach I should take.' "

6. *Difficulty in dealing with conflict.*

Women are uncomfortable with conflict. In their book *Between Women: Love, Envy, and Competition in Women's Friendships,* Luise Eichenbaum, C.S.W., and Susie Ohrbach, Ph.D., discuss anger, hostility, jealousy, and other unspoken feelings that exist in many friendships. They note that women friends rarely argue and that "selfish" feelings, such as desiring something for yourself or wanting to spend time separately, tend to remain hidden. So does any suggestion that friends are individuals who don't always agree. According to Eichenbaum and Ohrbach, women often believe that "difference is dangerous" and that it can end the relationship.

Friendship is seen as fragile and vulnerable—and it is, in a sense. It isn't protected in a way that other relationships are. You can't just walk out of a business partnership; it takes legal action. You can't stop being a relative. Even though you and your sister haven't spoken for five years, you're still sisters. You can, however, cease being a friend at any time. There is no ritual or written contract to begin a friendship or end it.

Because many of us feel we can't risk vocalizing upset in these circumstances, we allow issues that could have been resolved early on to grow and fester. Unexpressed resentment or hurt doesn't disappear, however. It builds—and often erupts inappropriately in one way or another.

Social worker Karin Schultz observes that women's friendships are often harmed by taking too much responsibility for friends' feelings and needs and by fear of envy, success, and conflict. In an article in the *Journal of Independent Social Work,* she concludes that these relationships are frequently characterized by selflessness rather than mutual growth.


## WHAT'S HEALTHY, WHAT'S NOT

Healthy friendships are easy to recognize: On balance, they improve the quality of your life. They are generally positive, supportive, constructive, sometimes intimate relationships that allow each of you to be as close or true to yourself as is comfortable and possible. They give both of you room to grow and enhance your self-esteem. Self-affirmation should be one of the key payoffs of friendship.

That doesn't mean that healthy friendships are free of tensions and uncomfortable feelings. We all feel annoyed or angry at, envious of, and competitive toward friends occasionally. Conflict can arise in any close relationship, and feeling good all the time is not necessarily a marker for a healthy friendship.

There's a difference, however, between friendships that generally add to your life, despite ups and downs, and those that consistently diminish it. Some relationships are toxic to your well-being.

A toxic friendship is *regularly*

- unsupportive
- unrewarding
- unsatisfying
- draining
- stifling
  and/or
- unequal

The toxicity is in the interaction, not necessarily in the individuals. Caring friends can, without realizing it, wind up in a relationship that does neither one any good. *Toxic* friends, on the other hand, are people who exhibit a pattern of damaging behavior and are rarely well meaning. Someone who consistently lets you down, puts you down, saps you with her self-absorption, is toxic. Someone who regularly rains on your parade and is unable to celebrate your successes is toxic. A friend who threatens your values or consistently lies is toxic. Someone who harms you or those you love (or who wishes you ill) is toxic.

Of course, there are varying degrees of toxicity, ranging from being merely upsetting all the way to being directly damaging to your life. The reality is, friendships change, people change. Sometimes they change in ways you can't tolerate. Sometimes changes in them (or in yourself) cause you to view them differently.

Sometimes you've outgrown a friend and have nothing in common anymore. The satisfaction is gone. Continuing a stagnant friendship prevents you from opening up to new faces and experiences. "It's great if two kids who went to the movies at age eleven are still doing it at forty-five and have a fine time together. But if the relationship is lifeless, you're clinging to a habit that was fortifying once but is now just dull," says Dr. Buxer. Such relationships soak up precious time and energy that could be invested in friends who *are* important to you.

Other friendships (and people) are more actively hurtful. A few years ago I stopped a new friendship in its tracks at the first sign of this. The woman invited my husband and me to a dinner party at her home. The next day she let me know that one of the guests considered me too inquisitive. "She said you were interviewing her," she told me. I thought that if she would say something hurtful to me so early in our friendship (when one tends to be on best behavior), what would happen later on? I immediately cooled our relationship.

A truly toxic person is someone who betrays you—who sleeps with your lover, hurts your child, steals your client, or tries to turn others against you.

"Some people have called betrayal the sin against the friend. *Et tu, Brute.* It's one of the classics," says Dr. Rawlins.

Toxicity turns up in different ways in different situations and phases of your life. The needs and the benefits of friendship vary as well, depending on whether you're at work, going through a divorce, adjusting to retirement, or raising a family. The chapters ahead explore these differences, identifying the kinds of relationships that support you and get your needs met—and those that do not. They guide you in maximizing the profits of friendship and minimizing disappointments.

We all have toxic moments when we feel (and even express) dark emotions toward friends, including those we love the best. But committed friends can face up to such issues and make constructive changes. Through adjustment and accommodation, they can take relationships to a new plateau.

"Friendships that work—in the sense of the richest friendships (not simply those that never have fights)—are relationships in which negotiation is an ongoing process. How much do you give, how much do you get, how much can you and can't you offer, what can you live with? These are all issues to be continually negotiated," says Dr. Satow.

Deep, lasting friendships can survive change and hardship. It takes two, however, to work things through. Often toxicity arises from the unwillingness of one or both of you to discuss what has occurred.

When a friendship no longer serves you well (and if change

isn't possible or feasible), the answer may be to downsize the relationship and see the person less often—or to end it. It's hard for women to let go; we tend to be "fixers" and don't want to hurt feelings. We're concerned with being "nice," sometimes at great cost to ourselves. It can be toxic, however, not to cut loose.

Everybody has struggled with low points in good friendships. Everybody's got a story of a friendship that failed. Friendship can be messy. Yet when you sharpen your skills in dealing with the downside, you can build better friendships and reap remarkable rewards. Why not make friendship work for you in changing times?

## Quiz

### DO YOU HAVE A TOXIC FRIENDSHIP?

Do you recognize toxic signs when you see them? Think of a friend, then take this test. (Circle the appropriate letter in each case.)

1. In this friendship I find that
   a) One of us does most of the giving and the other most of the taking
   b) One of us gives somewhat more than the other
   c) Give and take is balanced over the long haul

2. When I spend recreational time with my friend I
   a) Often come away feeling angry or depressed
   b) Sometimes have a good time
   c) Usually have fun

3. My friend tends to
   a) Try to change who I am
   b) Try to change certain things about me
   c) Accepts me as I am

4. If I had a life-threatening health problem, my friend would
   a) Withdraw
   b) Try to help minimally
   c) Provide essential support

5. When I get off the phone with my friend, I
   a) Often feel insecure
   b) Sometimes doubt myself
   c) Usually feel affirmed and valued

6. If I ask for advice on a romantic or work problem, my friend is likely to
   a) Berate me for getting into the situation in the first place
   b) Let her own feelings on the subject get in the way
   c) Give helpful, objective counsel

7. I can be candid with my friend
   a) Rarely
   b) Sometimes
   c) Usually

8. My friend often influences me to
   a) Engage in behavior that can get me into trouble, such as lying to my husband
   b) Stay in situations (such as a dead-end job) longer than I should
   c) Stretch and reach my potential

9. If my friend and I feel differently about the merits of a play we've seen
   a) One of us gets annoyed that the other doesn't endorse her view
   b) One of us changes the subject to avoid disagreement
   c) We hear each other out and accept that "Some people like vanilla, some like chocolate"

10. I feel mistreated by my friend
    a) Often
    b) Occasionally
    c) Rarely or never

11. When I show my friend the new condo I've just bought, she is likely to
    a) Say "Ohhh . . . it's so small!"
    b) Say "It's great, but why did you paint the walls green?"
    c) Appear with a smile and a bottle of Champagne to toast my new digs

12. My friend resents it when I spend time with other pals
    a) Often—and even if invited along
    b) Sometimes
    c) Rarely or never

13. If I ask my friend to keep a secret, I know she will
    a) Probably blab it to others
    b) Probably tell her husband or her close friend
    c) Keep it to herself

Your answers offer clues to the quality of your friendship and can alert you to toxic situations and areas that need work. If you circled mostly *C*'s, you seem to have a healthy relationship. Keep it up. If your answers are mostly *A*'s, you have a toxic friendship. Mostly *B*'s or a relatively equal mix of *A*'s, *B*'s, and *C*'s suggests your friendship could be more satisfying—and improved.

The issues raised in this quiz, along with skill building and myth busters, will be discussed in detail in the following chapters.

## 2

# *Friends on the Job: Will It Ever Work?*

THE SLENDER BLONDE sitting in the center seat watches my husband and me approach row 24. Would she mind shifting over, we ask, allowing us to sit together? Semigrudgingly, she moves to the window. I slide in beside her. It's 7 A.M. and I'm not in the mood to chat; apparently she feels the same. She opens a leather briefcase, pulls out a yellow pad, and jots down notes. She seems to be planning something. I assume she's on her way to a business meeting in San Diego, our destination.

An hour into the flight, the pilot announces that we are about to encounter turbulence. She suddenly turns to me nervously and breaks the silence. "Do you think we're going to crash?" she asks, quite seriously—and I laugh. Though I don't love flying myself, I reassure her: "It may get a little bumpy, but don't worry. We'll live."

"I'm Sandra," she says. I introduce myself as well, and we proceed to talk nonstop for the rest of the trip. I learn that she is an entrepreneur on her way to see a client. At forty-three, she owns a health care advertising-marketing business that bills $2.5 million a year.

How did she get where she is? "I did it myself," she tells me without hesitation, a response that would border on arrogance in anyone else. In Sandra's case, it's a statement of fact. She's a renaissance woman—an artist, a writer, a high-octane salesperson, and a former creative director for an international advertising agency. Although she's terrified of flying, she clearly doesn't fear much else.

"I'm just a killer. I've been through so much crap in my life that I'm more of a risk taker than most people. I have nothing to lose. If I don't have thirty possibilities on my roster, I'm not doing my job," she says matter-of-factly. But as she talks, she also mentions Ed. "Ed has always guided me and had tremendous faith in me. He's someone I've always looked up to and trusted," she says.

Sandra met Ed when she was in her early twenties and worked for a personnel firm. He was a client, the director of human resources for a bank. Although thirteen people were employed at the personnel agency, he chose to work exclusively with Sandra. It began a lifelong friendship. "We just clicked, and after I left to go into advertising, he was always there for me. I worked for one agency, then another, and we'd have lunch a lot. When I got to the point of 'I'm going to do it—I'm going to start my own business,' he'd say, 'You can do it. You can do it like the best of them can.'

"When someone knows you that long, it means so much to hear that reassurance that you're doing the right thing. To have it come from someone noncompetitive—who is always honest with you—it's the kind of support you usually get from family," says Sandra. But she didn't have a family. Her mother died when she was a teenager, her older sister died ten years later, and she wasn't close to her father. She'd been divorced. Sandra was alone; for her, Ed *was* family.

Because he had started his own business three years earlier, Ed could offer advice based on his own experience. "I didn't know the basics. I didn't know how much money I needed as a cushion. He told me it was less than I thought. I didn't even know what telephones to order. It was such a relief because he'd been through it all himself," she says.

Ed served as a trusted sounding board and reinforced Sandra's confidence in herself. Through the years he became a source of strength—and the positive effect of their relationship is not unusual. Work-related friends play a major role in our lives today. Friends can not only serve as support systems when you start your own business, they can have enormous impact no matter what kind of work you do.

"Friends are crucial to success in the corporate world. To advance in most organizations, you need the requisite skills to perform, but you also need relationships that have been developed and nurtured in order to open doors, get things done, and deal with the bureaucracy. It takes talent and skill *combined* with the resources you have to achieve results—and that includes friends," says Marilyn Puder-York, Ph.D., a clinical psychologist in New York who specializes in relationship coaching for executives.

Regardless of the field you're in, friends can help you find a job, move ahead, or connect with those who can do you some good. They can make your job easier and help you improve your performance. They may inform you of opportunities you otherwise might not have known about and can even warn of looming changes that may affect you, putting you in a better position to protect yourself.

Says a social worker, "On my last job I had a disastrous personality conflict with my boss. I couldn't stand her, she hated me—and she was about to lay me off. Then another supervisor I was friendly with stepped in and told her, 'She does a good job. Transfer her to me.' She didn't save my job just because I was capable and worked hard; she *liked* me and was a friend."

Research shows that friends enhance your self-esteem and affect job satisfaction, as well. They make your work life infinitely more pleasurable, relieve stress, and even prevent burnout.

But the workplace is a complex social environment with unique tensions and boundary issues, and there are thickets to negotiate. Work-related friendships need to be defined and managed differently from other friendships to protect you against potentially toxic situations. Never forget that there are economics involved at work. If a friend has to choose between a job and you, he or she will almost always choose the job.

## WHAT KIND OF FRIENDSHIP—AND WITH WHOM?

American employees now spend an average of forty-four hours a week on the job. Many of us see our coworkers more than our families. We may depend on friends at work for social connections—and the workplace is a wonderful place to meet people. When people *don't* make friends on the job, they often wind up leaving. They feel it didn't work out because they weren't able to establish the personal relationships so important to job success. Yet the dimensions and ramifications of workplace friendships differ from those in other areas of your life. The former tend to be "lubricating" friendships that help to get the work done but don't necessarily lead to intimate relationships.

The ground rules of workplace friendships are different. Trust is something that cannot always be guaranteed, especially where the environment is highly politicized. The workplace is not an ordinary gathering place; it's a setting where people assemble to get work done. We're all social creatures and we want company and people to go to lunch with, but the ultimate focus is the job. A healthy friendship at work gives you support and helps you perform effectively. That's different from a relationship with a confidant.

Introducing intimacy adds static to the relationship and can complicate your life. How complicated it gets depends on the people and the setting. Some fields and company cultures have competition built in: People are set up for rivalry. In other environments, familylike relationships are the rule. In general, however, it's smart to understand that friendships involving confidences may put you at risk for awkward situations on the job. They sometimes confuse boundaries, raise issues of allegiance, and increase stress at a time when the workplace is already stressful enough.

Treating someone as a confidant and socializing outside the workplace may actually *reduce* job satisfaction, according to research on friendship quality and job satisfaction by Barbara Winstead, professor of psychology at Old Dominion University in Norfolk, Virginia, and her coauthors. "It may pose a conflict between loyalty to the friend and what's required at work," she says.

In another study, the mostly female respondents reported that close work friends provided access to information, help with tasks, and an easing of frustration and anxiety. But they also cited difficulties with confidentiality, inequality, and other issues. The more formal the work setting, the greater the tension.

If friends at work are invaluable but also cause problems, what's the answer? Make friends, but be careful. Be cautious about an extremely close relationship in your life on the job. Consider it only in circumstances where you have a long track record together, a number of experiences where the person has been consistently faithful and loyal in work-related situations—and where there is no conflict of interest. Sandra's relationship with Ed deepened and he became her confidant *after* she left her personnel job and went into another field.

## FRIENDSHIP AND THE CHAIN OF COMMAND

When Barbara Winstead asked people to identify their best friend at work, only 13 percent chose a superior; another 13 percent named a subordinate; and 73 percent named a peer. This should come as no surprise. Friendship is a relationship between equals and there's a hierarchy at work. It's very hard to be personally close with someone over whom you have power—or who has power over you. When you have other roles and obligations besides that of friend, tensions are magnified. You can't be as expressive as you might be with your old college roommate.

The ideal of friendship is to be completely open and able to talk about anything. The more you have to censor what you say—or think in advance about how it will be received—the less comfort there is. But you don't know what can happen when you share certain information in a work friendship. The issue of watching what you say can be particularly difficult for women because we tend to disclose more to each other in our friendships than men do. Yet there may be information that you need to keep to yourself to avoid being seen as unable to do your job, or information that you can't reveal because of your position.

The flip side is, if someone reveals what they shouldn't, it can burden the listener with unwanted knowledge. A manager felt uptight after her boss came out of a meeting, apparently upset, and confided to her that she'd been asked to make staff cuts. "I didn't know how to take it. There had already been other cuts and I wondered, 'Is she trying to tell me something? And what am I supposed to do with the information? Should I start looking for another job?' It was inappropriate."

You can also be hurt by unrealistic expectations—that your boss loves you unconditionally, or that your employee will never take advantage of you, or that your client will always be there for you even though you stop providing a service that he or she wants. That kind of thinking can set you up for situations where you feel betrayed.

It's important to understand that colleagues have their own goals. If you accept that they have their own career needs, your expectations of friendships are more likely to be rooted in reality and you're less likely to be disappointed. People in your chain of command *can* become good friends—but it's dangerous and it shouldn't happen until you've understood and clarified the relationship.

Close friendship with your boss or supervisor is especially dangerous unless you realize it is possible that a supervisor may be planning to lay you off in three months but can't tell you now. Carol, a twenty-six-year-old assistant personnel manager for a Boston financial services company, has found that it's hard to be a subordinate and a friend. When she joined the organization, she and her boss, who is only three years older, instantly connected. Both are single at a time when many of their friends are married. They go out to dinner and on weekend ski trips, shop, and see movies together. Yet all is not well.

Carol feels let down at times. "I expected her support, but she takes credit for things that *I* accomplished. When we went up for raises and my salary was lower than industry standards, she got a big increase for herself but a lot less for me than I deserved. As a friend, I thought she should have asked for more or at the very least discussed it with me beforehand."

The reality is that bosses are primarily involved with their own careers and not the management of yours. Unless they own the company, they owe loyalty to their superiors. If you think otherwise, you'll usually be disappointed.

The hierarchy can also shadow your social life. Says Carol, "We'll be out on the weekend and she'll ask me, 'What are you working on?' That reestablishes the boss-employee connection. We're very good friends, yet there's always a sense that she has the upper hand." As previously noted, friendship is based on equality. When the balance tips in this way, the term "friendship" no longer fits.

"She knows how I perform at work," adds Carol, "that I have trouble speaking up and asserting myself—and in the friendship I tend to do similar things. She takes advantage of that. When we discuss something, her opinion is always right. She doesn't like it when I introduce her as my boss in social situations, yet she likes to play that role. She's bossy."

When they threw a joint New Year's Eve party, they agreed to share the work. Says Carol, "As soon as her friends arrived, she dropped everything to socialize with them. I had to make sure the food trays were filled and that we didn't run out of ice. She knows I'm reliable and I'll take care of it. I won't balk the way I would with my other friends. I tend to allow her to walk all over me because the bottom line is, she's my supervisor."

Other constraints arise, as well. When you rely on someone you work with for a lot of outside time together, you don't want to rock the boat. If Carol has plans with her boss for the weekend, she avoids any work-related disagreement at the office on Friday.

When you sit on your emotions and always say yes, it takes a toll. Carol has cut back on socializing with her boss and is looking for another job.

This kind of friendship can also wind up isolating you from your coworkers. Work is an interesting social setting precisely because it's not just you and the other person. If you're close friends with a superior, other people might wonder, "Will she tell her X?" You're aware you're being regarded, that your relationship is sensed and wondered about by your colleagues.

One of the things that goes on in the workplace and often bonds employees is complaining to each other about management. If your superior has become your friend, who do you align yourself with—your coworkers? Or do you become the boss's defender? If you elect the latter, you wind up alone.

When *you* are in charge, perceptions of favoritism by employees are always a possibility. No matter how much you and a subordinate like each other, it's your job to set boundaries, monitor and evaluate performance. When you cross the line between boss and subordinate, it's easy to feel torn between what works at work and real concern for a friend.

The co-owner of a fashion accessories company discovered how difficult it is to get the best performance from employees when they're friends. She comments, "Once you've got a very personal bond, people tend to take advantage of it, even if they're not aware they're doing it. This happened to me a few times. The person starts wanting time off when it's inappropriate, and you're expected to grant it because you're good friends."

At other times, subordinates have confided in *her,* though she did not confide in them. "It doesn't matter. Once someone tells you personal information, they feel they've crossed a line and are entitled to take liberties," she says.

On the other hand, she does presently enjoy a close friendship with a vice president. "We work so well together that we're more productive as a team than we are separately. She's the only employee I've confided in and she never takes advantage. It works. But that's highly unusual," she says.

Another dilemma is, how do you give negative feedback to a friend? It's natural to seek acceptance and approach the supervisor role by trying to be a nice person. Yet the very nature of the job means that you're going to have to set limits and say no to people. If you really want to be liked, that's very difficult to do. When you turn someone down, the person isn't going to like you for a while. When that someone is also a friend, the strain is compounded.

## CAN A MENTOR BE A FRIEND?

Friendship is reciprocal (or should be) and mentoring is usually one-sided. The goal of the mentor relationship is advancement of your career. It is usually specific to the situation and short-term. The mentor may be there briefly to help you become familiar with a new work environment. It's almost like hiring a fitness trainer. You book a series of sessions; then after a few months the person is no longer part of your life. But relationships can evolve and mentors *can* become friends after a while. If you develop a sense of comfort with each other, you begin to be helpful to your mentor and share things in common. At that point, the mentor relationship, which involves inequality, is over. For example, an attorney enjoyed a mentor relationship with a senior partner in her law firm. He helped her negotiate office politics and deal with difficult personalities. When she became a partner herself, the friendship grew and flourished.

## FRIENDSHIPS WITH CLIENTS

Many businesses depend on special relationships with clients. These relationships can be very good for business; they create customer loyalty. However, you must know how to control the relationship and, except in rare instances where you've known the person for years and have become close, it's a mistake to share your own sensitive personal or business information.

When clients become confidants, the natural boundaries shift. Olga, thirty-eight, owner of a training film business in San Francisco, had a client who was attempting to adopt a child from South America. As the process became an ordeal, the client began to talk about the emotionally charged details.

"There was constant turmoil. I got to know her day-to-day stuff. It was on; it was off. Every day was a drama. But I did not reciprocate; I maintained my distance. When someone gives you information, it feels like you should give information back. But I still feel the need to censor because I want to be as professional as possible. I don't ever want clients to question my ability to do what it is I do because I may have personal difficulties. I don't want to tell them I've got baby-sitter trouble. I don't want them to worry, 'Well, what if she can't get someone today? Will she meet the deadline?' I'm self-employed and I don't want someone to feel there's no safety net," says Olga.

Other tensions emerge when a friend becomes a client. There is a real risk of losing both the client and the friendship unless there is a clear understanding of the *new* relationship. It cannot, for example, be based on the fact that one friend feels *obligated* to give the other his business or that the other would not normally take him on as a client. Grief can be avoided by having frank discussions that cover questions such as "What do you expect as my client?" or "What about fees—do you expect a discount or preferential treatment?" or (if you're the client) "Will you be the one to handle my work or will day-to-day servicing be delegated to others?"

Clients need something from you and you need something

from them. Friendship can interfere with being straight and direct with each other. You may hesitate to say "Why haven't you paid my bill?" because you don't want to jeopardize the friendship. The client may hesitate to say "Your bill is way out of line" or "I didn't like the service that I received." Or you have expectations that get expressed as "I thought you'd give *me* this extra business because I'm your friend." Given the dangers, should we do business with friends?

## *Levels of Work-Related Friendships*

Because work friendships are different from social relationships, it's crucial to keep the boundaries clear. This breakdown should help:

LEVEL 1: Intimate friendships that involve personal confidences. You trust this person. If you're having breast surgery, or you hate your boss, or have political problems at work—you can speak freely. You probably socialize outside of the organization and may integrate the person into your family life.

LEVEL 2: You socialize outside of the organization, but there is little intimate discussion. Comfort and ease with each other is primary; trust is secondary. You share recreational or cultural interests like tennis or theater and you like each other. That holds you together.

LEVEL 3: People you're friendly with during a particular project. A specific situation brings you together; you discover you're compatible and grow to like each other. You enjoy each other, but maybe not as much as at Level 2.

There are also allies, colleagues, and people you deal with on a day-to-day basis. They're people in your internal network (your department or, when you are the owner, your employees) or in your external network (such as someone in another division or from your professional organization) you can call to get something accomplished. Although you may have lunch together once in a while, the connection is episodic. You tap each other as needed and know that you're both well-meaning and supportive. But the relationships come and go.

## FRIENDSHIPS WITH PEERS

The majority of on-the-job friendships involve coworkers. You can be more relaxed with them than with superiors because you are equals. Coworker friends help your job go smoothly, offer empathy and encouragement, and add fun and pleasure to your job. A friend's perspective can help you better understand the politics of the workplace. Research suggests that the support of others in the workplace buffers job dissatisfaction and noncompliant job behaviors when job security is at stake. In one case, a friend turned an unpleasant, stressful job situation into a tolerable experience.

"It was the craziest place," recalls a former administrator for an insurance company in Massachusetts. Previously a social worker, she had taken the job after layoffs due to budget cuts at a nonprofit organization. She was the only person in her department without a sales or insurance background and she was treated like an outsider.

Three months after her arrival, the company hired another ex-social worker in the same department. Both "misfits," they bonded immediately as two of a kind. She smiles as she remembers, "We both wanted more responsibilities and tried to get promotions, but partly as a result of ingrained sexism and partly because of our boss, we had a heck of a time.

"The boss viewed me as a threat. Not only was I a woman, but I also had degrees he didn't have. If he was ticked off, he was always threatening to reorganize the department—and a few times he talked of demoting me. It drove me nuts; I really needed the job. My friend would calm me down and say, 'Now, now. This is what he can do; this is what he can't do. Here's where he's making a threat; here's where he isn't.' She was a much smoother negotiator than I and she gave me a new slant on things."

In turn, when her friend tried to get promoted, she accumulated résumés from everyone in the department and amassed statistics. "I thought we had the makings of a class-action suit because of the way women were treated. When the boss balked at my friend's promotion, she read a few of my statistics to him. She got the job."

This was the ideal internal friend—a peer in a noncompetitive position. Even better is someone noncompetitive who works in another department, which avoids issues of "sibling rivalry." When you both work for the same boss, you may find yourselves vying for the attention of that person. This is especially so in a very bottom-line-driven business where the more sales you make, the more money you make.

## PROTECTING YOURSELF

Jennifer, a thirty-four-year-old management consultant in New York, changed her expectations of colleague friends as she progressed at work. She discovered there was competition all around her for position, status, and being well-thought-of in the organization—and that in situations where competition and money are involved, you have to be selective about whom you can trust.

The first time she got burned, her employer was restructuring staff. Rather than having a pool of consultants who worked on projects in the order in which they came in, the plan was to align consultants by industry (such as consumer products and financial services). Jennifer became friendly with a coworker and the two of them had lunch together three or four times a week. Over tuna sandwiches one day, the friend asked Jennifer her opinion of the restructuring plan. Thinking it was just an intellectual exercise, Jennifer said it would be most workable if the company

solicited staff members' feedback on which industry team interested them. Perhaps if they were asked to give their top three
preferences in order of rank, it would ensure that people would
feel they had a say in the process—and in their own futures.
There would also be fewer complaints about team assignments
down the road.

Two weeks later, Jennifer attended a staff meeting where the
changes were discussed. The managing director moved around
the table, asking each person's opinion of the plan. He reached
her friend first, and to Jennifer's shock, her opinion had suddenly
become her friend's. The managing director thought it was a
splendid idea. When he got to Jennifer, she could only concur
that it was a splendid idea! She felt used and resented it on both
a personal and professional level. The friend gained the recognition that should have been hers. "It dawned on me that if I'm
generous as a friend, some people might take advantage of me.
That's happened to me a couple of times with both men and
women," she says.

Sometimes, however, a competitive relationship can be trans-
formed into a positive friendship. Imagine being hired on the
same day as a coworker for a similar job but receiving $2,000 a
year less than this person. The woman to whom it happened said,
"Why should she get more than me?" Fortunately, she saw that
the real issues were the boss and more money—and she dealt
with him to equalize the salaries.

"It also become clear that our approaches to the job were
different. We could learn something from each other. Each of us
brought something else to the table. We could be leading the
same seminar in the same room and she'd approach it from a
technical skills point of view; I'd focus on relationships and interaction. So there was no vying for the last word—we both had
the last word."

Though work friendships are usually transient and end when
one person leaves the company, this one blossomed and continued even after both had moved on to other jobs. Because they

had a lot in common, they forged a bond that has lasted fifteen years.

When a work friendship is already established, the need to compete at times can shake the relationship. Can your friendship survive when both of you are candidates for the same promotion? Rarely, though it depends on the people involved. "In general, women have a lot of difficulty with conflict. To avoid it, they frequently don't express a lot of real feelings early on and there's a lot of pretending everything's okay. You're not dealing with what's going on and that starts to eat away at the friendship," says Susyn Reeve, Ed.D., a corporate consultant on workplace relationships.

Some might be able to handle it by saying beforehand, "We're playing by the rules—let the chips fall where they may. The final decision is out of our hands, anyway." But even with a frank conversation there are likely to be negative feelings when one person loses out and the other moves up. There's likely to be a lot of acting as if the loser *isn't* jealous and angry. For the winner, there may be guilt. She'll want to celebrate but won't want to hurt the other person's feelings. That detracts from the ability to savor an achievement.

Matters grow more complex if the promotion makes you your friend's supervisor. Due to the dynamics involved, there's an authority relationship that adds a lot of stress. The ability to be explicit about the boundaries between a subordinate and a boss is crucial. For example, when you're talking about performance, it may be helpful to identify which role you're playing and say "I'm having this conversation with you as your supervisor" or "I'm talking to you as a friend." Then say what you really mean, instead of tiptoeing around touchy issues, as in "Your work has really gone downhill lately. I'm concerned about what's going on with you." That doesn't guarantee the conversation will go smoothly, but it helps to frame the conversation. If the friendship is to survive, it's important to recognize that there are times when things get uncomfortable.

## UNCOMPLICATED WORK
## RELATIONSHIPS

These problems can disappear with a close friend who works outside your organization but within your field. Because industry friends usually aren't competing for the same position or recognition, they can be more objective and issues of trust often become clearer. This kind of relationship helps keep you informed of what's happening in (and what's typical for) the industry. Be careful, however, not to mention plans your company is making or engage in gossip. It's important, too, to create rules between you.

Says Dr. Reeve, "Sometimes you *do* want to air dirty laundry to someone who doesn't know the people involved and can be objective, but it must be a person you can trust." You have to say to (and get an agreement from) an industry friend that "When I tell you something, what's said will be kept just between us." Often we don't make the rule explicit; the other person can think the information is open.

Jennifer learned to rely on a friend who once worked at a competitive firm. Over the years both their lives have changed, but they still have a lot in common. They meet for lunch twice a month and talk on the phone every three or four days. Because Jennifer has known her friend for ten years, she's had a chance to observe her behavior and to test out her advice. "I know how good and objective her counsel can be. We're not competing for the same piece of the marketplace. I have three to five friends like that—professional-personal friends. They are, with one exception, people with whom I've never worked."

Professional organizations and industry groups can be sources of friends who serve specific needs. A state educational consultant found it was hard to have a good friend at work because she supervises people and must keep her own counsel. She needs women friends outside the organization as sounding boards and usually talks to people in the same field whom she has met through coalitions and interagency organizations.

On the other hand, noncompetitive friends can disappoint you, too. A sales promotion executive befriended a woman in the printing business, also a heavy hitter, and brought her in as her printer. She spent numerous lunches giving her ideas on how to do direct mail campaigns and quick sales. She sent friends and suppliers to her.

Then she learned the woman had a new client—a company that would be a perfect client for the executive to work with, too. When she asked "Didn't you tell them about me?" the answer was "I never thought of it."

"I helped her so much, but she was so self-absorbed it never occurred to her to help me. She also didn't offer to refer me to the client even at this point. I stopped being her friend. I saw she wanted to drain me of my skills and give nothing back. After that, when she called, I was always busy."

It's in cases like this one that the issue of "Is this a business relationship or is it a friendship?" causes trouble. In a professional relationship, much of what occurs is surface. When you assume that there will be reciprocity and equal trust, you may be disappointed. It's not personal or evil; you just can't expect it.

This is why friends with whom you have no business ties at all are crucial components in your support system. They come without baggage. As you negotiate your career, they provide emotional support, stability, and perspectives that broaden your vision. They're also the ones in whom you can comfortably confide all those unflattering anxieties, fears, or mistakes you can't tell anyone else, as in "I really mishandled this project."

Many find that siblings and longtime friends serve this purpose well. They have seen your life unfold and understand you, and you know if they've been supportive and constructive. Says Sandra, who has three or four close women friends, "One has no idea what I do and how, yet I want to know what's going on in her life and I tell her what she can understand. I talk about the loves of my life with her. Though she celebrates my success, she's also been there during the down times. It's a gift to hear someone say, 'It will turn around. You'll see.' That kind of support is priceless."

Support can also be found by cultivating relationships with people in different careers. This allows you to talk after hours about topics other than business and to hear other people's perspectives. Investment clubs and book clubs are great sources of such relationships.

## THE BOTTOM LINE

The business world is so complicated that there is no way in this day and age that you can move through the complexities alone. Organizations don't run that smoothly, and somewhere down the road you're going to need help from others. Friendship is a powerful force at work. Just manage it smartly.

## Opposite-Sex Friendships and Romance at Work

Women like to have access to the male perspective, learn how men think and operate—and with most women now in the workforce, we're exposed to more opportunities than ever for friendships with the opposite sex. Although these friendships tend to be less intimate than those with female friends, there is comfort in the "big brother" relationship. (Men like women friends because we provide emotional support to them, which their male pals don't.)

Psychologist Linda Sapadin found, however, that 62 percent of women (and 65 percent of men) reported sexual feelings and tensions in many of these friendships; 50 percent of women (76 percent of men) said they liked flirting and teasing; 46 percent of women (66 percent of men) said friends can become sexual partners.

They sometimes do, especially today. Because so much time is spent at the office, there often isn't any other place to meet somebody. The risks, however, can be steep. Romance adds yet another layer of complication to your work life and is likely to be grist for the office gossip mill.

I know firsthand. Back in my single days when I worked as a copywriter in a corporate advertising department, a friendship with an art director who sat at the next desk progressed to a dating relationship—and eventually an engagement. Then one Saturday morning he called to tell me, "It's off. I don't want to get married."

Being dumped by your fiancé (who also happens to be a colleague) gives new meaning to the term "exquisite pain." There is not only rejection to deal with and the humiliation of knowing that everyone else you work with knows—but also the torture of sitting a few feet from him all day, every day, for months afterward. It requires a superhuman effort to put it behind you and move on.

As it happened, he did me a great favor. If I hadn't been jilted, the life I enjoy today would never have unfolded. I wouldn't have met and married my wonderful (and far superior) husband. But the point is, you can save yourself a whole lot of grief by drawing the line and refusing to ever make that date in the first place.

Romances and careers can each travel on very bumpy roads. It is difficult to navigate both at the same time. You're sitting in a meeting with someone who is your lover and also trying to concentrate on the client. The energy is different; the dynamics are different. It's not clear-cut. There are all kinds of communication going on. Or how are you going to feel when you had a big fight last night and must work with him today? If you're already involved, you have to deal with the complications, but if it hasn't happened yet, be aware of the potential difficulties.

The reactions of other people are a consideration, too, and

they're usually negative. Romance on the job has been called a kind of incest. It has an impact on everybody's behavior, particularly when others you work with know about the liaison.

If your company culture permits it, dating a peer (preferably in a different department) probably won't hurt your job. (Some companies actually encourage employee dating.) Romance with someone in the chain of command, however, is a strategic career error.

One woman who married (and who is now divorced from) her supervisor told me, "It's okay if you're in different areas of an organization and your job doesn't in any way affect what he's doing, but it's a great mistake to get involved with your boss. Coworkers think you can get whatever you want and they don't trust you. If you don't get the cooperation of coworkers, it can really hurt your career."

If you're falling in love with your boss or subordinate or client, some very serious thinking is in order for another reason, too. When you date someone who has control over your career (or whose career you control), or if there's a big financial connection between you, there are ethical and possibly conflict-of-interest concerns. The smart move is probably to look for another job in or out of the organization.

Sandra makes it a strict policy not to get involved with clients. Her view: "A woman in business has to be very careful, and if you have an affair, things get clouded. Do I hate him because we're not sleeping together anymore or because he didn't pay me on time? Am I doing this work because I'm so infatuated with him, or do I really want to do it? From the client's perspective, it could be, 'I don't want to see her anymore, but do I want her to keep doing my marketing? Should I pretend I desire her so she'll keep up the work? Or am I keeping her because I'm sleeping with her?'

"Once or twice in my career I really wanted to start something with a male client and I held myself back. This is where my female friends were very important. They said, 'Put your business first. Whatever you want to do with him, do it in your head. Don't get involved.' "

## FRIENDSHIPS THAT WORK AT WORK

To enjoy the advantages of job-related friendships, yet protect yourself:

1. *Limit what you talk about.*

You're less likely to get hurt when you keep your private life separate from your work life. Whether you go out on Saturday night for dinner together is not the issue. It's what you talk about—to a boss, a client, or anyone else. You can spend eight hours on the golf course with somebody talking about golf, not your child's school problems or your marital woes.

Be friendly, of course, but don't confide sensitive personal data—including dislike of a subordinate—unless the person has proved to be completely trustworthy. Assume that you're on record and that there's a possibility that everything you say could get repeated or otherwise used without your knowledge. You also don't want to share problems that make you look weak, vulnerable, or could hurt you if repeated to anyone else.

Beware of discussing your ideas with colleagues who are competitors, too. That doesn't mean you have to be distrustful all the time. You can be competitive, yet cooperative. You might want to work on a project together at some point; colleagues are each other's best resources for contacts. Competitors sometimes recommend each other for speaking engagements or assignments that they can't (or don't want to) take.

Competition turns toxic when you can't relax with anybody and remain on guard about all you say or do, afraid the other person may steal and use it. When competition becomes a barrier or turns into one-upmanship, it's a problem. Clearly it's not fun, either.

2. *Know what you can confide.*

Ideally, your personal life should be kept private, but if we look at what's true in the real world, many of us spend most of our day in the workplace. Our work is affected by our personal life, and vice versa. It's appropriate to confide in your boss if performance is affected by a personal problem and the problem is presented as something you're trying to solve (not as an indication that you're out of control or venting).

If you have a child-care issue, there's nothing wrong with saying, "I'm having baby-sitter difficulties. Do you have any resources or is there any way I can create a more flexible work schedule?" Some companies have employee assistance programs or a child-care information hotline.

You can also say, "I've got a problem with my mother—she's having surgery and I have to be at the hospital. I know there's a big report due. How am I going to do this? Can you help me figure this out?" Your supervisor may be able to point you to elder-care resources through a company program, or you may agree to delegate some of the tasks involved in generating the report. It's when personal difficulties start getting in the way of performance that they're a work problem. If the boss stops confronting you about issues such as missed deadlines because he feels sorry for you, you're in trouble. You're not getting the feedback you need.

Other problems cross the line. Your superior really can't help you with (and doesn't want to know about) something like "My boyfriend and I are not getting along. He doesn't understand my needs."

3. *Set clear boundaries early.*

If you're a supervisor, you have to do a balancing act between nurturing and supporting subordinates while also allowing them to grow. To a large degree, your employees project you in a parental role. When you have that level of responsibility, you have to be very careful about the line between being a good boss and being someone's therapist or guardian.

It's flattering when people confide their personal problems. If you set a precedent by being an employee's counselor, however, at some point you're going to get resentful at spending unproductive time managing this person's life. Another danger is taking on serious problems that may be beyond the scope of what you can deal with. You may know someone is an alcoholic or has a drug problem and you may want to be supportive, but do you have training in this regard? Giving unqualified advice or help can harm your employee and you; there might even be legal repercussions.

That's why knowing your boundaries and not getting involved in others' minutiae are important. There are times when you may have to say, "I can't help you with that." A key question is, is this an ongoing problem or a onetime occurrence? Let's say an employee goes back to school (with your blessing). She no longer gets her work done because she stays up late to do papers—and she's counting on you to understand. You can set a boundary by telling her, "You have to take personal days or vacation time to get your papers done."

Conversely, if you're a subordinate, don't mistake your boss for a confidant. What you want is a superior who gives you support and the information you need to perform, who listens when you say you need help to do your job. You want someone who encourages your efforts to grow, teaches (if possible), and is balanced and fair—who gives credit when you do something, rather than rushing off with it himself.

Maintain boundaries with clients, as well. Let them use *you* as a sounding board, rather than the other way around. If a customer confides a personal problem, he won't be in crisis forever. When the problem has been resolved, bring the focus back to where it belongs—the work relationship—as soon as possible.

4. *Take your time.*

One senior manager told me, "If someone walks into your office your first day at work and is instantly your best friend, that's the person to watch out for. People don't fall in love that quickly and they don't make friends that quickly."

Trust and intimacy are hallmarks of friendship, but at work everyone has his or her own personal temperament and job-related needs. You can't take people at face value; some are going to prove more supportive than others. Give yourself time in any work relationship to determine whether this is someone you want to trust. You're not going to know that right away.

Watch people's behavior for clues to who may become trust-worthy (or toxic) friends at work. Do they treat other people well? How much vicious gossip about others are they bringing you, hoping you'll trade gossip back? If someone is willing to talk with you about your colleagues, they're likely to talk about you to others. Be wary—and avoid initiating gossip, too.

5. *Don't put all your eggs in one basket.*

Make sure you have a network of people in your profession outside your office. Ex-bosses, ex-subordinates, and ex-clients can become wonderful close friends. The dynamics change when they don't work for you (or you don't work for them) anymore.

Make time also for purely personal friends. These are people who *want* to hear from you and share with you on the phone at night. If your career is your life, these friendships can suffer. But there are ways to stay in touch, even if it's through E-mail or a funny card. Make it a priority to get together in person, too. Balance in life benefits most people.

6. *Know when to speak up.*

If you feel you've been betrayed, consider confronting the person. You may be surprised. Sometimes there can be a mis-interpretation. In the case of a stolen idea, the fact is, it's not unusual for ideas to be "in the air." That's why inventions tend to appear around the world at the same time. The situation is ripe for a new idea and you are not the only one who sees it. The person may already have thought of the same basic concept, though she may be wrong in adding your slant to it. People can do such things, however, without realizing it. You might say, "Are you aware that you presented my idea as your own at the meeting? This is the way I feel about it." The other person may have another perspective and respond, "I was thinking the exact same thing all the time." On the other hand, if it happens more than once, be wary of that person.

Clarify (in your own mind and with friends), too, "What is the basis of our relationship? Misunderstandings occur because we usually don't talk about what we expect and need from each other." One possibility is to say, "I enjoy helping you with your business planning and I expect that if you can ever help me out, you will." If the person is unwilling to reciprocate (and is honest about it), at least you'll know that up front. It's a valuable piece of information. You want to be wary of people who are likely to use you, and keep those relationships casual.

On the other hand, do not share too much information such as "The company is thinking of folding our division and I'll have to lay off people" with someone who reports to you. It doesn't benefit the person and leaves her wondering whether she's about to lose her job. If you *know* she's likely to be laid off, it's helpful to say something like "Things are uncertain around here. If you hear of anything else opening up, you might want to look into it."

### 7. Beware of "difficult" friends.

It's especially hard to put up with someone who gets upset easily or often becomes annoyed or jealous on the job. It takes time and effort to have to watch what you say or to deal with repeated misunderstandings—and it may interfere with your work.

What you do about it depends in part on how often it happens and where the emotion is aimed. If a friend repeatedly gets angry at you, for example, set a boundary and say, "You can't talk to me that way." Friendship *does* require a certain level of mutual respect and emotional maturity—and if an unwarranted accusation has been made, you do have to protect yourself. If anger erupts at someone else, you might want to try to calm a friend down.

Assess the situation. Is it a rare loss of cool—or does the person have a pattern of difficulty in controlling emotions? In the latter case, steer clear of the person as much as possible. A healthy friend helps reduce job stress—not add to it. You don't want someone volatile to affect your value in the workplace.

# 3

# Friends Who Boost Your Marriage:
# What Nobody Ever Told You

I T STARTED WITH a missing pair of navy wool socks. Karen's husband, Doug, left them in the laundry room dryer and they wound up in Ginny and Phil's wash. In the search for the socks, the two couples (newlyweds who lived in the same Atlanta apartment complex) met and quickly meshed. Doug and Phil were both jokesters who constantly kidded each other. Karen and Ginny found they could talk to each other about everything from feelings to fashions. The couples became inseparable. "We didn't have any money, so we played Michigan rummy for entertainment—and laughed," says Karen.

Ginny was the first to become pregnant. After the baby arrived, she and Phil felt pinched for space. Six months later they moved into a larger apartment forty minutes away. Yet the couples' relationship stayed strong. They spoke on the phone, they shared vacations and New Year's Eves. Through the years, they were there for each other's health crises, hassles with family, and business setbacks. When Karen and Doug celebrated their twenty-fifth wedding anniversary, Ginny and Phil wouldn't miss the 4 P.M. mass, even though Ginny's father was going to be buried that morning. Said Ginny, "You're too much a part of us for us not to be there. Life must go on."

Ask Karen and she'll tell you that Ginny and Phil—and other close friends—have nourished and strengthened her marriage. Research confirms her experience. Studies show that friends are sources of support, connection, and pleasure for couples throughout the course of married life.

Friends can lighten things up and take some of the heat off marriage, so you don't feel overburdened in meeting *all* of your partner's needs. Couples' friends provide creative ideas for problem solving and can be models, allowing you to see that others have conflicts and work them through. Friends help ease the stress of major life transitions. They can make up for losses, too. Some couples stay together longer, despite lack of intimacy, because they have friends with whom to spend satisfying time.

Despite all the benefits, however, certain kinds of friendships are negative influences that weaken bonds with your spouse. It's important to recognize friendships that enrich your marriage—and be aware of those that can divide.

## FRIENDS AND THE STAGE OF MARRIAGE

Individual and couples friends can have a positive effect on you and your spouse, but the nature of their impact shifts, depending on the stage of the marriage cycle. Early in marriage, strong mutual friendships can help prevent divorce, according to a study of people under fifty-five by Alan Booth, Ph.D., professor of sociology at Penn State University. He found that the more friends shared by couples who were married seven years or less, the less likely they were to divorce. Couples with many mutual friends had one-third the divorce rate of couples who rarely socialized. Even young couples with a moderate number of shared friends were twice as likely to stay married as socially isolated couples. What explains this powerful impact? Adjustments in the early years of marriage create enormous strains between spouses, and couples with role models for long-term intimate relationships were less vulnerable to divorce.

Friends are less important in keeping longer marriages together. These are more likely to be sustained by the couple's mutual investment in "capital" such as children and home ownership. Yet friends still perform key functions. In midlife, they serve as sources of wisdom and advice on raising children. At times of stress, friends provide empathy, information, and affirmation.

Take Karen and Doug's kitchen remodeling—the kind of project that tests the best of marriages. As the mess seemed to overtake the entire household, patience wore thin. Old friends Jan and Bob, who had survived a similar renovation, just let the couple "scream and holler."

Karen recalls, "The whole kitchen was torn up and I was ready to scream because I couldn't stand the chaos. I'd call Jan and want to cry. She's known me since sixth grade and she'd say to me, 'It's horrible. But it's not going to last forever. Soon it will be over with and just think about how gorgeous it's going to look.' That put things into perspective."

Friends help fill up your life when the kids leave home and during other life-cycle changes. For retired couples, socializing with friends helps predict marital satisfaction. Long-term mutual and individual friendships enhance the well-being of couples married more than fify years. Friends from as far back as childhood provide continuity in their lives and share activities. Couples without friends (usually because the latter have died) are more dependent on their families or socially isolated.

No matter how old you are, friends can encourage you and your mate to grow, stretch, explore new interests and activities you wouldn't have tried on your own. Sometimes they change your entire life, as they did for Evelyn, a forty-three-year-old New York photographer, and her husband, Joe, fifty-five, a corporate consultant. During a trip to Colorado, they met lifelong residents Pete and Susan, who introduced them to possibilities they'd never considered. One day Susan invited Evelyn to go backpacking with a group of women friends. It started simply enough. Evelyn was a city girl through and through who had never hiked before. She recalls, "I felt a lack of leisure in my life and I decided to take a chance. I went out in the woods for three days with these wonderful women who could walk with forty pounds strapped to their backs."

Unaccustomed to the altitude and physical strain, Evelyn's stamina was depleted quickly. After four miles, she virtually collapsed in the woods. She says, "I felt like a total failure. Then two of the women just scooped up my backpack and carried it along with their own forty pounds. Off they went to the campsite, with me trudging behind. It was an amazing experience to be with women who all work, who are all wives and mothers but somehow know how to put up a tent, make gourmet meals in the wilderness, filter water, and pee in woods on a pitch-black night. Part of me was exhilarated and the rest of me yearned for a hot bath and Chinese food."

In the meantime, Joe went on his own packing trek with Pete. His excursion was far more demanding than Evelyn's. They walked forty miles in five days.

When the couple returned east, Evelyn felt a profound change. "It hit me in the face. I couldn't live anymore in an urban canyon of high-rise apartments and screaming ambulances with few trees and no mountains. I was also stuck in the 'never enough' club. If you work ten hours a day, why not work fourteen. If you make $50,000 a year, why not $75,000? You always raise your own ceiling. I thought, 'I have to make a change but I don't know how to do it,' " she says.

It was done for her. The phone rang one day and it was Susan, excitedly announcing that a terrific house in her area was available for rent. The location and price were right; it sounded perfect. After a conference with Joe, who had been seduced in his own way by the Colorado lifestyle, Evelyn told Susan they'd decided to move. "We called the owners of the house, negotiated over the phone, and rented it. Then we called the movers, packed, and left," says Evelyn.

It worked because Evelyn *and* Joe had shared their first experience of Colorado. She explains, "If I had come back myself and said, 'I had this great time,' he would have said, 'That's nice but you're back in the city now, so let's address our concerns.' And we had lots of concerns. Joe's business involved tremendous pressures. If he hadn't gone on his own walkabout and cleared his own head, he wouldn't have been able to extricate himself from that." It also made it easier that this is a second marriage for both, and that Joe's children are grown and out on their own. They had no schools to worry about.

Two years have passed and Evelyn's life is very different. As she describes it, "I work, but I have a garden. I hike and ski and write letters. I play with my cat and I lie on the floor and stare at the sky, which is cobalt blue. Joe does business here. We're happy. But we couldn't have made the transition without these friends who showed us a lifestyle we didn't know could be ours."

## THE SPECIAL ROLE OF WOMEN FRIENDS

Major contributors to Evelyn's contentment are her friend Susan and other women who share her passion for the arts, as well as the great outdoors. Women friends actually do enhance wives' marital satisfaction, adding pleasures that go beyond the limitations of socializing as couples. A thirty-eight-year-old sales manager devotes much of her time to what she calls "Noah's ark friendships."

As she puts it, "It's you and your spouse and them and their spouses—couples going to some overpriced Italian restaurant. That's nice. I enjoy that. But those relationships don't have the depth and dimension of my relationships with women friends. Four people don't sit around and have intimate conversations. It's hard to talk about aspirations and fears and qualms with three other people. You talk about superficialities, which are nice and fun—but you're not going to say, 'I'm worried about getting pregnant,' or 'I really don't feel professional fulfillment when I'm doing what I do.' "

Close women friends fill wives' needs for intimacy and understanding and actually strengthen wives' commitment to their marriages, according to Stacey J. Oliker, Ph.D., author of *Best Friends and Marriage*. She found that wives without close friends often felt depressed and lonely.

But isn't your husband supposed to be your best friend? "The concept of an ideal marriage where husbands and wives are perfect best friends and avid communicators is relatively new. It's only since the 1960s and '70s that intimate communication and empathy between spouses have been emphasized. Though there *were* spouses who became intimate best friends before that, it wasn't necessarily the expectation," says Dr. Oliker, associate professor of sociology and urban studies at the University of Wisconsin–Milwaukee.

And today's expectation is frequently at odds with reality. Research suggests that only 30 percent of wives consider their husbands their best friends. Many men aren't willing (or able) to satisfy wives' needs for intimacy. The availability of women friends to fill the gap eases the pressure on husbands. Wives wind up making fewer demands that might lead to fights.

Women friends provide what even the most sensitive and communicative of husbands cannot—empathy for and validation and understanding of the experience of being a woman. Imagine the stress of a breast cancer scare without a woman friend with whom to share your feelings. One wife who lived through weeks of uncertainty about an ambiguous mammogram reading told me, "I felt like a sword was hanging over my head. I don't think a man understands what you're going through the way a woman does. It's not the same. My friend was a constant source of encouragement, and having her to talk to meant the burden wasn't all on my husband's shoulders. It turned out to be a false alarm, but I don't know what I would have done without her. She's the first one I call when something goes wrong. She helps me to see things in a more positive light."

Talking together is a key component of women's friendships; in contrast, men tend to *do* things together. Women discuss emotions, as well as parenting, homemaking, cosmetics, and clothes. Who but another female can fully appreciate the frustrations of frizzy hair in July or commiserate with your sister-in-law problems? Only another woman *wants* to listen *at length* to your PMS stories, or to the details of your cousin's wedding, or to the drama of your search for patent leather sling-back heels. Dr. Oliker observes that men often belittle this kind of conversation—especially when it's conducted on the phone—and that we women tend to reinforce this devaluation ourselves. Yet such conversations bring texture, pleasure, and connection to our lives. They affirm us as women.

Women friends also help you solve conflicts with your husband. Some husbands don't want to talk about problems, or they don't talk constructively or they become angry. Friends empower wives by helping them to strategize and figure out how to get what they want in their marriages. They also help you understand your mate better.

A social support network is particularly important in military marriages. Friends and family help army wives adjust to separation and reunion when their husbands are deployed abroad. When you face disruptive moves every few years, it means everything to have a friend stationed nearby. Mara felt overjoyed when her husband, Stan, a U.S. Army sergeant, was assigned to a school in Texas.

"It really helped my marriage that my friend Amy and her husband, Bob, were stationed close to us. She's loads of fun and was available to spend time with me while Stan was at school. We have the same philosophy: We both want to get to know a place while we're there and we love to explore a new area. We shop together, have lunch, go sight-seeing. No one person can provide every single thing you need in your life, not even your husband. Amy helped provide other things," says Mara.

Amy helped the marriage go more smoothly in another way, too. Stan and Mara are very different types of people. She's a Type A, very structured and logical, a perfectionist. Stan is a free spirit, spontaneous and fun-loving. As Mara puts it, "I'm a recovering worrier; he knows how to relax and just take things as they come. Amy is exactly like him, and you might say she acted as a sort of translator for me. She could identify with what he was thinking and feeling and explain it to me."

Amy also reframed problems and created empathy for Stan. Mara remembers the time Stan returned from an assignment he'd gone on alone. "He wanted me to drop everything and pay attention to him. I was in the midst of a project for my mail-order business and couldn't do it. I told him, 'I've got to get this done. It's a deadline,' " says Mara. When she recounted this to Amy, rolling her eyes and adding an acerbic "Can you believe it?," Amy responded, "I'd feel the same way he does." Mara was surprised. It never occurred to her that there could be another point of view.

"Amy couldn't fathom *not* giving up your work for your husband who just got back—and I couldn't imagine *doing* that. It helped me to see there was nothing 'wrong' with my husband. We simply had different personalities and saw things differently."

At other times, Amy would tell her, "This is probably what your husband wants from you right now." Says Mara, "That helped tremendously because I never saw it. For example, I'm not very demonstrative, but sometimes my husband needs a show of affection. She'd overhear me finishing a long-distance conversation with him and I'd be about to hang up. She'd whisper to me, 'Mara, say you love him.' It didn't occur to me that it was important. He *knows* I love him. But she understood he wanted to hear that."

Friends help cool down marital fights and encourage wives to think rationally when nerves are raw. Allison, twenty-eight, credits a friend with helping her to prevent a conflict from escalating. Married three years, Allison resented that she and her husband, Vince, thirty-three, never had time alone together.

"He's a workaholic and at the top of his career track in computers. We also have loads of friends and socialize a lot. Either he was working late or we were out at dinners and parties. It was as if our private life had slipped away. There was no time for *us*. I felt I needed more face-to-face attention and my resentment kept building," says Allison.

When a wife discusses her husband with a friend, some of what she is doing is figuring out how to approach him. It's a conflict-avoiding strategy to sort through, identify the issue, then decide on the best way to handle it. One day Allison told a married friend how unhappy she was. The woman validated her feelings, saying, "Hey, you're not being unreasonable. I couldn't stand so little private time with my husband. You two need to get lost together. Tell him how you feel."

The support helped Allison tell Vince, "We have to sit down and discuss this." To her surprise, he agreed that they had a problem and needed to schedule more time alone. He cut back on late nights at the office. The couple has also learned to say no. They've stopped automatically accepting every invitation and are careful about overcommitment. "Things have changed," says Allison.

## TOXIC SITUATIONS

Not all friends are positive influences or bridges between you and your mate, but toxic situations may not be readily apparent. Some friends can subtly or overtly torpedo a marriage unless you're alert. Lydia, a fifty-two-year-old office manager and mother of three, learned that someone bitter about men can encourage marital conflict. Years ago she joined a women's consciousness-raising group, along with a neighbor down the street. As a result of the group experience, she pushed for change in her marriage, and her relationship with her husband became more equal. She went back to work, assumed a stronger role in financial decisions, and grew in other ways. Her husband was tolerant of the shifts and gave her the room she needed. But her neighbor's marriage couldn't take the strain. She and her husband broke up.

"She thought mine would, too, and she never missed an opportunity to criticize my husband. If he asked for a glass of water, she'd say, 'Don't let him talk to you like that. Tell him to get it himself.' But he wasn't barking an order; he was asking. She was trying to drive a wedge between us, so I finally stopped seeing her," says Lydia.

A thirty-six-year-old vice president of human resources finds that some of her single friends project their own issues with men onto her relationship with her husband. She's had to count to ten to stop from exploding at their remarks. "If I complain that I had to fall over three days' worth of dirty laundry in the bedroom, it doesn't mean my husband is trying to oppress me. But one friend of mine invariably interprets it as a sign that he wants to turn me into his hausfrau slave. She's been divorced three times and has never been able to sustain a relationship with a man."

Other friends have invited her to go on shopping trips and spend $5,000 at a trunk show. Describing a typical scene, she says, "I'll decline by saying, 'No, that's really not where I want to put my resources.' And they'll question, 'Well, is your husband really cheap?' No, that's not it. He doesn't hold the purse strings; we both do. There's always a feeling the man is oppressing the woman in a marriage (especially financially), and that's not true at all in my case. Because I've known these women a long time, I know they don't mean to criticize me or my marriage. They're just speaking out of their own experience. But this kind of talk really makes me mad."

## DANGERS OF OPPOSITE-SEX FRIENDS

Cross-sex friendships have long been considered a potential threat to marriage. A friendship with a person of the opposite sex can be especially tricky these days as women are exposed to more contact with men on the job.

"If you're not careful, such friendships can lead to affairs of the worst kind. They're more likely to destroy a marriage than an encounter at a convention because the relationship has depth. The people know each other well, and it's based on more than just sex," says Patricia Hudson, Ph.D., a marriage therapist in Grapevine, Texas.

One couple socializes with several women who used to work with the husband. They generally see him as a "safe" man, someone who makes no sexual demands because he's happily wed. But his wife bridles at one woman who comes on to him. She says, "We go out with her and her husband, but there are times when he's away on business and it's just the three of us out for a drink. Suddenly her body language changes and becomes so obvious. She buttons and unbuttons the top of her blouse, for example, but my husband doesn't see it. It annoys me. It also bothers me that he's more solicitous to her than to me on those occasions. We go to a restaurant and he holds the seat for her but not for me. He hands her the menu, not me. When I point it out, he says I'm imagining things. I don't think anything's going on, but it makes me feel he takes me for granted. What am I—chopped liver?"

Pangs of jealousy are not necessarily unfounded. At age fifty-seven, Lily didn't think anything was going on either, but her husband walked out and married a mutual friend. The other woman was her college classmate. When this woman was widowed, Lily's husband, a Houston lawyer, was executor of the estate. He spent a great deal of time at her house, ironing out the details for months. During this period, Lily's father had a stroke. Since her brother lived abroad, she bore the full burden of her father's care.

Although Lily needed her husband's support, he was consumed with his own problems. His power at work was waning; his body wasn't what it used to be. He was depressed. Feeling that he was totally self-centered, she had no patience with him.

"I couldn't hear that he was hurting. But he was her white knight. He took care of everything. He did the taxes, gave her advice, made her feel secure—and she loved it. What middle-aged man, married to a wife who's telling him 'That doesn't match,' could resist a woman who thought he was wonderful? She took advantage of his depression," says Lily.

When the friend's thirty-year-old daughter died in a skiing accident, Lily was the first to comfort her. "I even went to the funeral home to pick out the casket—and she was already having an affair with my husband."

When her husband left, he spoke of his need for freedom and his feelings of confusion. He never mentioned there was someone else. Months later, he wrote a note to Lily: "To avoid embarrassment, I want you to know ahead of time I'm moving in with Kate."

It took Lily two years in therapy to deal with the pain and rage. "It was the ultimate betrayal. They wrecked my life and destroyed my trust," she says. She believes her own over-confidence helped create the climate, however. "I was too secure and sure of myself in my marriage, and that's a big mistake," she says.

Such betrayals are more common than we realize, according to Dr. Hudson. At other times, however, it isn't *your* problems but the fallout from your friends' troubles that can be toxic for you and your mate. For example, your friends' separation or divorce can rock *your* boat, too. You tend to compare your marriage to others, and when your pals split, it shakes you up. Etched forever in my own psyche is the phone call I made to an old friend on a Sunday evening one May. "Happy Mother's Day!" I announced cheerily, settling into a comfortable chair for a long chat about our respective family celebrations. Instead, I heard silence—then finally the whispered words, "Steve left me. He's gone." After twelve years of marriage and two children, he had walked out. That phone call was the final irony of a Mother's Day neither my friend nor I will ever forget.

My first reaction was simple shell shock. As that wore off, I felt deeply threatened. I hadn't had the slightest inkling that their marriage was in trouble. My friend didn't confide such information. Sure, they had fights with each other, but so did my husband and I. Theirs seemed no worse than ours. You fought and then you patched the differences. Why were their differences less fixable? And if it had happened to them, could it possibly happen to us?

Six months later, their split was followed by that of other close friends. In one fell swoop, our social life had been decimated. The couples we went out with on Saturday nights were gone. We felt devastated. If one divorce leads you to ask questions about your own relationship, two feel like a brutal assault. One woman told me she felt so frightened when her best friends separated that she changed her own behavior. "It may sound silly, but I really worried about being a good wife. I was much more diligent about cooking meals. The husband left for someone else, and it made me take a hard look at whether I was doing enough to please my husband," she says.

There's reason for concern, because divorce can be "catching." Dr. Booth's research found that couples with one divorced friend and one divorced sibling had nearly double the divorce rate of those with no divorced friends or siblings. The trouble is, divorced peers may not only cause you to reevaluate your own marriage but may also (like cheating peers) relax *your* inhibitions and reduce the pressure to make a less than ideal marriage work. When you know someone who is experiencing divorce, you gain an understanding of what to expect. It shows you that divorce can be survived and that divorced individuals are not bad people. It also means that you have friends who won't object to or criticize you for a split. If they've been divorced, they're more understanding—they're kindred souls.

When your friends separate, there's also the potential for conflict with your spouse if you identify with one partner and he feels close to the other. In a variation on this theme, one woman described the turmoil when her best friend's mate was unfaithful. "My husband and I constantly talked of what she should do. He was on her side, but his attitude was very cut and dried—'If he cheated on you, leave.' She wanted to stay and try to work it out, and I felt that all I could do was support *her* decision." The couple did reconcile, but it was difficult for the foursome to get back together as couples again. "My husband resented what her husband had done to her and it was harder for him to put it all aside than it was for me. I felt it was for the good of the couple," she says.

If your friends' rift is permanent, you frequently must decide which half of the pair gets your loyalty. Rarely can you maintain friendships with both parties for long. Divorce among friends makes for hard choices. Some people find it so painful, they withdraw from both partners.

My husband and I chose the wives when it became clear that there was no chance of reconciliation for our friends. The men had left with other women waiting in the wings, and it was unthinkable to me to socialize with them. It would have been a betrayal of my women friends, and I had no desire to make polite chitchat with the men's new romances. The wives also *needed* us more, and my friendships with them were much stronger than my bonds with their husbands. (To understand what a separating or divorcing friend is going through—and how to be appropriately supportive—see Chapter 4.)

In view of all the complications, friendship can have its price. But despite the real possibility of toxic situations, friends are usually good for your marriage. With a little awareness and sensitivity to potential dangers, you and your spouse can reap the benefits of friendship. Says Karen, "Our friends are like family. There's an unconditional acceptance of the people we were and the persons we have become, with no strings attached. They're a constant source of support for us."

As times change and the pressures on marriage continue, we can use a little help from our friends.

## ARE YOUR FRIENDSHIPS
## MARRIAGE-FRIENDLY?

Do your friendships measure up? It's important to recognize and appreciate those that enhance your bond with your partner—and be alert to relationships that threaten it. Here's how:

1. *Look at friends' reactions to your marital conflicts.*

Positive, healthy friends cool you down when you fight with your husband, rather than stoke the fire. When you're furious at him, does a friend listen and let you vent, then say something like "He *does* help around the house. He *does* coach the kids' soccer team. He *is* crazy about you"? When someone points out your spouse's good qualities, the problem seems less enormous.

In contrast, beware of friends who encourage you to dwell on your spouse's faults—who say "I wouldn't put up with that" or denigrate him. When you hear negatives often enough, they can eventually take a toll. If you say, "My husband said _____," and your friend replies, "He's a jerk," after a while you may start thinking, "Maybe she's right." Be very cautious about friends who do this.

I complain selectively myself. When I need to blow off steam about my husband, I do so only to trusted friends who champion "the couple" and who have the best interests of our marriage at heart.

There is, however, another issue. By supporting and making bad relationships tolerable, good friends may sometimes prevent you from making changes you need to make. According to Dr. Oliker, best friends can encourage wives to put up with destructive marriages because they're so concerned about survival outside of marriage. Despite the great numbers of women in the workforce, women are still very economically dependent on marriage, and when they leave a marriage with children, they're likely to be extremely overburdened financially. Given that most of us know someone who's a struggling single mother, friends tend to take the side of keeping a marriage together rather than risking conflict.

Yet there are times when a friend *should* speak up—such as in cases of abuse and/or when the spouse is addicted to gambling, drugs, alcohol, or other destructive behavior. If the wife has done everything possible, such as going to Al-Anon herself, and it hasn't helped, then it's time for a close friend to say something like "This is hurtful to you (or the children). When you made your marriage vows, I don't think this is what anyone had in mind."

### 2. Be cautious about opposite-sex friendships.

On-the-job opposite-sex friendships can be especially dangerous. Many romances start in the workplace, where spouses meet other people. To head off problems, set boundaries at the start. If your best friend at work is a man, the relationship, even if sex isn't involved, can become very intense and threatening to your mate, especially if you begin to discuss intimate things. The big question is, could you comfortably bring this person home for dinner with your spouse—or do you have to be secretive?

Keep your life very open with a male friend. Avoid activities that could be construed as a date. Instead of going out for a long dinner, why not meet for breakfast or lunch to avoid even the perception of crossing boundaries? Keep your spouse comfortable with the relationship, avoiding cause for suspicion—such as secret phone calls. Some spouses may not feel jealous but they can feel excluded from that kind of secret existence.

It's not all bad, incidentally, if an opposite-sex friend arouses a competitive instinct in your mate. A little awareness that you're attractive to others can be good for your marriage—as long as you don't make it into a game where you're deliberately trying to provoke him.

What if your husband has a female friend? You can often (though not always) tell whether she is after your spouse. If the three of you do things together, it's usually a sign there's nothing going on—but be alert regardless.

3. *Count up the singles and the divorced.*

There's nothing wrong with single friends, and we all have them. But exposure to an oversupply of opposite-sex singles can be threatening. Research by Scott J. South, Ph.D., and Kim M. Lloyd, Ph.D., of the State University of New York at Albany implies that exposure to too many unattached people can lead to temptation and put your marriage at risk. The lowest risk of divorce for young couples was found in areas with 129 eligible men for every 100 eligible women. Risk rose by 13 percent when there were 162 eligible men for every 100 women. When surrounded by all those options, it seems, people may be enticed to leave their spouses for someone "better."

Certain single women friends can be negative influences, too. One question to ask is what *kind* of single are they? Be aware of those on the hunt who prod you to "Come out to the bar or club," where you'll be exposed to the mating scene.

Having too many divorced friends can also be threatening. We may become less willing to invest fully in the marriage, which can lead to increased dissatisfaction. Perhaps not surprisingly, divorced friends who are miserable pose no problem in this regard. But if a divorced friend looks happy, the situation can seem tempting. You may think, "Well, it's not so bad. Maybe I should leave."

4. *Agree with your spouse on boundaries.*

Discuss what both of you will and won't talk about with friends—which topics should be off-limits to others. If he doesn't want you to talk about his income, his mother, or your sex life, his wishes should be respected.

Sex and money are usually hot-button issues. Some people never talk about either topic with friends. Americans consider income a very private matter. Some might not talk about sex as routinely as they did when they were single, yet if sexual problems seemed threatening to a marriage, a woman might feel it was important to talk with a friend as a way to solve the problems.

5. *Avoid "overdoing" friends.*

There is a balance. When your friendships compete for time and intimacy with your spouse, there is danger of diminished interaction with (or competition stirred in) your mate. Research shows that husbands report more conflict and ambivalence when their wives interact frequently with friends.

If your husband has a sports obsession and spends most of his free time with his bowling buddies, you may feel that all his intimate needs are being met somewhere else. He may feel the same if you and your best friend (or your sister) are inseparable or go off on vacations together, telling him, "You don't like the beach, so we'll go ourselves." One husband felt so threatened that he told his wife she had a choice: her friend or him. She chose him.

On the other hand, if a single friend expects more of your time than you can spare, reassure her that she is important to you, but explain that you do have other obligations. You might say something like "You're my dear friend and that hasn't changed. I care about and value you. But Brian is my husband and time with him has to come first." Singles' conflicts with married friends will be discussed in depth in Chapter 6.

6. *Avoid friends with different values.*

Friendship is easier and likely to be more comfortable if you feel the same about issues like monogamy and commitment. If those around you feel there's nothing wrong with having affairs or switching partners or think that open marriage is okay, the result can be relaxed inhibitions and the temptation to weaken your own standards.

7. *If your husband dislikes your friend, don't insist that he spend time with the person as a courtesy to you.*

Don't impose a friend on your spouse. See the friend alone. It's rare that spouses' interests totally overlap, and it makes for a richer marital relationship to have some friends you see on your own, such as those who share your interest in tennis or antiques or other specialized hobbies. As previously noted, having lots of friends is a way of strengthening marriage because you don't demand so much from one another.

## Difficult Situations

Consider this scene:

Two couples—you and your husband and another couple—have rented a condo near San Diego for the weekend. The four of you are out on the patio on the last day, when you feel chilly. You go to your room to get a sweater. As you toss it over your shoulders and turn to leave, you're confronted by your friend's husband, standing there in the doorway. Arms stretched high and wide, his body blocks your exit and he stares at you intently. Seconds pass, then he growls, "I want you. Since the day we met I've wanted you."

This may sound like something out of a grade-B romance novel, but it really happened to one woman, who still relates the story years later with an air of disbelief. "His wife was my close friend, and I felt so stunned I just blurted out, 'No, no, no! The answer is no! She's my friend. I love her. She's your wife.' "

"I love her, too," he insisted, although that statement did not deter him from the matter at hand. He wouldn't budge from the doorway. It was only when someone could be heard approaching that he finally turned and left.

He never bothered her again. Her relationship with her friend continued, although she admits it wasn't easy to behave as if nothing had happened. "But somehow I was able to push the whole thing to the back of my mind and feel, 'It's over. It's done with.' I'm good at doing that. We occasionally went out as couples, but if I so much as went to the ladies' room, I made sure I wasn't alone."

Wives can be approached by friends' husbands. A man might say, "Why don't we go to lunch?" and make flirty, seductive comments, for example. Or, after a few drinks, he might grab, kiss, and beg, "Please, pretty please." What do you do in such situations? Deal with the husband. In the "pretty please" case, the woman pushed him away and told him, "Stop it—and stay away from me," then avoided him the rest of the evening. Later, she wrote him a letter, saying, "Jean deserves better than this. Don't be such a jerk." He subsequently wrote back, apologizing for his behavior.

In general, women I talked to opted not to tell the friend as long as force was not involved. The reasoning: These things come out in good time. In the case of the condo incident, the husband had greater success with other women, and within a year, the wife found out. The couple eventually divorced. Says the friend, "She's still close and I've never told her. I never will. It's so humiliating. Why do that to someone? I've never told my husband either."

An inappropriate gesture is one thing, but knowledge that a friend's spouse is actually having an affair is another. In the latter case, you might feel that a caring friend is doing a disservice by keeping silent. On the other hand, speaking up might force the wife into an action she doesn't want or isn't yet prepared to take. Chances are a wife knows on some level that her husband is fooling around.

One wife clearly remembers the call from her friend announcing that her husband was having an affair with a co-worker. The caller had seen him in a restaurant with his arms around the woman. Says the wife, "I wish she'd kept it to herself. That hurt. I don't believe there's any woman who doesn't suspect the truth. But you may not be ready to do something about it. You have to go at your own pace. I never forgave the friend who told me."

However, without hitting a friend with a hammer, you *could* drop hints, such as "How would you feel about it if Pete was having an affair?" It's rare, but there are wives who don't consider a husband's philandering a big deal and who would never consider breaking up a marriage because of it.

One friend asked, "Do you really think he's working late every night?" The wife finally said, "Do you know something I don't know?" The response was, "Yes, I do. He's propositioned me many times." The wife knew the marriage had problems, but this conversation tipped her off that her husband had actually hit on several of her friends.

What do you do when a married friend confides that *she's* having (or considering) an affair? Let's say your friend is browsing through a bookstore when a man stops and asks her the time. The encounter starts what could become an affair. Because she's been married a long time, she resists, but she sees him, speaks to him on the phone—and asks you for advice.

One woman listened, but refused to tell her friend what to do. "If I really told her what I thought, I felt I would be judging her in a way I didn't want to because I understood how exciting it was. When she pressed me, I said, 'You have to decide. The decision isn't up to me. I understand what you're going through and how difficult it is. You'll somehow work it out. It will become clear to you.' What would I do? If I cared about my husband, I would not want to hurt him because I wouldn't want to be hurt in that way."

Another option is to acknowledge her feelings, saying, "I know it must be hard," but stay gently on the side of the marriage (assuming it isn't abusive) and advise that she work on her marriage first. Says Dr. Hudson, "I'd say things like 'You don't want to be five years out of this and be saying, "I wonder if I could have trained old Jim to do this." ' " Point out the consequences, as in "Just try to keep the big picture in mind. If you *did* leave, think of the effect on the children and on your career. In this community, it wouldn't work at all."

4

# Separation/Divorce: Will Your Friends Deliver—or Desert You?

M<small>Y HUSBAND GOT</small> married because it was expected of him and yet he was pulled by the desire to come and go as he pleased and not have to spend time with the kids," Shelly recalls. "Alcoholism was also involved. I grew up in a town in Massachusetts where the men went to bars to drink after work. My husband did, too. It was the normal routine and I thought when we dated, 'That's what everyone does. It's all part of being young. When you get older you establish responsibility and change.' It never changed."

At times Shelly's husband would try hard to be a family man. Instead of working late at his auto repair shop and going out drinking with the boys, he'd come home, play with the kids, help with homework and around the house. Then the old familiar routine would start all over again. "Deep down, I knew from the beginning that he didn't want to be married," says Shelly. "He said I was too dependent on him. He told me I was too fat. When I became pregnant with our third child, he didn't want the baby. But I was determined to make this work and be the kind of wife he wanted."

They went for counseling. After a few sessions, he announced over coffee that he wanted a trial separation. "I felt so frightened," Shelly recalls. But she was determined that one more time she was going to fix it. "I accepted that it was my fault and I needed to change. I had no idea he already had someone else."

At the time, Shelly was thirty-nine, had three children, ages two to fifteen, and a part-time job. "It was a nightmare. My life was crumbling and I felt like I was going crazy."

Little help came from her family. Her mother couldn't accept the idea of divorce, and remained on the sidelines. Her two brothers never called. She felt deserted and cheated. "I couldn't have pulled through without my friend Rose. I was obsessed with what was happening. I felt I had to tell my story one more time, one more time. Rose always listened and never judged."

When your marriage breaks up, your entire world comes crashing down, especially if you're the one who's been left and you have children to worry about. You're living a major life crisis—and it can feel like the end of the world. It is, in a way. It's the end of one world—the one you inhabited as someone's wife.

Getting through the process of separation and divorce takes a superhuman effort. The trauma is devastating; your whole idea of what it is to be a family is crushed. But nobody (including the person who leaves) gets off scot-free. It is friends who are turned to most often to help people cope and make the enormous adjustments required at this time. Women I've talked to confirm: There's nothing more powerful than peer support. There are, however, threats to that support that you need to recognize. A marital breakup can also disrupt friendships.

## THE DYNAMICS OF SEPARATION
## AND DIVORCE

Whether you're the leaver or the left, the support of friends is so important because you're assaulted by change and stress. The most difficult emotional time is usually the preamble—the struggle to decide whether to stay or split—and separation itself, according to Constance Ahrons, Ph.D., associate director of the Marriage and Family Therapy Program at the University of Southern California at Los Angeles and author of *The Good Divorce.* "Some people get divorced quickly after separation; for others, it takes years. 'Separation' is really what most people label their divorce. They usually don't remember the date of their legal divorce but they'll tell you what day they (or their spouse) left home," she explains.

The entire process is charged with ambiguity, ambivalence, anguish, confusion, and other emotions. If you've been left, there's enormous anger and feelings of rejection. Self-esteem plummets. Leavers tend to experience profound guilt. A thirty-year-old lawyer who opted out of a five-year marriage remembers, "I felt like such a failure. I'd always succeeded at everything—in school, at work. I was a problem solver. If something was wrong, you worked at it. But nothing I did worked to repair my marriage."

Because divorce remains a stigma in our society (even today), deep feelings of shame are common, causing some partners to hide their marital difficulties from others. One wife couldn't confide in her best friend. "I didn't tell her I was separated at first because I couldn't bear the disappointment I knew she'd feel in me. In her eyes I could do no wrong. She always told me I was the best, the smartest, the most capable, the funniest. She looked up to me. How could I tell her my marriage had collapsed?"

Loss—what the toll of a marital breakup is all about—is pervasive. And it is emotional, financial, and social. You lose your husband, your role and identity as a wife, and the status and respect that goes with it. Like Shelly, who had to sell her house within a year of her divorce, you may lose your home and have to move. That means losing your neighborhood, your daily routine, even your Monday night aerobics class (it's now too far away) and your regular PTA meeting, if your children have to change schools.

Odds are you lose economic security. Even your job may become a casualty if you have to move in with your family in another locale. In some cases you may lose custody of your children.

Although the degree of stress depends on the circumstances and varies from person to person, it's serious enough to put both spouses at risk for developing emotional and physical ailments. Health problems frequently show up a year or two following separation.

## WHERE FRIENDS COME IN

Friends are the most important source of support for women during the first six months of a marital breakup. They can act as sounding boards and confidants during the preseparation period. Once one of you leaves, they can give you perspective, provide empathy, and help fill up your life. Shelly's rock was Rose, who had been divorced from an alcoholic husband a few years earlier. Shelly had minimized the impact of alcohol on her marriage, but Rose encouraged her to go to Al-Anon. "She went along with me, educated me to what alcohol does to the mind, and gave examples from her own life. It meant everything to me when she'd confirm, 'Shelly, it's not you—it's the alcoholism.' The blame and anger my husband heaped on me (and my willingness to absorb it all) is a typical pattern of an alcoholic and codependent. The codependent assumes responsibility and says, 'It must be me. I'm not capable of having a male-female relationship.' "

Rose validated Shelly, supporting her emotionally throughout a three-year-long separation, then a divorce. "She never minimized anything I did, or said 'You shouldn't feel that way.' She'd tell me, 'You have a right to be mad.' "

Rose also shared Shelly's values and provided intellectual stimulation. "She made me think. She had interests. She took courses in politics and history and discussed them with me. When I decided to go back to school for my master's degree, I could share with her what I learned. It made everything so much more meaningful."

Friends play other roles, as well. A forty-nine-year-old Los Angeles footwear buyer feels that her married friends saved her life when her architect husband walked out of a twelve-year-long second marriage—at about the same time her older brother succumbed to a stroke, a college friend committed suicide, and her sister-in-law, with whom she had become very close, had her second mastectomy. "This was all in the space of six months," she explains. "I thought the losses were never going to end. There I was—my children lived in other states and the only people around were my friends.

"One never wanted me to be alone on the weekend. Every Saturday or Sunday she'd call and say, 'What are you doing? I don't want you to be by yourself.' When I was really in the depths, the other one would say, 'I'm coming over to stay with you.' My husband had never wanted me to see my friends—we saw only his. Fortunately, I stayed in touch with these two women in spite of him."

Friends also help ease you through transitions like holidays and birthdays. One woman can't imagine what her first Christmas would have been like without her couple friends down the street. "My kids were with their father. Tom and Muriel invited me and my father, who is a widower, for the day. Since then, I've spent many Thanksgivings and other occasions with them."

They also supported her children, particularly her youngest, who was devastated by the split. Often kids can talk to a family friend about their feelings, especially if the person can be a good listener and not take the side of either parent. Later, her friends slowed her down when she started thinking about remarrying, helping her to be much more thoughtful in her mate selection the next time round. "They were very cautious, urging me to look out and be careful," she says.

Because you have specific needs at this time, different kinds of friends serve different functions. You need:

## Divorced friends

Married friends who stick by you are invaluable, yet they aren't enough. They can feel sorry but they can't help you through it. Shelly's were supportive, but none of them had personally experienced divorce. It was hard for them to appreciate the emotional roller coaster involved, the feelings of being out of control, the rage and the guilt.

"I was hurting and they'd come back with pep talks like 'It will be fine' when I wanted to hear 'He's a son of a bitch.' They didn't understand the process I was going through. It seemed to them it takes two people to make a marriage. I'd say, 'It only takes one to break it up.' They still cared for me, but were limited in what they could do for me. I thought, 'I've gotta find somebody who will speak my language because I'm going crazy here.'"

It was then that she thought of Rose, a former coworker she had always liked but had lost touch with. Rose understood. "When she told me her own woes, I could relate to them," says Shelly.

## Playmate friends

Single friends can share activities and leisure hours, so you don't feel so lonely and can get some of your intimacy needs met. We live in a couples society and it can be uncomfortable when you're the odd woman. Weekend evenings are the traditional time for couples—and the time when divorced people feel most in need of company.

Playmate friends help structure your time and can accompany you to the movies and other events. They can also introduce you to activities you wouldn't have known about on your own, such as a class or a club.

## Feisty friends

Feisty friends encourage you to get what you're entitled to. Says a separated wife, "One friend of mine is really strong and gutsy, the kind of person you wouldn't want to oppose in a fight. She's been very important in encouraging me to insist on decent child support. She helps me to set limits and not just be 'nicey-wifey.' "

Other friends have also mobilized her. When her husband moved in with another woman who worked for him in his office equipment business, it was very hard at first to accept what was happening. She just couldn't believe it. "In some ways their outrage helped move me from my 'deer in the headlights' stance. They said, 'Forget it. It's over.' This was his second affair. If it was the first time, you figure the marriage might make it through, but I don't think it can survive two betrayals. These friends handled details for me and sort of took care of me."

## Spiritual friends

These are the really deep friends who have something wise to say. If you're lucky enough to have one, he or she can be a great comfort. The woman above told me, "A friend of mine is very religious and I always had trouble relating to it. She had considered becoming a minister. But her spiritual perspective was very effective. She said things like 'There's a reason for this. There's something else out there for you to do, whether it involves another man or some purpose in your life. I think in the long run it's going to be the best thing that ever happened to you and that God is really working in your life.' That was a good thing to hear—the idea that there's a reason for this happening, a sense that it is karma."

## Friends who provide information

Some friends can steer you to sources of help, such as job contacts or support groups, and sometimes they provide material assistance themselves. One wife got legal information from a lawyer friend. "I know I was taking advantage of her expertise, but we're good friends and I felt I could reciprocate in other ways," she told me.

A Virginia computer consultant needed advice on how to tell her children about an impending separation. She called someone who was divorced with two children and who belongs to the same women's business organization. "I felt okay about contacting her because she isn't a client. I didn't have to worry that she might think my work would be affected by all the upset. First I talked about the organization's business; then I said, 'I really don't know your personal situation and you don't need to get into it if you don't want, but how did you tell your own children?' She was very nice about it and extremely helpful."

A client took the initiative and called *her*. "She said, 'I understand you're having personal problems.' And I thought, 'Oh no, she's going to be worried about the work getting out.' But the first thing she said was 'I just want you to know that underneath this calm collected person is a once divorced lady.' I knew her as someone in a happy marriage with a child; I didn't know she'd been married before. She started laughing and said, 'I know you need support. If you're a little late on deadlines, don't worry about it.' "

Also helpful: a friend of the opposite sex. For Shelly, developing a friendship with a man was like learning to walk again. She'd never had platonic friends in high school or college. Her only picture of the male perspective was filtered through her spouse. "I had to see men as friends," she explains, "because when you add romance, it changes the whole relationship. I learned I was capable of having an intelligent conversation with a man; he was a peer, not just a date and not an authority figure. I found that men suffer, too, from divorce and that my ex-husband was also hurting; he just showed it differently. It was so helpful. I can tell my friend Charley anything."

## FRIENDSHIP LOSSES AND STRAINS

All the heartwarming stories, however, can't paper over the fact that separation and divorce alter friendships—and some relationships don't survive the aftershocks. The changes in your marital (and probably financial) status, plus other external tensions, can drive wedges between you and some friends. It may be harder to get together. Dinners, movies, fitness classes, baby-sitters, all are expensive.

Many people also don't know how to respond when a marriage goes sour, since there are no norms for this situation. Even before an actual split, some married friends may withdraw from couples socializing if sparks fly openly between you and your partner when you're all out together. Some people *prefer* to socialize with other pairs and may fade away now that you're not part of a twosome anymore. If you had mainly couples (rather than individual) friendships, *your* friendship patterns change. It's common to distance yourself from some couples, especially if the friendship is associated with your husband's business or recreational activities.

If you've been divorced before, friends may not have as much empathy for what you're going through, feeling it's not as hard on you the second time around. Their reactions tend to depend on the length of the marriage and how long ago the last divorce took place. There's less empathy, too, if there are no children. The feeling is that it's easier.

Even if you've wed just once, you may be viewed as a threat by some married women—and fair game by some married men. Abby, a forty-year-old auditor, was propositioned at the first sign that her marriage was in trouble. Her best friend's husband informed her, "If you ever break up, I want to see you."

Abby recalls, "I was so raw and vulnerable and he came in and put his arm around me inappropriately. He danced too close. I said, 'Stop it, that's disgusting. Joan is my best friend.' I've never told her to this day."

She watched a similar incident happen to someone else. Her friend's spouse, a womanizer, left six months after Abby's husband did. "Mine was the upstanding conservative guy and when he left, her husband thought that gave him permission to do it, too. My friend, a total wreck by now, stayed at my house for a while. A neighbor's husband came over and asked her, 'Do you want to go nude swimming with me?' "

Less lurid but even more hurtful is being dropped by your close friends. Abby's husband, a real estate broker, moved out after a long period of upheaval; he was involved with another woman, a client. When Abby started to tell people he was gone, among the first ones she called was a couple she'd known since her newlywed days. Very close as couples, they often vacationed together in Maine. "She was aghast at the news," says Abby, "but after I told her, I never heard from her again. I finally called her and asked what was going on. She told me, 'I don't think it's healthy for me to get sucked into your marital problems.' I felt so furious and hurt. I couldn't believe it."

After a two-year separation—and therapy—Abby and her husband reconciled. The woman who had dropped Abby wanted to rekindle the couples' relationship. "My first reaction was to remember all the good times. I was glad to see her. Then I asked her, 'Why did you abandon me?' " To her shock, the real reason went back over twenty years. The woman had been depressed after the birth of her second baby and felt that Abby hadn't been there for her then. She had held this grudge all those years.

"I told her, 'I was twenty years old and didn't know anything about feelings or depression. I felt so scared. I didn't know what to do. I didn't know how to listen." Abby had been supportive in other important ways. "But all she did was point and blame. I knew I would never see her again."

## DISAPPROVING FRIENDS

If you're the leaver—and your husband didn't beat you (or drink or gamble away the kids' college money)—you may pay a big price. Friends may make a moral judgment that you've made a bad decision and feel you've taken the easy way out. Bernice lost her whole support system when she left her husband of fifteen years and relinquished custody of her seven-year-old daughter. Everyone around her felt threatened.

"I left because I felt comatose," she says. "I was a thirty-four-year-old New Jersey hospital administrator who hated her job—and I was getting nothing out of being married. It was so boring. There was no real intimacy. My husband was very regimented. He wanted to plan everything. We had to know where he would pee on vacation. There was no spontaneity, no excitement. We had to go out with other couples every Saturday night to do things I didn't want to do. He also could be verbally abusive and sarcastic. I felt that I hadn't smiled in twelve years."

When she left, her husband wanted custody of their daughter. He had no interests or friends of his own—and no life without the child. Since he kept the condo and Bernice had no family to baby-sit, she agreed. "I'd never found me. It was my chance."

The impact on her friendships was swift and dramatic. Her married friends disappeared. They were raised with the philosophy "What is life without a man?" and she was saying "I'm happy on my own."

Says Bernice, "I left my job and got into the publishing business. It flipped them out when I talked about loving my life. My closest friend since I was three years old forbade his wife to speak to me. The last time I called, he said, 'You can't talk to her for more than a few minutes. This is a very happily married couple.' "

The biggest disappointments were her sister and her best friend. The latter, who lives in California, never called to see whether Bernice was okay. "I was afraid to ask," the friend admitted later. "It was awful that you got divorced. I thought, 'How could she leave? She doesn't have a terrible marriage. Why isn't she sticking it out?' "

Says Bernice, "She couldn't say that, so she ignored me. I felt so sad and hurt that she didn't know what friendship was all about. It wasn't until she went through her own divorce later that she understood.

"Today she and my sister apologize. They tell me, 'We just figured you're strong; you'll handle it. You'll survive without my support.' "

The mythology is that men leave women, but in general it's women who leave men, according to Dr. Ahrons. "Women initiate more divorces than men do. They're less satisfied with marriage and expect more. Women want men to be their best friends. They expect them to be emotional and understanding—all the things men often cannot be to women.

"It's always been this way. What's changed is that women are economically independent today. They have the means to get out if they choose to. There's more freedom for them in the world and it's more acceptable," she says.

One Atlanta woman left her husband after twenty years because they had nothing in common—not a basic philosophy, not a lifestyle or friends. "I didn't like him. I'm a social-worker type and he was a financial consultant who had a lot of highs and lows. He had tons of energy and people were drawn to him. He was an extrovert who needed people around. If you're married to someone like that, you have to take care of these people, feed them, remember their names. It didn't leave much time for my own friends. It kept eating away at me. It took me so long to leave because finances are a big thing."

When she made her decision, some friends were sources of comfort. "They said they understood, so I didn't think my feelings were unique and isolated. Some shared their own experiences. One said to me, 'You feel the terrible pain in your stomach one month for every year of marriage.' It made me feel that I could do it. It wouldn't last forever. I thought, 'This is manageable.' "

But she lost one set of good friends in the process. They chose to side with her ex-spouse—and it hurt. When her husband needed someone to talk to about *her,* he found the wife a willing confidante. "She excluded me and talked only to my husband about the marriage. I think she liked the attention—or maybe she thought I was all wrong."

## WELL-MEANING FRIENDS WITH TOXIC IMPACT

Other friends may stand by you, yet make your adjustment to separation or divorce more, rather than less, difficult. They include:

1. *Downers.*

Says marriage therapist Patricia Hudson, Ph.D., "You have to be careful about contacting people who keep saying, 'Oh this is so awful, this is so awful.' These are people who are chronically depressed. They're very hard on you. That doesn't mean you should drop all your negative friends, but be very much aware of them."

2. *Angry friends.*

There can be a downside to feisty people. Someone who is mad at your mate during the divorce process—who feels your split is almost a violation of her, too—can upset you unnecessarily. One woman told me, "I occasionally think I'd better not call one friend because she's going to go ballistic when she hears what my ex-husband wants to do. I don't want to get that riled."

3. *Bitter friends.*

Bitter friends are negative influences because they're stuck in resentment about what happened to them and haven't moved on. Or, they have avoided processing it. They don't learn how to discover themselves—who they really are and what their strengths are. They may drag you down to their level.

4. *Pushers*.

People who try to immediately push you into a relationship will say, "What will help you through this is to find somebody." It's a common response if you've been left, since your self-esteem at that time is so low, you may feel you have to prove you can still attract men. The best thing for self-esteem is a new relationship, but it isn't a good idea to start one too soon. If you get into a relationship too fast, you can repeat the same mistakes unless you take the time to find out what happened and come to terms with your own part in the breakup.

5. *Projectors*.

Some people project their own issues on you, which can add to the ripple effect of breaking up. One wife received a lecture from a male friend: "The problem is that your parents paid for too much stuff and he could never feel like the man in the family."

In fact, that was something the couple never had conflict about. Says the wife, "There *were* other things we clearly had problems with, but that wasn't one of them. It was a totally rude thing to do. He did it because he wanted to save the marriage, but it was wrong."

6. *Friends who help you remain a victim*.

They don't help you solve your own problems. They tell you what to do rather than drawing out *your* plan—or just allowing you to have the feelings you have and express them in a healthy manner (assuming they don't include stalking your ex). The way to stop being a victim is to find your own solutions and realize that you have the ability to survive on your own.

## LIFE DOES GO ON

Separation and divorce rank just behind the death of a spouse in the magnitude of stress caused by life events. Friends are crucial resources prior to a split, as well as when people actually move apart and the news becomes public. They help make life manageable, especially since it may be wiser not to involve some family members in all the details. Parents or siblings may still have a close relationship with the spouse because of the children—or for themselves.

But breakups also place new demands on friendship, as we've seen. Although you can't avoid all disappointments, good friends stand fast. And as Shelly and others have discovered, new ones are out there if you look for them.

## SURVIVING SEPARATION AND DIVORCE— WITH FRIENDS

1. *Establish support and emergency networks.*

They're essential to help you hang on when you think you're falling apart and to remind you that you're stronger than you thought. Knowing that she needed friends who had been through the same experience, Shelly asked herself, "Who do I know who's divorced?" Rose came to mind and Shelly looked her up. They connected instantly.

You also need single friends pretty quickly to share activities with; otherwise you'll have nothing to do on Friday and Saturday nights. One way to meet people is to identify an interest and follow it. After her long second marriage broke up, one woman had to find out what she wanted to do because she'd been doing what someone else wanted for so long. She started hiking and seeing offbeat movies and she met other women through these activities. "I wouldn't say they're enduring friends," she comments, "but they're fun. Some of them are younger than I am."

Shelly joined a local support group for separated or divorced men and women. Such groups help by giving you the opportunity to meet new people, hear yourself talk, and realize that you're not the only one who has problems and that yours aren't nearly as bad as some others'. A support program can also take you through the grieving process, which is healing. When your marriage breaks up, you grieve not only for the loss of your daily life but also the loss of being a couple and the death of your dreams: "Next year, we're going to go on a cruise." "When we retire we're going to buy this gorgeous home in Florida." All the things the two of you were going to do are now gone. Support programs help you look at trust and forgiveness of yourself for your part in this. Some resources include:

New Beginnings, Inc.
2711 Covered Wagon Way
Olney, MD 20832
*Phone:* 301-924-4101
*Fax:* 301-924-4102
     Support groups for separated and divorced men and women in Maryland, Virginia, and Washington, D.C.; devoted to easing the transition from being one half of a couple to becoming a whole person.

DivorceCare
P.O. Box 1739
Wake Forest, NC 27588
*Phone:* 1-800-489-7778
*Fax:* 919-562-2114
*E-mail address:* 72603.1341@compuserve.com
*Web site:* http://www.divorcecare.com
     Nondenominational support groups in 4,500 churches and counseling centers throughout the country.

North American Conference of Separated and
Divorced Catholics
P.O. Box 1301
La Grande, OR 97850
*Phone:* 541-893-6089
*Fax:* 541-893-6089*51

*E-mail address:* nacsdc@pdx.oneworld

Support groups and other resources for separated and divorced Catholic men and women.

For resources geared specifically to single parents, see Parents Without Partners and other organizations listed in Chapter 5.

### 2. *Expect to lose some friendships.*

Some friendships will probably fold after divorce, especially if your husband's friends and their wives were your social circle. It's often hard for couples friends to relate to you, particularly if you're the one who initiated the separation. Sometimes another woman in a bad marriage may envy your decision to get out. Sometimes a husband says to a wife, "I don't want you to be friends with Jane now that she's single and running around."

In her book *Just Friends: The Role of Friendship in Our Lives,* psychotherapist Lillian B. Rubin also observes that married couples will spend time with a single man because wives tend to participate in the conversation or listen to it. An unattached woman is a different commodity. It's common for husbands to roll their eyes at women's discussions (or feel left out of them)— or to take them over. As a result, women alone may not be included in the first place—or they themselves will opt out.

Your own behavior, however, can increase your isolation. Sometimes women don't confide in their friends because they want to maintain their self-image or because they don't want to burden others. Shelly admits, "Lots of times I found it difficult to ask for help. I'm the one who helps other people. I'm the do-gooder. To ask someone else is to admit, 'Hey, I have needs, too.' It's a lot easier to meet others' needs—you don't have to look at yourself."

### 3. *Beware of being too dependent too long.*

The divorcing person has to do much more talking, even repeating herself, for a while and most other people get bored with it. I always admired my friend Martha's solution. From the day she and her husband split, she consciously decided not to over-burden any one friend. She spread her need around. She'd call me one day, someone else the next. "I didn't want to become a drag and a drain," she says. It really worked. She got the help she needed, given most willingly. Nobody felt oppressed.

If you get mired in neediness and complaining, friends can turn off. In his book *Friendship—Developing a Sociological Perspective,* sociologist Graham Allan, Ph.D., notes that it's the exception, not the rule, that friends stick by you through thick and thin over the long haul. Friends tend to give short-term help.

One wife finally had to wean a divorced friend who's still whining after two years. Her husband perceives it as complaining and gets furious when the friend keeps calling. Long-term im-balance in a close relationship does not work.

*4. Pick (and handle) confidants very carefully.*

Everyone needs a place to vent some of the anger at a spouse—and you don't want to explode to your children, putting them in loyalty conflicts. Talking to a good friend during the separation (or preseparation) period is the perfect answer. Unfortunately, however, it can sometimes backfire. An advertising copywriter told me sadly, "My friend called and asked me to meet her for dinner, where she proceeded to pour out all the details of her unhappy marriage. She talked for three hours about how she had to leave her husband. Ever since, she has refused to take my calls. She cut me off completely. It's the end of a nice friendship."

This is not a unique experience and is sometimes referred to as "truth dumping." It often happens on airplanes. People will talk to a total stranger and reveal things they've never told any-body else. But it's done with the comfort and knowledge that they'll never see each other again.

In cases like the one the copywriter experienced, someone will reveal a lot of secrets and then not go through with the split. There's a sense of embarrassment and shame. The friend-ship often breaks down at that stage. You've said all these ter-rible things, then decided that you're going to stay after all.

How do you retract all the private stories you've told? Every time you have contact with the person, you also have to confront your feelings.

Or a wife may expose her husband's affairs to a best friend. Then she and her husband get back together and the husband says, "You mean Josie knows all this about me?" He's embarrassed and wants nothing to do with the friend. The wife pulls away, too.

Knowing full well that you'll be saying some awful things about your spouse and marriage, a good friend will realize that you can change your mind, despite all the bitter words you spewed—and understand why. To protect the friendship, talk about it with her. It's important to say "Look, I thought lots about this and I feel differently now" or "I've decided to make a compromise—and it's better to stay with him for the sake of the kids" (or whatever).

An explanation smooths out a difficult situation, includes the friend, and avoids a potential rift.

If you want to vent, "He's a bastard," pick someone who doesn't know your husband. That's the safest person to talk to—and the one who can safely agree with you.

5. *Watch out for other toxic situations.*

Don't call chronically depressed friends if you're down yourself. You don't want to reinforce negativity. As noted, know when not to call feisty friends, too. They can encourage you to take a more aggressive stance when it isn't in your best interests. For example, if you want to try to cooperate with your spouse, no matter what, for the sake of the children, it isn't always helpful to talk to a friend who says "The best thing you can do is never talk to that creep again."

Realize, too, that you adjust and accommodate in relationships—and often you lose yourself in a marriage. You want to go into a new relationship as a person confident of who you are and what your gifts are. Take the time and opportunity to discover that. Abby chose not to date because she wanted to get stronger and know herself before she got involved again.

## HOW TO BE A GOOD FRIEND TO SOMEONE DURING SEPARATION AND DIVORCE

Because there are no rules for separation and divorce, nobody is sure how to behave. We often don't understand what friends are going through and may withhold support or give the wrong kind. Here's how to do your best for a friend:

1. *Don't take too strong a stance in separation.*

Separation may or may not mean the end of a marriage. It can also be a time-out to cool down. Some couples, like Abby and her husband, reconcile. If a friend is separated, don't make the mistake of saying "Ugh, good!" If they get back together, they may both be mad at you. Once someone knows you don't approve of her husband, it can affect your friendship. Instead, say something like "I'm sure you'll make a good decision. Take your time. Don't rush."

2. *Keep your balance.*

If you're friendly with both partners, stay neutral. When you give a party, don't invite just one. Let them know they are both invited and leave it to them to decide whether they're comfortable attending. Be prepared, however, to learn that one or both may resent your neutrality.

A separated wife felt angry when a friend told her in advance that she planned to invite her husband and his girlfriend to social events at her house in the future if they remained together. "Why tell me? I didn't ask. Why rub it in?" says the wife. On the other hand, letting her know seems to be a kind and wise thing to do.

3. *Listen.*

Be a good sounding board. The most supportive friends, says Abby, were those who listened and said, "I hear you. If you need me, call at any hour." Or, "Take baby steps—one step at a time to get yourself stronger."

If you're friendly with both spouses, you can listen without adding to or reinforcing negatives. You may have to set boundaries, however, and possibly say, "I'm friends with Joe, too, and I don't want to hear that. It makes it very difficult to be with both of you."

Incidentally, if a friend confides in you about an impending separation, then changes her mind about leaving, don't say, "Gee, but last week you said you were going to dump him." You don't want to fuel the embarrassment that can hurt a friendship.

4. *Understand what the person is going through.*

When an old friend recently told me how she felt when her husband left years ago, I was astonished. I'd had no idea. It sounded like post-traumatic stress disorder. "I felt like I was sleepwalking," she said. "One minute I was cooking hamburger for his supper and he suddenly said, 'I hate the way you make hamburgers.' Since I'm not a great cook, I let it go. But then he said, 'I hate your hamburger. I'm leaving.' He got up and walked out the door. That was it. For the next week, I'd walk my son to the school bus every morning, put him on it, then go back to the house and dust. I'd stand at the window and dust the sills. Just dusting."

I know now that her reaction was a common one. But if she'd told me then, I probably wouldn't have understood. If you haven't been through the process yourself, it can be helpful to get a book on divorce to try to understand what's happening. What may seem to you to be strange or crazy behavior is often normal for a divorcing person. One day she loves him, next day she hates him—normal ambivalence. An extended period of grieving is normal, too. People often say, "Oh my God, how come it's three months and she's still crying?" Three months is actually pretty routine for tears.

Says Dr. Ahrons, "We often don't allow divorced people to grieve, especially when it's the leaver. But there are a tremendous number of losses. The best thing you can do is help the friend understand, 'You'll get through it.' "

5. *Know when to speak up.*

If a friend is still acting like a victim after two years, she is probably stuck, and it may be tied to depression. But she may also be stuck in a role—playing the scorned person who is hurt— which brings some goodies in the form of attention from others. You can help by saying, "You know, it's been two years. You really need to get out of this. It's ruining your life. Maybe it's time to get some professional help." You can also add, "We have to have a relationship about other things besides talking about John all the time."

One woman was more direct with: "Enough. I don't want to hear any more bitching about him." The friend was taken aback and hurt at first. She felt, "Doesn't she understand?" But later she said, "Thank you." It was time to move on.

Early on in the process you can also say to a distraught friend, "I understand that it's probably going to be like this on and off for the next few months—and I'll be there for you. You're going to survive; everybody does." That's a way to offer normalizing acceptance of where the friend is.

Be careful about sharing your experiences, however. If you're divorced yourself, you can say, "I felt ———— ," but realize that your friend may not feel exactly the same way you did. People can react to situations differently. You may have a friend who is still tied up in rage and anger. One of the best things you can do is help the person or couple de-escalate.

Realize, too, that giving advice all the time perpetuates victim behavior. Positive friends help the person to problem-solve, saying things like, "What do you think you could have done differently?" Or "What do you think the options are here?"

6. *Talk smart to children.*

If you want to help a friend's kids, realize that it's important to stay neutral toward both parents. A child won't talk to you if she knows you don't like her dad. Depending on the age of the child, you can take him or her out alone and give a friend some relief. Then you might ask, "How's it going? It's a hard time for you." This provides the opportunity to talk because there are things the child can't say to the parents.

# 5

# Friends Can Make You a Better Mom (Most of the Time)

I BECAME PREGNANT WITH my first child at age thirty-one, *before* it became fashionable to postpone parenthood. Although I'd baby-sat for children in my neighborhood since the age of ten, virtually all of my charges were toddlers or older. I felt totally inadequate handling and caring for a tiny baby. The idea of giving an infant a bath seemed particularly daunting: What if the baby wriggled? What if my soapy hands slipped?

I sighed with relief when I spotted an ad in the newspaper for a Red Cross course in baby care, signing up immediately. In the back of my mind, too, was the desire to meet other pregnant women. I needed to connect with women who shared my fears and joy and anticipation, who could get as excited about the subject of cribs and layettes and baby carriages as I did. When I arrived at the class, I found a candidate in the back row—a tall lady with glasses and light brown hair. She flashed me a quick smile, immediately making me feel more comfortable. Her eyes sparkled with intelligence and there was something about her face and body language that radiated energy. As the instructor demonstrated diapering techniques on a plastic doll, the woman and

I traded comments. "I feel like an idiot," I whispered. "I don't know what to do with an infant."

"Me, too," she laughed. We bonded instantly. When I returned the next week, I looked for her. We sat together again, went out for coffee, and discovered how much we had in common. Both of us were older than the rest of the class; we were both career women—she was a fashion consultant. Both of us came from ethnic backgrounds in Brooklyn (she was Italian, I Jewish). We shared the same streetwise sensibility—the same dark sense of humor. We both lived in Manhattan apartments and were married to struggling professionals. We fancied ourselves sophisticates, loved theater and museums, and valued education. Ambitious and full of high hopes and dreams, we had big plans for our babies. We were determined to be the very best parents, the most informed, providing our children with every emotional and intellectual advantage.

We read all the baby books, researched the best crib mobiles. City girls, we wanted to bring up our children in Manhattan— an unheard-of choice among people I knew at the time. *They* all moved to suburbia. But we were goers and doers; the idea of walking our strollers through Central Park seemed wildly exciting. Our due dates fell within six weeks of each other. Later, even our husbands hit it off. We were a match.

We both had boys. Janet's Sean arrived a month before my son. I lived downtown, she was uptown, but we visited back and forth and talked on the phone several times a week, trading information, experiences, and play-by-play descriptions of our infants' progress. When our babies were four months old, we vacationed together in the Adirondacks in adjoining motel rooms. What joy to have someone to share it all with!

Janet was my first parenting friend. And although she moved to Atlanta a year later and we gradually became twice-a-year-phone-call friends, her impact on me was enormous.

At the same time, I had also sought the company of other mothers in my neighborhood. I had waited a long time for motherhood and arranged my job schedule to work three days a week at first. I *loved* sitting in the park on a bench, chatting with other mothers about baby food and sleep patterns. I became part of a quartet who regularly met at the playground. They told me which pediatricians were most desirable, what to do if your baby had an ear infection, where to get the best buys on baby clothes. They became my parenting pipeline. How could I possibly have survived without them?

How, indeed, when parenthood is mined with insecurities. "My daughter is in the terrible two's. This is what happened this morning. Do you think I handled it okay?" "Am I going back to work too soon (or not soon enough)?" "Will my son *ever* be toilet trained (or learn to read)?" It means everything to have friends you can call for answers, advice, and understanding through all the stages of your child's life. Friends empower you and boost your satisfaction as a parent. They strengthen your skills and build your confidence. Their support has grown more crucial than ever.

Women face complicated choices, pressures, and guilts that didn't exist a few decades ago. Approximately 72 percent of mothers with children under eighteen (and almost 59 percent of those with children under one year) are in the workforce* today, stretching themselves between job demands outside the home and family demands within. National Institute of Mental Health research shows that women are particularly vulnerable to chronic stress because of their multiple roles. They need support in juggling tasks and reinforcement that they're doing a good job at home. But grandparents, aunts, uncles (or even concerned neighbors) are often unavailable to lend a helping hand. If you're a single parent, the stresses are only magnified.

For these reasons, friends have assumed a new function for women who are mothers. They're a basic support system, sources of know-how, assistance, and connection that used to be taken for granted. Utilizing friends wisely and well makes parenting a whole lot easier—and can make you a more effective mom.

*Employed or seeking jobs

## THE FUNCTIONS OF FRIENDS

"A depressed mood can affect how you interact with children and the ability to parent. So support that makes women feel more optimistic helps parenting—and the ability to look out for and interact spontaneously with kids," says Sharon Telleen, Ph.D., research associate professor, School of Public Health, University of Illinois at Chicago.

For a new mother, friends are especially vital because a baby isolates you from your previous life, even if you take only a brief maternity leave. Many women don't know what to expect. "When you want to drive a car, you get lessons. When you want to get married, you get a license and maybe precounseling as well. But people have children without knowing what they're getting into. Women have no idea that once a baby arrives you can no longer soak in the tub or chat on the phone or spend half a day at the mall whenever you choose. Your whole life revolves entirely around this helpless creature you've created. It's a stunning awareness. For information and sharing experiences, women rely on books and peers," says Janet Weisberg, Ph.D., a New York psychologist who specializes in children and families.

Friends who are moms calm you down, reassure you that others have the same worries and concerns, and offer creative input. Without them, you can feel alone. For Ruby, twenty-five, the adjustment to motherhood became that much more difficult when her husband's career needs dictated a move to Chicago. Leaving her friends, family, and job behind, she found herself alone day after day with her two-month-old daughter. Immersed in his new job, her husband had little time to spend with her. She hungered for conversation, for someone to talk to about whether she'd had a good or a bad day, as well as what was and wasn't normal for an infant. She wanted companionship. Stay-at-home moms need playmates, just as children do.

"I didn't know a single soul. I felt so desperate for company, I'd strike up conversations with virtually any adult who crossed my path. I talked to shoppers on line at the supermarket. I spoke to clerks at the drugstore and the post office. I tried to meet other mothers when I took the baby to the park," she recalls.

Through one of them, Ruby heard about a support group for stay-at-home moms. It changed her life. "What an experience it was to meet other women and discover that they were going through the same struggles and triumphs I was. We could compare notes on everything from teething to toys—and brainstorm ideas. I've made close friends and the group even has a babysitting co-op. I can go to a doctor's appointment *alone*. It's made me a better, happier mom," she says.

Formal groups (like Ruby's) tend to provide information and, sometimes, concrete assistance. Although emotional support usually comes from informal networks of friends and family with whom you're in daily contact, individual relationships often develop from a mothers group.

In or out of a group, friends assume added significance for older mothers. When I gave birth, no one I knew had ever had a first baby so late in life. Today, many women become first-time parents in their late thirties or in their forties—and face unique challenges. At that age, you may no longer have your own mother around for nurturing support or to baby-sit. It's also possible to take your child to a playgroup and have people ask, "Is this your grandchild?" A friend in the same situation who understands what you're going through—how awkward and strange and tentative you feel—is a blessing.

For working moms, connections with other women in the same situation can be lifesaving. They're even more in need of information because they have less time to do research and experiment on their own. A thirty-year-old accountant on maternity leave feels truly fortunate that two close friends had babies at about the same time she did. "It's so wonderful to be able to call and say, 'Is your baby doing this, too?' " she says. She has also met other new moms in her neighborhood.

But a money manager with a school-age child laments how hard it is to see her friends who are parents. "In my case they work full-time, too, so time is scarce, and they don't live around the corner. I try to read parenting magazines and research parenting on-line. I talk to the parents of my daughter's classmates. But it's a few minutes in the morning when I drop her off on my way to work. The baby-sitter picks her up."

This woman does have her husband to turn to. But if you're a single parent, you're usually on your own. In such cases, it can seem as though the camaraderie of others in the same situation protects your sanity. Some single parents raise their children virtually together. They may live in the same neighborhood, get together, say, every Friday night and for holidays, and look out for each other. One will say, "I'm going to the supermarket. Can I pick up anything for you?" They don't necessarily share their deepest feelings and have the most intimate relationships, but their friendships are a very important part of their lives.

After her divorce, Carla needed all the help she could get when she moved from Ohio to Pittsburgh to be near her parents. She found a job and an apartment and settled her five-year-old daughter and nine-year-old son in school. Her parents agreed to pick up her kids after school. Everything fell into place—until the calls from school began. Her daughter was throwing up every day in kindergarten. Medical examinations found no physical explanation. "She was afraid we wouldn't go get her," says Carla.

This reaction was not so unusual. After a divorce, kids experience the same separation anxiety their parents do. They're afraid they'll be left, too, and they constantly need reassurance. There are so many changes, especially if they must go to a different school and leave their friends behind. Fortunately, Carla had joined Parents Without Partners, the national organization that serves as a support group for single parents and their children. Other members gave her the information and advice she needed. "They suggested I put her in counseling. I did—and it made a tremendous difference. It helped her understand I wasn't going anywhere."

For any mom, friends also come in handy for practical help. Can I borrow an egg? Can I borrow cab fare? That old neighborliness reduces stress and enhances a woman's sense of well-being. So does help with child care. Baby-sitting swaps with other parents not only give you a break, they deepen your friendships and are good for your marriage, too, according to Stacey Oliker, Ph.D., author of *Best Friends and Marriage*. She found that child-care exchanges reduced wives' demands on mates for help with the kids—demands that caused marital conflict.

Says Oliker, "Women who exchanged child care also felt it was a bonding exchange. They saw giving another person the one you love most to care for as a huge act of trust. It increased intimacy. When one new mother had to stay in the hospital after her baby was born, her friend took the newborn home. The best friend of a mother who worked full-time picked up her child at school every day."

## FRIENDS AND OLDER CHILDREN

As children grow older, it continues to be important to have other adults around to share the experiences, joys, and heartaches of parenting—and to advise on increasingly complex issues. How do you handle a dispute with a teacher? How do you deal with bullying—or with a peer-group problem in the neighborhood? Friends can help.

Monitoring children's behavior is important, especially during adolescence. Are they buying beer at the grocery? Are they smoking? You can ask a friend, "Would you keep an eye out?" Friends who also become your kid's friends make parenting easier. The last person teens may want to talk to is Mom, but another adult can make a major impact and become a positive influence.

Friends whose children are older than yours are sources of wisdom and expertise. One mother recalls ongoing fights with her kids over issues like clothes and curfews: "My friend Esther never told me what to do. She helped by telling me what *she* did. She'd say, 'When your son comes down the stairs in green hair and you think 'Why me?' it isn't easy. But I bit my tongue, kept quiet, and he's turned out all right.' I'd start laughing and it would put everything into perspective."

When her children left for college, this mother had a hard time accepting that they were on their own and that she couldn't expect a call every night. "Esther told me, 'You've given them a good foundation, the right values and morals. Now you have to trust and let them grow and develop.' It helped me let go."

Male friends play an important role, too, especially for single moms. Male members of Parents Without Partners helped Carla's son learn to play baseball and other sports, activities he couldn't participate in with his faraway father. When her son started talking back to her, one of the men told him, "You have to treat your mother with respect." It shocked her son. Says Carla, "He backed off. He was willing to listen to a man."

If you're lucky, some friends who aren't parents (often singles) may become part of your family—pseudo-aunts and -uncles who enjoy standing in when necessary and who add dimension to your home life. One working mother will never forget the single friend who insisted on baby-sitting every Wednesday night for her two young children, allowing her to have a night out alone with her husband. "She gave the kids dinner and played with them. They loved it, she loved it, we loved it. It was a wonderful gift."

Sometimes a friend touches your child's life and your own in a very special way. For Katya, such a friend enhanced the miracle of motherhood at forty-four. Always a free spirit who felt that marriage would fence her in, Katya had never expected to settle down. An adventure lover, she served in the Peace Corps, traveled the world, and treasured her freedom. Then at forty, to her shock, she found herself living with a man she dearly loved and thinking, "I'm really ready. I can sink my roots down with this person and live the fullest life I can imagine."

When she became pregnant a few years later, she could hardly believe it was happening. "Here I had this marvelous husband and it was like proving to myself and the whole world that I was truly a woman. I was carrying on the tradition of giving birth and it was really the right thing to do," she says.

Katya's network of women friends, who had been her family through her adult years and who were always in touch, shared her bliss. But it was Ann, her friend since high school and her deepest soul mate, who stood out.

Ann's only child had died of a brain tumor at the age of eight. Katya's child became a sort of substitute. Says Katya, "It was amazing that I had a baby after all those years, and Ann loved my daughter. There was an intensity to it—my child being almost like her child. She had kept her son's little rocking chair and she gave it to my daughter. She gave her his doll, which was unusual. Not every boy would have been interested in dolls but he was a very artistic child, full of love and life. So my daughter inherited these things, and when Ann came to visit, she'd give her toys and play with her in the bathtub."

Now this chair sits on the front porch of her daughter's playhouse. Recently Katya asked her, "Can you still fit in this chair?" "Yes," said her daughter with conviction. She sat down and began to rock, then looked up and conveyed wordlessly, "I will always fit in this chair."

Says Katya, "Today I have this wonderful child. There is a sense of continuity. Ann sends my daughter gifts, talks to her on the phone, and plays with her when they're together. Ann has been with me through it all and now she's there for my daughter."

## THE POTENTIAL FOR PROBLEMS

When friends have such a profound effect on your life as a parent, can there possibly be a downside? The reality is that, as in all relationships, tensions and conflicts can erupt. Emotions and differences can get in the way of cooperation and mutual support. For your child's well-being as well as your own, it helps to understand what's going on.

## How motherhood alters friendships

When you become a parent, all of your previous relationships change. It's harder to conduct the relationship if you and a friend are in different life stages, and strains may appear in some friendships, at least at first. Tensions can begin the moment you become pregnant. You drift from those who don't have kids and don't want to hear about your morning sickness and weight gain to those who do.

After the baby arrives, it's normal to lose contact with some friends and become less close to others. Either they're not comfortable and don't want to talk about kids—or you're not comfortable. If they want children but can't have them, for example, you may feel as if you're rubbing a raw wound when you rhapsodize about *your* baby.

Says Jean Kunhardt, M.A., coauthor of *A Mother's Circle: Wisdom and Reassurance from Other Mothers on Your First Year with Baby,* who leads parenting groups at the Soho Parenting Center in New York City, "It's not unusual to take maternity leave and find that your close friends on the job withdraw. They may not visit—or make only a token appearance and give you the impression they don't want to be around. Friends in your work life often are competitive if you're doing something different."

Regardless of what choice people make—to have a baby or not—they feel ambivalence; each tries to justify her own choice. Many women who want to be pregnant themselves feel envy. Others may find it difficult to understand what a huge change in your life having a baby makes. They may feel jealous of the time and attention a child claims—and the fact that when you do get together, it's clear they've dropped a few notches in your list of priorities.

Says Kunhardt, "There's something so intensely intimate about the mother-child connection. If it's going well, it's a tie that excludes others and stirs feelings in others." She sees many moms so disappointed in the negative reactions of friends that they start to cry when they talk about it. Some moms tell her, "I feel I have to pretend I'm not in love with my baby," or "I have to make a date and go out with my friend when I want to be with my baby and my friend. But she doesn't want that."

## Friction between working and stay-at-home moms

Friendships with singles and childless couples aren't the only ones affected by your motherhood. Strains turn up in relationships with other parents, too. A forty-year-old corporate vice president finds that other mothers at her five-year-old daughter's school resent her demanding career.

"One of the most explosive underlying tensions with women now that you're older is 'How much do you work?' I feel pressure on me because I put in long hours. It's not just nine to five. At my age, a lot of women have made other choices. They either stop working, take care of the kids, and devote themselves to their husband's career. Or they have come up with a way to work two or three days a week. They're jealous that I have a serious career. I'll never forget the mother who dabbled in real estate and asked me, 'Do you really have to work so much?' I felt angry at the attitude. I don't particularly want what they're doing."

Her use of the word "particularly" is significant, reflecting the fact that few women feel totally confident in their decision, whatever it is. For their part, stay-at-home mothers tend to feel out of the loop and unrecognized. In one group, moms talk about feeling undervalued and unappreciated by family and society in general and about the dreaded question "What do you do all day?" Or what to write under the heading "Occupation." There's a tendency for each group to band together. "Often there is tension between the two. It's almost two camps," says Jean Kunhardt.

## Strains about reciprocation

Exchanges of child care, while they are a great help and an excellent way to allow parents time out, can also be a burden. There are expectations and obligations created by exchanges that can cause stress and conflict.

Dr. Oliker found that women don't want to impose on each other's time or ask too much of friends. Those who can afford a baby-sitter usually hire one. They prefer it because exchange increases the likelihood they'll be asked to reciprocate in a way (or at a time) they can't or don't want to. If you have to take care of someone else's child during dinner or on Sunday, the exchange may impinge on family time and can create conflict with your spouse.

Dr. Telleen believes it's the conditions of the exchange that count. "There's something bonding about watching someone else's child or taking your turn in a car pool. You may chuckle about car pool antics and it's nice to see these people around years later," she says. But if you're in a child-care exchange that requires you to go out at night and baby-sit in someone else's house (as opposed to daytime sitting, when the children can come to you)—leaving your own children home with your spouse—you may feel that is too stressful, especially if you're working. If you occasionally get a call saying, "I can't find anyone for this mother. Can you rearrange your schedule to do it?," you may desperately look for a neighborhood teen you can pay so you don't have to do it.

On the other hand, a daytime neighborhood baby-sitting co-op where the kids are all the same age and you take care of four children once a week for four hours in return for a break on other days, may be well worth it. Says Dr. Telleen, "You have to handle reciprocity with great care. What makes a group work is planned, reliable, predictable reciprocity where everyone truly shares. You know when your turn is and have agreed to it."

Another frequent issue is resentment felt by stay-at-home moms because they're always driving everyone else's children around. Employed moms need help with carpooling, but if you made a sacrifice to stay home, you might resent it when one of them calls upon you to pick her child up. The thinking goes, "If I'm making less income, why should I subsidize her?"

Issues can get even dicier if a *close* friend participates in your car pool. Expectations can spill over between the dual roles, creating tensions. People rely on a car pool. If your friend says at the last minute "I have to go out of town on business" (without arranging for a substitute), that's a problem. She assumes that because you're her friend, you'll understand—and you want to. But such behavior also violates the rules of the car pool and inconveniences you.

## Different parenting styles

Different values or strategies in child rearing may also get in the way of your friendship. Are you keeping close tabs on nutrition, while your friend serves her kids chocolate doughnuts for breakfast? Do her kids watch TV after school, while yours are restricted to weekends only? What happens when your children visit her house and then start to resent your rules?

Friends may also disapprove of the behavior of each other's children. If one mother can't stand children who won't share and another won't tolerate shoving, it may be hard to spend time together.

"If you can't work those things out (and friends don't think they should impose their values on friends), it really does put distance between you. Some friendships eventually wither," says Dr. Oliker.

I remember dreading the visits of some of my children's playmates, especially Timmy, who not only often behaved like a wolf child, but whose parents were my friends. The problem was my need to please. Because my mother was always mean to my friends when I was a child—and thought nothing of yelling at (and therefore humiliating) me in front of them for transgressions like failing to dust my room—I thought twice about inviting them home rather than risk my mother's being provoked by their behavior. When I became an adult, I decided that things would be different for *my* children and went out of my way to be gracious to their guests. I wound up tolerating behavior I didn't approve of and feeling like a prisoner in my own house. It took me a long time to learn that setting rules is not the same as being inhospitable.

Another issue that can chill relationships: differences of opinion on when it is and isn't appropriate to include kids in adult social activities. Some working parents, strapped for time with their children, want to bring them along to Saturday night get-togethers. But that doesn't mean everyone else likes the idea. As wonderful as it is to find friends who can talk about the joys and challenges of parenthood, it's also refreshing to talk to someone about something other than parenting and children. Stories abound of couples who have dropped friends who never get a baby-sitter. An attorney told me, "My husband and I would go out for dinner with these people and you couldn't have an adult conversation. The focus was on the children at the table. They talked about nothing else but their twins. We were so turned off, we finally stopped seeing them."

## Jealousy, envy, and rivalries

Perhaps because motherhood is surrounded by so many performance expectations, issues of competition, jealousy, and envy are rarely acknowledged, let alone discussed. We're supposed to be perfect mothers who raise perfect children and possess the patience and grace of a saint. Yet the reality is, everybody feels competitive about their children (or jealous of someone else's) at one time or another. If such feelings aren't understood and dealt with, they can divide friends. Says psychoanalyst Roberta Satow, Ph.D., "People are sometimes even more competitive about their kids than themselves. Parents invest their hopes and dreams and fantasies in their kids. They want them to achieve and reflect on them. If someone else says, 'Isn't *my* kid wonderful?' it can stir competitive feelings."

It can start when one baby walks or talks earlier than the other. Says Jean Kunhardt, "Some comparing is natural. At work you're assessed all the time and you assess others; in school you have grades; but in parenting, there's often no way to determine how you're doing as a parent except to look at how your child seems to be. Frequently parents look at the books for guidelines on what to expect, but they also look at friends' children. Mothers tend to get anxious if a baby rolls over in the group. Some think, 'Why doesn't my baby do that?' " But development is quirky and sporadic. It's important to accept your child's own pace and rate.

Children, like the rest of us, also have their strengths and weaknesses—which can be hard for parents to accept. One woman, whose daughter was a poor student, was horrified at the idea that she had a child who wasn't at the head of the class. It had to do with competition with her brother and her need for her child to be as bright as his.

I confess that I've always been a competitive mother, very ambitious for my children to achieve. When my son didn't get into the college I had my heart set on, I felt crushed. I felt rejected. It reflected on me. (Interestingly, my husband, who is a competitive businessman, shared none of my feelings and was perfectly happy with the school our son ultimately attended.) When the son of a very nice casual friend was accepted by the school that rejected my son, I felt so jealous. I threw tantrums in my head. Why her child and not my wonderful son? I felt ashamed to feel that way. It wasn't pretty, but there it was. It was a painful struggle to live with my feelings. Every time I saw my friend, my jealousy stirred. It took two years—and the realization that my son was happy at his school—before I could lay my feelings to rest.

Says Dr. Satow, "Everybody is competitive. If your child didn't get into a selective nursery school, of course you'll feel competitive if you wanted it. That's normal. The same thing can happen when your friend's child gets 1500 on the SATs and yours does not."

On the other hand, some people constantly tell you how advanced their child is and make you crazy because *they're* always competing. They can become really toxic because we start to worry that our child isn't doing as well as our neighbor's is.

*Envy* is much more toxic than competitiveness and jealousy because it makes you want to spoil things. It's "I hope the other person falls on his face," or "I wish your daughter hadn't been chosen as a cheerleader." And that's the stuff of ending relationships.

Some people enjoy having their child envied. Their child's accomplishments are their own badge of honor. They may brag about the child, which can stir feelings of anger and upset in the listener. Why? Because bragging is not the same as expressing pride. It implies superiority over others.

## Unasked-for advice

Moms can feel that they're magnets for advice. It's annoying because it can really be masked criticism (or it can sound like criticism). A school principal who is an older mother recalls a friend who kept giving her unsolicited advice on subjects like spoiling the baby and getting the baby to sleep: "If I was twenty-five, it might not have bothered me, but I was forty-five, a professional, and a new mother. I didn't appreciate it. I felt supercompetent. What I wanted was not advice but someone to come in and cook dinner, because I had so much juggling to do. I needed loving support and the friends I kept gave this. Toxic friends gave advice I didn't want. They use you for their ends, not yours."

Advice can backfire even when given out of genuine concern. A travel agent watched a friend literally collapse from exhaustion because she insisted on ferrying her son back and forth an hour each way to a special music program every day—while also working a full-time job. The program was superb, but the price was the mother's health.

The friend spoke up and told her, "What are you doing? It's crazy!" To her amazement, the mother was offended. "It was a toxic situation. I meant it in a caring way but her reaction was 'Who are you to tell me how to raise my child?' It almost destroyed our friendship, but I wouldn't let it go. I explained I wasn't trying to tell her what to do; I was concerned and worried that she was in over her head. I kept saying, 'Look, it's not worth the friendship.' Since then, I bite my tongue."

## Let's be friends

Motherhood revolutionizes your life. It changes your relationships; it changes your needs. It's a boon to have friends who enrich your experience, educate and guide you, calm your doubts, and act as reality checks. But there are friends who empower you as a parent—and those who reinforce your insecurities. Instead of buffering stress, they boost it. There are also situations that can pull friends apart and reduce support. It's important to understand what's going on, help each other, and be alert to our own potentially negative behavior. In times like these, we need compassion for ourselves and others.

## MAKE FRIENDSHIPS WORK FOR YOU

1. *Check the kind of support you have.*

Do you have someone you can confide in, borrow a cup of sugar or get advice from, relax or laugh or swap child care with? Has anyone told you that you're a good mother? Positive feedback like that is important to your sense of well-being. You need supportive peer relationships in all these areas. If something's missing, it's time to mobilize.

But this is not always easy. One mother describes her attempts to make friends as "worse than dating." She comments, "It's hard when you're an adult. You have to be motivated and take the initiative. You're exposing yourself—and you have to overcome the fear of rejection. I'd call people for the first time and ask them to come over, and think, 'What if they say no? Or if they say yes, will they really want to?' I also didn't click with every woman I met or have enough in common." Yet she *did* connect. It takes effort.

Be consciously open and talk to everyone—at your child's school, in the supermarket, at the PTA, in baby-sitting co-ops, while volunteering to bake cupcakes at kids' soccer games.

Support groups are available to help. Women used to gather in the park, talk, and watch each other's kids while someone ran an errand. It was built into the daily routine. "But when women went to work in huge numbers in the '70s, it tore apart these informal network systems and destroyed the support. It took time to adjust to this change, and formal support groups grew out of it," says Dr. Telleen.

Some possibilities include:

FEMALE (Formerly Employed Mothers At The Leading Edge)
P.O. Box 31
Elmhurst, IL 60126
*Phone:* 1-800-223-9399
*Web site:* http://www.femalehome.org

Offers support to mothers making the transition from full-time employment to caring for their children at home—and connects moms with each other. After one woman gave birth to her second child, FEMALE members took turns bringing meals to her home for five nights. "I never felt so supported. Just getting the visitors made me feel good." About 150 chapters, which meet twice monthly for discussion, are available throughout the country. There are also two regular weekly chats at its Web site.

Parents Without Partners
401 North Michigan Avenue
Chicago, IL 60611
*Phone:* 1-800-637-7974.
*E-mail address:* pwp@sba.com
*Web site:* http://www.parentswithoutpartners.org
   Offers support meetings, social and recreational activities for single parents and their children through approximately 400 chapters in the United States and Canada. Its Web site includes chat rooms for members.

The Single Parents Association
4727 E. Bell Road, Suite 45-209
Phoenix, AZ 85032
*Phone:* 1-800-704-2102 (outside Arizona)
   602-788-5511 (Arizona)
*E-mail address:* ed@singleparents.org
*Web site:* http://www.singleparents.org
   Offers educational opportunities, including support groups, and activities for parents and kids. There are chapters in eleven cities, including three local chapters in Phoenix, Arizona.

PRISM
1111 Tower Road
Schaumburg, IL 60173
*Phone:* 1-800-266-3206
*Web site:* http://www.info@rainbows.org
   Offers support groups in churches, synagogues, and schools for single parents and stepparents; over 6,000 chapters world-wide.

You can also meet people *and* learn at parenting groups (including some specifically for older parents) and classes at Ys, hospitals, and community colleges. Referrals may be available though your local library, family physician or pediatrician, or organizations like the United Way. Ask around.

"There's something about these formal meetings that increases mothers' feelings of support and reduces stress," says Dr. Telleen.

2. *Realize there is no one "right" choice.*

Appreciate that the choice to stay home or go to work is a difficult one. We all need to listen to and support each other and realize that everyone is afraid of being judged. Whatever you do, the question is, "Does it work for you and your child?" Every case is different. If you're comfortable staying home and your child is fine, that's great. But if you're unhappy, that's a problem. If you go to work in tears every morning and come home exhausted, that's also a problem. Some people find new careers. They develop home businesses or choose part-time work.

If someone challenges your choice and you respond badly, it's usually because you have a certain amount of guilt about it. If you feel ambivalent, maybe you need to look at what you're doing and what "musts" or "shoulds" you're following. Then make a decision based on what's best for you.

3. *Work out terms of reciprocation.*

The best way to avoid conflicts about baby-sitting is to establish these guidelines ahead of time: the best times to be asked, when you are most likely to say yes at a moment's notice, and the worst times to be asked, when you are most likely to say no. Then nobody has to feel burdened or guilty or hesitate to participate in a swap for fear of being trapped by a sense of obligation.

Talk about issues of inequality in carpooling, too, instead of harboring anger. You can say, "Look, we have to do this in a way that's fair. It's true that working parents don't have as much time to drive the kids around, but maybe the baby-sitter can do some dropping off." One mom who works full-time picks up kids at soccer practices after 6 P.M. and on weekends. If she can't make it, her father, who is retired, fills in. She also does weekend sleepovers.

Consider alternatives as well. If you regularly ask another

mom to pick up your child, you might pay her for her services (depending on the relationship, of course). Or give a gift. Or offer expertise in return—plant her vegetable garden or set up her new computer.

### 4. *Check with others about bringing the kids.*

The situation has to be child-appropriate and other people's feelings must be considered. Ask the other couple how they feel about including children. In one case, parents who did not do this brought a toddler along for what turned out to be a very disruptive dinner with adult friends. The parents constantly popped up and ran after the child. Their friends, who wanted a relaxing evening away from *their* children, never went out with them again.

Conversely, if you want no-children-allowed time, set boundaries and speak up, rather than sit there and stew. You can say, "We didn't consider bringing our kids along, so we hope you won't be offended, but let's make it another time," or "See if you can find a baby-sitter." It can be hard for some of us to say that. We're *supposed* to be accommodating, especially when children are involved. But the alternative is to spoil your own good time and possibly jeopardize what might otherwise be a strong and supportive friendship.

### 5. *Deal with competition, jealousy, envy, bragging.*

Understand differences in child development. Kids develop in their own way. Every child is wonderful, each has strengths— and ideally we should appreciate them and not compare, say experts. The kid who walks and talks (or has a vocabulary of twenty words) at one year of age isn't necessarily going to surpass your child down the road. Walking or talking early aren't necessarily the most important thing. Some kids have wonderful personalities; some are good at sports. Look at your child's best traits; encourage and be happy with them.

It's often easier said than done, however. Says Dr. Satow, "It's helpful to realize that the reason you're so upset has to do with your feelings about *yourself*—that you feel not smart enough (or popular enough or athletic enough) and need your child to be so that *you'll* feel good. When you realize that you're using your child for a function for yourself, it starts being helpful. *Then* you can think, 'Well he's not an *A* student, but he's got a great personality.' "

We're all human with human frailties. It's okay to say "I feel jealous." Then you don't have to cover it up and the other person doesn't have to feel defensive. Jealousy is part of any relationship and it's going to happen sometimes, especially if your children are the same age. It's easier not to compare them if there's an age gap.

We're all capable of envy, but that doesn't mean we can't get past it. What if your child is the object of your friend's envy? One way to handle it is to talk about successes, but share your child's vulnerabilities, too (such as extreme shyness)—and/or stress her child's strengths, as in "Your Linda is so good with people. She has so many friends."

How much bragging bothers you depends on how you feel about your own child. If you feel fine, you can just sit there and smile as the person goes on and on about hers. If bragging makes you angry, you might want to deal with it with the friend, depending on how close and important the relationship is to you. If your son is having trouble in school, while another parent constantly extols her child's *A*'s, one response might be: "I appreciate the fact that Louis is smart and I'm happy for you, but it's painful for me when you brag about it. It ignores my trouble with John's learning disability." You're not saying "Don't talk about your child"—just "Don't brag."

6. *Set rules in your own house.*

Tell your friends' children (and any other kids), "In my house there are certain rules. If you can't play by those rules, you can't play here." Of course, if the child breaks your rules while the parent is there, it's very awkward. We all have different intolerances; she may not be sensitized to the things that bother you.

She may not care much that her child roughhouses, for example, or whether he or she takes turns or says please and thank you.

In cases where extreme diplomacy is necessary, you can say something sugary, in an exaggerated way, to the child, like "Sweetheart, in our house we don't let the sink overflow. I'd rather you didn't play in the bathroom"—so the parent knows how you feel, but you can't be accused of being inhospitable. My own rule is *never* to criticize a child to the parent.

Let's say you don't allow cursing in the house and your kids come home from your friend's house using unacceptable language. You can say, "That language isn't allowed in this house." What if your son retorts, "But Johnny talks like that"? Simply reply that there are rules for the bus and for school, and kids have to learn that there are rules for your house that may differ from the rules at other houses.

Distinguish, too, between a different environment for your child—and a dangerous one. Does a friend's parenting style (such as little supervision) or rules put your child in an unhealthy situation? If so, remove your child. On the other hand, a chocolate bar once in a while isn't harmful.

7. *Handle advice giving (and getting).*

There are consequences if you give unsolicited advice. When you're on the outside looking in, it's easy to see things that you feel aren't appropriate and think it's your duty as a friend to speak up. But even with the best of intentions, doing so can cause a rift.

Sometimes, however, a parent needs a friend to tell her about a problem—something she's unaware of (or has underestimated or denied). In such cases it's right to say, "I'm concerned about Joey. I think he has a problem with hitting and I think you should do something." But always talk positively about the child. We tend to think of our children as extensions of ourselves. If you criticize or dislike my child, then you're criticizing or disliking me. You may feel, "Your Susie is a monster," but if you say that to Susie's mom, chances are the relationship between you will never be the same (and it may be over).

If you receive unwelcome advice, Jean Kunhardt's suggestion may help. She tells mothers, "You are your baby's expert. If you feel things are going fine, put on some armor."

Or you can say what you're really feeling, such as "It's disturbing when you give me this advice. I prefer that you just tell me how you're feeling toward me." You can add, "What I really need is someone to make dinner." Your friend is not a mind reader. Chances are she means well and would be happy to help you if you directly stated your need. It's unfortunate if you feel really angry and don't discuss it. You can lose great friendships, and they're hard to come by.

8. *Be sensitive to friends without children.*

If a friend resents that you have eyes only for your baby, you don't have to make believe you're *not* preoccupied. Reassure someone you're close to, "I'll be back. For a while I *am* preoccupied, especially for the first three to six months of the baby's life. But it doesn't mean I care about you less." If the friend can join in, great. If not, sometimes relationships have to go on hold for a while. It's easier to do that if the other person doesn't feel you've totally rejected her.

Realize, too, that some people make a conscious choice not to have children. One woman told me, "Couples who have kids are suspicious of those who don't. They think something is wrong with you—that you *can't* have one or that your marriage is in trouble. You're looked at as a misfit. Or they assume you hate kids. I *like* children; I just don't want any of my own. I adore them for a weekend, but not twenty-four hours a day. It really annoys me when people say 'You'd make a great mother—how come you don't have kids?' Everybody thinks it's their business. It cuts to the bone of your sexuality and feelings about being a woman."

## 6

# Friends and the Single Life: Uppers and Downers—Why You Must Know the Difference

How do you feel when you've just sold everything you own at a garage sale and are about to move halfway across the country to launch a new life—alone? "Like a kid jumping off a high diving board for the first time," says Denise, recalling her leap into the unknown. "All I had left were my clothes and my cat."

It had taken Denise two years to find the courage to leave Iowa. When she finally made the decision to move to Los Angeles, she was taking the biggest risk of her life.

"I sublet an apartment sight unseen through a friend of a friend. But I had no job yet—just leads—and the only person I knew well on the Coast was my old college roommate.

"Everyone thought I was crazy. 'How can you live there?' they kept saying. 'Riots and crime and all that smog.'

"Well, I'd had it with cornfields, frankly. I was a thirty-four-year-old medical technician, still single, and there was nothing going on in my life. Out there were all those possibilities," says Denise.

Only her best friend, Lila, understood, even though she had the most to lose. "I was leaving, probably for good. Yet she knew I'd never be happy unless I got it out of my system. She never tried to stop me; she just let it happen and said, 'I know this is important to you. Go for it!' She even borrowed a van to drive me out to the airport," says Denise.

When the time came to go, Denise was close to hysteria. Her heart pounded the wall of her chest and sweat soaked her palms. She had a case of diarrhea.

As they headed for the highway, she announced, "I don't feel good. I'm having a gigantic anxiety attack." Lila stared ahead, silent. Then she whispered, "You're going to be okay."

When Denise blurted, "I'm going to throw up," Lila stayed calm. "If you feel *that* bad, get in the back and lie down," she replied.

It took an hour to get to the airport and Lila talked her through it like an air traffic controller guiding in a crippled craft. Always in command, Lila soothed and cooled her down. "At times I thought, 'She's not being very sympathetic.' But the fact was, she did what she had to do to get me there."

A few years later, when Denise decided to move to London for a time, Lila broke down and told her how much it hurt that she was leaving again. "I count on you. It's too hard to call you there," she said. "California is bad enough, but this is too much."

"It was the first time I realized how much I meant to her, that she really needed me," recalls Denise. "While I was away, I made an extra effort to call her more often."

The capacity to free the other person to expand and grow is a hallmark of deep friendship. Good friends do that for each other—and when you're single and on your own, such support from someone who puts your welfare before her own emotional comfort is very special. Friends nourish in other ways as well. They're number one (along with family) in making life meaningful for single women, according to research coauthored by family therapist Karen Gail Lewis, Ed.D.

Friends often become your near and dear, replacing spouses and family ties you don't have. They're people to turn to when you're in trouble—and have fun with when you're not. Largely because friends are nonjudgmental and are available in a way family isn't, they help make it possible to feel good about yourself. The challenge is to build a community of friends as satisfying as possible—and invest in it.

## SINGLES' FRIENDSHIP NEEDS

Postponement of marriage and the prevalence of divorce have fueled an explosion of singles of both sexes in the United States since the 1970s. Friends have assumed a powerful new role, helping many women get their needs met without marriage. They can help you feel settled and whole if you don't while you're looking for a mate (if you want one). When Dr. Lewis interviewed always-single and single-again (divorced or widowed) women ages thirty to sixty-five, she found that their friends served these functions:

1. *Companionship.*

Friends are an antidote to loneliness and isolation, providing a sense of connection. We all need someone with whom to share what's going on in our lives.

2. *Social life.*

Whether you're going to the movies, bowling, to brunch on Sunday, or on vacation, your life is enriched when you have people you can count on to do things with. Women have always focused on the opposite sex to share activities, but most single women wind up doing things with other single women. Even if they have men in their lives, they still need women friends.

3. *Intimacy.*

Most single women think in terms of intimacy with men. Studies show, however, that women turn to other women to confide in and get their emotional needs met.

4. *Daily contact.*

Friends provide the continuity of contact with one person that married women take for granted. Daily contact is more than security; it's regularity and a point of reference for your life. There's something missing without it.

5. *Touch.*

Physical contact, including hugs and cuddles, is life-affirming. Explains Dr. Lewis, "Therapists have known for years that without touch, infants fail to thrive and become depressed. They may actually die. Nobody has thought about the implications for singles who have no touch in their lives. One woman in her mid-sixties said that when the doorman at her condo helped her out of a taxi it was the first time someone had touched her in a week. A widow said she intentionally bumps into men because she misses the male touch so much."

6. *Family.*

Due to our increased mobility, kinship ties have changed for many of us. Friends offer the same sense of connection that family provides. They serve as family for holidays when you live far away from relatives (or have none). As one woman puts it, "I come from a large clan, but everyone is strewn through many states and I have no relationship at all with my parents. Friends are a layer in my life that approximates family."

There are different kinds of friendship families. Some are emotionally close; others are more utilitarian, perhaps living in the same neighborhood, getting together socially, and helping each other in ways like watering the plants when someone is out of town on a business trip.

The implications of being single (and the functions of friends) shift, depending on the stage of life you're in. In their book *Single in a Married World*, Natalie Schwartzberg, Kathy Berliner, and Demaris Jacob trace the course of singlehood through the life cycle. In your twenties, friends help you grow up and separate from your family, acting as an accepting support system. They share similar career and dating interests and provide a way (other than getting married) to learn about intimacy.

In their thirties, as women begin to see singlehood as a long-term or permanent state of affairs, career and love life tend to prevail. Friends add balance, so the focus isn't exclusively on work and finding a mate. By the forties, companionship is the top priority if you're not in a committed relationship. After fifty comes the fear of finding yourself sick and alone. Friends represent a safety net.

There is no one profile of a single woman, however. According to Dr. Lewis, there are more than thirty types, whose lifestyles and needs vary when you consider factors such as whether the person has been married before, has children, is in a committed relationship. Life is very different for a twenty-six-year-old with a boyfriend and a roommate than for someone like Ava, twenty-nine, a single working mom who has been divorced for ten years and who works full-time as an office manager in Wisconsin. Ava depends on her sister and on a circle of friends, including one from high school who has two children and lives an hour away. "We don't see each other often. We talk on the phone maybe once a month, which isn't enough. But I can call her anytime, no matter what, and she's always there for me," says Ava.

Ava has also been a member of her local volunteer ambulance corps for the last six years. A fringe benefit is a nucleus of buddies—other volunteers. They go to the movies together or out for a beer and some laughs. But there is also much more. A male volunteer has virtually adopted her son, playing sports with him and attending all his soccer games. Ambulance corps friends have come through now that Ava's father is battling leukemia. They pull her weight, without asking.

"I'm on ambulance duty once a week from 7 P.M. to 4 A.M. and every fourth Sunday. They know what to do when I feel overwhelmed. It's 'She's been there for us, let's work together. If I take ten hours of her duty, that's ten hours' less pressure on her.' They also understand if I say 'Let's get together Friday' and then I can't make it at the last minute because my dad's back in the hospital.

"My friends also pick up when I get depressed that I don't have the money to take my son on a trip—or that I don't have someone to tell me he loves me. When we talk about my ex-boyfriend, they'll say, 'I can't believe he let you go. What a jerk.' "

If you're in a committed relationship, friends provide stimulation and entertainment and save you from complete reliance on your lover for all your emotional needs. One thirty-two-year-old insurance executive observes, "My friends are *more* important now that I have a boyfriend. I feel it's very dangerous to put myself totally in the hands of one person.

"Part of the reason I won't live with anyone is that it's important to me to have my own nest. I have many interests that have nothing to do with my romantic relationship. I paint, I sing, I have a great job. I make big money and meet lots of people. Then I have a core group of friends that is my true support system," she says.

Such networks are even more essential if you're *not* in a committed relationship. One woman, forty, told me, "Everyone wants to share their life, have a context, and feel somebody knows when they don't come home at night. I have a large group of casual friends and then I'm close to three or four people. If I want to share news or something's bothering me, I call a friend I've known and trusted for fifteen years. Neither of us have biological sisters, so we're it for each other."

It adds up to a community, which includes people you can rely on, identify with, trust, and feel safe getting feedback from. Being part of a community helps you find your own identity *before* you marry, providing a reality check on how you behave and affect others. It ensures you're not operating in isolation.

Greta dropped all her friends when she got married. Now fifty-five and divorced, she fiercely appreciates them. "A man had better be more terrific than my friends, but I think that's hard to do. Even my married friends say they have more fun with their girlfriends. We really have a bang-up time."

They also stick around. Says Greta, "My great fear in life is being incapacitated and alone. It scares the hell out of me to have no family physically close. But my friends were really there for me when I had a breast biopsy and was in denial. One of them went with me. Others called and asked if they could come along. They didn't want me to be by myself. I understand how lucky I am and I'm very grateful for that. I'd never move because now I understand how devastating it would be to be far from my friends."

## Platonic friends fill a gap

Friendships with the opposite sex can also be extremely satisfying. Ava's ambulance corps colleague Mack has become a brother to her and her son. "He's the only man ever in my son's life that I'm not afraid will leave. I've never had a male friend like him."

He's there for life's little emergencies, too. When Ava was sick with bronchitis and desperately wanted a can of soup and her can opener wouldn't work, Mack was the friend she thought to call. They talk on the phone several times a week, sharing laughs and horror stories. Since he lives nearby, they regularly walk around the local lake together to exercise and relax.

Even a former boyfriend can make a terrific buddy, especially if he's a nice guy who doesn't threaten your lover. A forty-three-year-old sales manager considers her ex her best friend. She's known him for twenty years and sees him every week. "My significant other is my partner, but we're too different to be soul mates. There are times when he's not the best person to talk to about an emotional issue and he's the last one I'd turn to for business advice.

"In contrast, Frank is handy, smart about money, emotionally savvy, and anticipates my needs in a lot of ways," she says. She'll never forget one experience they shared a few years ago: the

Thanksgiving they spent with her failing mother. "We knew she was dying and she said, 'I love lobster.' So we forgot about turkey and brought over three four-pounders instead. It was just us— and we pigged out. What a special time."

By the next Thanksgiving her mother had died—and so had his brother. "It was the end of both our families and we felt pretty sad. He loves the shore, so he made two giant turkey legs, sweet potatoes, and brussels sprouts. He took chilled Champagne and his mother's good dishes—and we drove to the beach for a tailgate Thanksgiving. We watched the waves and toasted his brother and my mother. That's how friends become your family."

An actress's favorite male friend, a sculptor, fills her need for intellectual stimulation. "I love to go to museums with him because he's very bright and knows so much more about art history than I do. I love to suck that knowledge out. I can also share with him, 'Hey, I'm going through a rough time in my relationship with my mom,' because he has the same issues with his mother that I do with mine."

How about sexual undertones? How can you get closer to a guy when you want friendship, not romance? If you have to ask the question, there's already a sexual undercurrent, according to Dr. Lewis. Sex doesn't get in the way for some people, but we all have different emotional and biological drives; sometimes a platonic relationship is not possible. One woman finds any man she really enjoys being with sexually appealing. "If he's not emotionally attractive, I don't want to be with him, period. So I rarely have single male friends. I can have married ones, however, because the boundaries are there."

If you do have a male friend without all the sexual complications, you have the potential for a wonderful friendship. Men offer a unique perspective. A bear hug from a male pal or his arm on your shoulder adds touch to your life. It's great to have a male body sitting across the table from you. Often men are also able to be more emotionally giving when they feel real safety—when you're involved with someone else (or not romantically interested in them).

The issue of sex takes care of itself when he's gay. A journalist met her friend Gary when she wanted to rent part of her house to help defray expenses. Referred by a neighbor, he became her housemate.

"We're different and we're the same, so it's easy to talk. He's bright, fun, smart, loyal, and there's no jealousy. He has his own companion. He reads, loves theater, and he got me actively involved in community affairs. He cares about me. When he felt that my stockbroker bombed, he sent me to his."

Gary even kept her boyfriend under surveillance when she went to Europe for weeks on assignment. The man (who had talked about marriage) started dating other women, leading Gary to behave protectively. He called him to ask, "Are you getting married, or what?" Obviously it was the right question. The couple wed shortly after her return.

## FACING TENSIONS

Friends help you lead a fulfilling single life and enhance your personal and professional growth. But sometimes life changes and other factors get in the way of relationships.

### When friends marry or commit

When one of you gets married or finds a serious boyfriend, the change in status can test the relationship. There are demands for support that you may not be able to meet, even when both of you mean well. One person becomes less accessible and free to socialize, due to added obligations and responsibilities.

Many married people also gravitate toward other couples as they look for friends who share their experience and validate their life choice. Because there is no recognized social role for a single woman, she may be excluded from gatherings like dinner parties. Some hostesses are embarrassed for her that she doesn't have a partner. There's an awkwardness that doesn't exist for an extra man.

Loretta's relationship with her best friend of thirty years hit a low point when the friend decided to remarry. Says Loretta, forty-five, a Denver divorcée, "She's a wonderful loyal friend, but she became so wrapped up in her engagement and so self-absorbed that she wasn't there for me. At one point I had major surgery and really needed hand-holding. I was terrified I was going to die. But she lives a thousand miles away and didn't call for three days; she was busy. When my significant other dumped me, I called crying hysterically. She didn't get back to me for a week. I felt I had no support from her that whole year."

The friend's wedding was the worst time. Loretta had planned to go but felt so stressed by a series of work crises that she told her sister, "I'd give anything to skip it." The reply was "Then why are you going? Put yourself first." Loretta canceled her plane reservation and left a message on her friend's machine that she was sick.

When the bride called from her honeymoon to find out what had happened, Loretta blamed the flu. Six months later she visited and decided they had to talk honestly. She said, "I have to tell you the truth. Had you been a friend to me, nothing would have kept me away from your wedding. Instead, I put myself first, which you've been doing all year." Her friend cried and admitted, "You're right." Even her husband agreed. When she told him, he blurted, "Good for her."

Painful as it was, talking things out strengthened their relationship. "After that, we can get past anything," says Loretta. "Real friendship is about being able to listen and understand and move ahead. We don't keep tabs. We love and trust each other. If I can do it, I will—and if not, you have to be friend enough to realize there's a reason why I can't."

A lawyer, thirty-one, still smarts at her experience with a friend who moved in with a boyfriend. "She feels the need to bond with his mother. When the mother came into town, she canceled *our* plans together at the last minute. She's done this before. She feels I'll understand. I do understand, but in this case she changed plans several times with me, then said, 'We're all going to a restaurant. Do you want to stop by and say hello?' I felt outraged. 'Stop by' said 'You're not very important.'

"I wouldn't have minded if she was honest and told me, 'Listen, I want to make points with his mother. I'll be out of commission for a week. Please bear with me. I'm scared and nervous.' I would have felt, 'Fine. I'll see you in a couple of weeks.' But the way she handled it made me feel lousy and angry."

When issues aren't talked about, they can fester—and sometimes turn a friendship toxic. When women don't have a man, they spend a lot of time and emotional energy together; if one becomes involved with a man—and they don't discuss it—trouble may follow. An excluded friend who has few other social outlets may experience deep feelings of abandonment.

Some people react to exclusion either by withdrawing and becoming very shy—or by becoming enraged. An assistant advertising manager actually became the object of a malevolent rumor campaign when she began spending lunch hours with her boyfriend, rather than with her friend in the next cubicle at the office. The friend overreacted, spreading vicious stories at work about the young woman. Human nature being what is, many people believed them. The atmosphere became so uncomfortable, the manager finally left.

Though this incident is extreme, it's not uncommon to have a problem adjusting to other people and priorities that have become part of a friend's life. Carol Anderson, Ph.D., coauthor of *Flying Solo: Single Women in Midlife,* found that single and married friends occasionally had trouble accepting each other's lifestyles—and criticized each other's choices. If both of you have exciting careers and travel the world, for example, you may not understand why she would give it all up for a guy who (in your view) is boring and a major compromise. Her choice to marry and have kids may be threatening if there is no one on the horizon for you—and your biological clock is running out. "These issues can be worked out over time if both friends are willing, though you may wind up seeing each other less than you used to. Some people, however, can't tolerate the differences," says Dr. Anderson.

When friends do things differently from us, it rocks *our* boat. One woman wanted to buy her own house—and found her friends did everything they could to discourage her. She was told "That should be something a couple does together" and "I'm older than you and I don't own a home." Fortunately, she resisted the pressure and stuck to her plan. She told me proudly, "I bought my first house at age twenty-eight."

The lawyer whose friend canceled plans at the last minute admits that she felt a bit threatened. "I didn't want to see how important it was for her to have this relationship with this guy and be close to his mother—because I was struggling to be independent and free and wanted her to be, too."

Single friends are threatening to some marriages. Many husbands get jealous, thinking, "If my wife goes out with her, are they looking for men?" Some wives look at a single friend and feel, "She has all this freedom and here I am doing diapers. Did I make the right decision?"

Another kind of strain occurs when you don't like your friend's partner—or he doesn't like you. One woman, who is in a committed relationship, rarely wants to see her friends' husbands. "Most spouses are dull. The woman is the one who is my friend and I'd rather spend time with her alone. Fortunately, most are smart enough not to say, 'Oh, the four of us should get together.' You're trying to shoehorn four people into a contrived situation."

She detests one husband. "Once I had to break down and say to a friend, 'Never put me in the same room with him. He provokes rage in me.' Everyone who meets him feels that way and she knows it. It's a little awkward because there are times when his path and mine might have to cross—like at her birthday party." Should this occur, she'll just have to grit her teeth, say a quick hello, and circulate.

## FRIENDS AS DOWNERS

Instead of enhancing the quality of life, friends' attitudes can detract from it. For example, some single women feel defeated together, instead of taking pride in their relationship. They drag each other down.

"When two women go out to dinner, the dialogue can go something like 'There are no good men out there . . . it's all women.' It's as if they're two losers and here they are on Saturday night. But you don't *have* to have a man sitting there with you to enjoy yourself. It's very irrational," says Bonnie Jacobson, Ph.D., a New York psychologist.

The problem is, society tends to devalue time spent with other women—and so do women themselves. You may want a man in your life, but why can't you *also* have a good time in a restaurant with a person you enjoy?

Friends who project their own issues with men can have toxic effects, too. Sometimes they may contaminate a promising romantic relationship. Let's say you meet an intriguing new man at a party. You immediately feel a mutual attraction, talk together nonstop, and enjoy a wonderful evening. You can't wait to tell your friends about him. When they cluster around to hear the details, however, they proceed to rip him apart. They call him a sexist and barrage you with statements like "I'd never go out with anyone like that." You seesaw from feeling a strong connection to thinking he's the worst male chauvinist. By the time he calls about a first date, he's been demolished to the point where you're ready to dump him.

Such behavior by friends has happened. It may be a defensive reaction that can be traced to their own feelings of rejection.

They feel spurned by men so they reject in advance of being rejected. They're beating him to the punch.

In a case similar to the one just mentioned, a married friend, who was able to be more objective, saved the day. Cutting through all the peer pressure, she sensibly advised, "Why don't you give him a chance? You can't tell from just one conversation at a party."

Of course, the ultimate downer is betrayal by a friend. Camille, a forty-two-year-old art consultant, remembers her painful experience all too vividly. Living with a man who had a history of fooling around during his previous marriage, she was convinced he had changed. In fact, he was having an affair—and took the other woman to get-togethers at the home of Camille's friend.

"She entertained frequently and I couldn't always attend. When they showed up together, she knew what was going on. She accepted them. I finally found out about it when I unexpectedly stopped by at one of her parties and saw the two of them there. I felt so humiliated. The entire town knew—everybody but me. I would have appreciated a friend saying, 'I'm afraid you may be hurt over something. I don't know how much to say, but you might want to ask him point blank what's going on,'" says Camille.

The friend, who was very embarrassed, was struggling against her own deep need to please people. The man would have been angry at her if she had informed Camille—or if she had told him, "Don't bring her here." So she didn't set a boundary, even though she knew her own moral code was being jeopardized.

Later, she tearfully apologized, "I don't expect you to forgive me. Staying friends with everyone, no matter what, is how I've operated all my life—and I don't like it much. I'm so sorry."

But it was too late. Camille left town shortly after. "When I moved, she told me, 'I wish you weren't going now. I feel we're becoming closer friends.' I didn't say anything but I could never trust her again. Her loss."

## FRIENDS LINK YOU WITH
## A REWARDING LIFE

A forty-year-old manager of information services, who has never gotten close to the altar, muses, "I'd still like to marry. If I meet someone I can see spending my life with, of course I would. But if a guy is just okay, I'd rather be single. I can be happy without a man. I'm not afraid to be alone. I think it's because my family moved so much when I was growing up."

Others love being single and aren't willing to give up their freedom. And for many, finding "Mr. Right" is the ultimate goal. Regardless of where you fit, you've got a life to live for as long as you *are* single—and friends help make it work. There may be hurts at times. But when your friendship world is generally satisfying, you're less likely to say, "I'm lonely and depressed because I don't have a man."

## MAKE FRIENDSHIPS AS A SINGLE
## MORE REWARDING

1. *Check your satisfaction level.*

Fulfilling friendships are extra important if you're single because they help keep you feeling good about yourself—and because (unless you're in a committed relationship) you don't have that continuity of contact that married women have. Friends fill out your world.

Are your friendships satisfying? Are you getting enough intimacy and emotional support? Do you need more touch in your life or more regular social contact? People you bump into and talk with every day—such as a neighbor who also walks a dog at 7 P.M. and regularly stops to chat—add structure and a sense of stability to your life.

Do you need more action-oriented friends—pals to jog with or go to the theater with, who aren't necessarily confidants? A married college friend may be your soul mate, but she may not be available to go to dinner or a museum, especially on weekends. Research shows that life satisfaction for single women thirty-five and older is correlated not only with good health, but also with not being lonely and with having many casual friends. Dr. Anderson believes that the women she interviewed probably felt good about so many friendships because they didn't depend on any one relationship to fill all their needs. "They sort of spread it around," she says.

When you have many social outlets, you're also less likely to get involved in pathological or highly charged negative relationships. If one friend becomes less available because she's got a guy, you always have others who *are* accessible to you.

2. *Prune your friends.*

Over time, you may find that you want to deepen some friendships and make others more casual. Sometimes you outgrow friends.

Dr. Lewis compares friendship to a garden. "You plant a garden and all the flowers you like best are in the middle. But over the years you may decide you're a bit tired of roses. You still like them, but they aren't your favorite anymore. You move them from the center to the edge of your garden—and maybe you bring in a new variety that wasn't there before. You may need to get some flowers out of the garden altogether because they may turn into weeds."

If you want to add friends, the best way to make new ones is to do what you like doing. Ava has always been interested in medicine and once considered a career in nursing. Becoming an ambulance corps volunteer was a natural step for her. Do politics turn you on? Get active in a local campaign. Some say, "I love going to singles dances because I meet the best women." You have to work at meeting women the same way you work at meeting men.

Groups, such as book clubs, where members meet regularly and have dinners together afterward, are a good way to build a community, which involves reciprocity and interdependence. Some older women have mah-jongg or bridge groups. They save the winnings at the games and go on trips together. A group initially revolves around something external, such as taking a course together, but then eventually you start to branch out and develop friendships. If the activity involves giving back to society, it has a secondary gain. It's empowering to feel you're contributing to making the world a better place.

3. *Respect and negotiate boundaries.*

You do have to respect the primacy of a friend's marriage and family—and understand that your married friends have other obligations. It may be difficult to get together when your friend is juggling. You can't have your feelings hurt all the time and sometimes you may have to do more of the work. If a friend has children and you like kids, think of ways you can be helpful. A forty-year-old city planner volunteers to baby-sit. "It fills in a gap for not having children myself," she says. "I like to do it only occasionally and in small doses, but I enjoy the time I'm with the children and they enjoy me because I'm not an old fogey."

She also stretches in other ways. "When one of my juggling friends forgets to call to confirm an appointment, I say to myself, 'Look, all you have to do is get out of bed in the morning, and she's got three kids, a dog, a husband, and a job.' I have to be understanding of people whose lives are more complicated than mine. I don't know why anyone would *have* three children and a dog, but to each his own."

"I don't understand when people say, 'My friend got married and I lost a friend. She spends all her time with her family.' I've never lost a friend that way. Either I see the couple or I have lunch with the woman or a whole group gets together. She's still my friend and I intend to see her as much as her schedule allows. Sometimes that means I go to her neighborhood to go out to dinner, rather than her coming to mine."

Some people do have trouble with boundaries in relationships, however, and there may be jealousies. If a friend always brings her husband or kids along, you may feel, "Oh, no, not again!" But you're not always going to get undivided attention. In a really comfortable relationship, you can be pretty honest when you want time alone and say, "Can we get together, just you and I? Sometimes it's nice to talk by ourselves."

4. *Discuss problems as you would with a lover.*

We put much less energy into nurturing close women friends than romantic attachments, even though these friends give us so much. We take them for granted because we've been told that only marriage provides intimacy and security.

Says Dr. Lewis, "If you have a problem with a woman friend, you might not call for a while, then phone in a few weeks and pick up as if nothing ever happened. You'd never do that with a man. You'd call and say, 'Hey, we've got to work this out.' It's important to use the same emotional energy in dealing with close friends as with a lover. When women don't talk about problems, friendships fade away."

Refuse to tolerate toxic behavior. You wouldn't let a man repeatedly cancel plans on you. Why would you accept it in a female friend? The lawyer who was dumped by a friend when her boyfriend's mother came to town spoke up. She told the friend, "I'm furious. How dare you speak to me like that? Don't ever treat me that way again or I'm gone." She explains, "One of the cool things I've learned is that when a girlfriend does something that pisses me off, I can tell her, 'Wow, I'm angry.' It's up to me to take responsibility—and not be a victim."

What if *you're* the one with the boyfriend? If you really care about your friend, you can head off feelings of abandonment by reassuring her, "I'm still going to spend time with you."

If you feel a friend is pulling away from you, discuss that, too. Sometimes *you're* actually withdrawing yourself. You may think, "You have a partner now and I don't," and call less frequently, assuming the friend is too busy. She may be feeling, "I'm out in the cold. She doesn't want to be with me."

Unfortunately, however, some women *do* drop everyone

when a guy comes along—and that's too bad. Friendships don't replace love relationships—two different kinds of needs are being met—but they're just as important and deserve the same respect. As women get older, they have more realistic expectations of friendship. Many have learned to value other women, too.

5. *Show married people how to deal with you.*

We have an image of what we want married life to be like but there is no model for single life. It's up to you to teach married friends how to act with you. Tell them, "I've got theater tickets. Do you want to come?" If you enjoy being a hostess, invite married friends to dinner at your house. Why wait for them to ask you?

Women often say, "I can't because I don't have a partner." So what? If more singles gave dinner parties, some of the tentativeness that married people feel toward them would be gone. Although she can't afford to entertain in the same style her married friends do, one divorcée makes a point of having them over to dinner with other couples.

Leading your life exactly as if you were married is part of grounding, one of the developmental tasks single women must negotiate. Grounding involves doing all the things you need to live a full life, rather than spending it waiting to get married. It involves feeling part of (and comfortable in) your own home, your neighborhood, and your social life (as well as in your career and in finances).

## 7

# Making Family Your Friends, If You Can: The In-law Dilemma (Siblings, Too)

LORRAINE REMEMBERS THE night her sister-in-law (a schoolteacher) asked how Lorraine's daughter scored on a city-wide exam. When Lorraine proudly told her, her response was: "That's all? My class did better than that."

A few years ago, Lorraine would have exploded at the remark and a battle might have ensued. But her attitude has changed. Says Lorraine, "If you have a relationship to preserve for a greater good—like the stability of the family—I think the answer is to ignore everything. My sister-in-law is nuts, so I held my tongue and just walked away. I've seen too many family fights do damage and I refuse to participate anymore. The price is too high."

Other women speak of mothers-in-law from hell and brothers-in-law who drive them crazy. Clearly it isn't always easy for family members to get along, yet we need each other. Extended families (warts and all) offer benefits and supports—for our children, our mates, and ourselves—that we can't afford to toss away today. Dealing with each other, however, can sometimes require all the skill and patience we can muster.

Can we find a way to get along without shortchanging our

own needs? Here's what you must know to prevent, resolve, or diminish conflict with your husband's or partner's parents, his siblings, and their mates—and the spouses of *your* siblings.

## IN-LAW DYNAMICS

Positive relationships with in-laws enrich family life, multiply your resources when you feel overwhelmed or need assistance, and may even make up for missing connections to your own parents or siblings. Despite all the mother-in-law jokes, many women like (even love) their husbands' relatives. But it takes time and adjustments on all sides to develop relationships and keep them on track. It also helps to realize that in-law problems are most likely to arise at certain transition points in the life cycle, such as when you marry or become a parent.

"These transition times often involve the entry or exit of family members," says Israela Meyerstein, LCSW-C, director of clinical training, family and marriage therapy program, Sheppard Pratt Hospital in Baltimore. "Imagine the family as a boat. When people step on or get off, there's unsettlement. Relationships need to be renegotiated."

*Marriage* is the major point for development of problems. In-laws are born when you wed—and it takes time to get comfortable. You enter a strange new family, feeling sensitive and vulnerable. Marsha, a newsletter editor married two years, has learned that first impressions can be misleading and that it's wise to give people a chance. "You never get a family where every single person gets along well. There are always a few people who are hard to take. But our little segment does well. At first I thought my husband's sister, who has a brusque manner, was mad at me. But we're getting closer."

After Marsha and her husband became engaged, they went away for a few days to celebrate. When Marsha returned to her office, there was an envelope from her sister-in-law. Inside was confetti and a banner emblazoned with "Congratulations." "She had mailed it before she knew for sure that I'd accept his proposal. She was that confident I would say yes.

"She's still abrupt, but I realize that it's not that she doesn't like me—it's just the way she is. She's so thoughtful. She remembers things about you and then does something caring. She remembered that I love the color purple, then made me a purple stained-glass rose in a frame. I felt so touched."

She admits she had to adjust to the rest of the clan, too. "When you get married, you think you're the center of the universe. It's so easy to get hurt. I remember going to my husband's family reunion and coming away feeling rejected because everybody ignored me. But he has a huge family and they can't keep *each other* straight, let alone his new wife," she says.

At thirty-five, Marsha is a mature woman, but some younger adults run into problems associated with leaving their families. The traditional way to leave is to pick a mate and move on. For some, however, it's hard to separate from family. Instead of working through their own process of becoming independent, they unconsciously choose the kind of spouse who will help them do it. For example, someone obedient and compliant because parents always had high expectations for him or her might marry a mate who can say no to those parents and set limits. The spouse may then be the one who gets enmeshed in in-law conflict.

*The birth of a first child* is another transition point. Some in-laws may be seen as interfering—or aloof and uncaring. When the relationship works, however, it can be a magical time when grandparents are welcomed and can help care for the baby without threatening your independence. They (and other in-laws) can become wonderful resources for children—and supports for you.

Susan, a thirty-year-old medical receptionist, grew close to her sister-in-law when they both got pregnant at the same time and discovered they had much in common. They both had boys and shared the same philosophy of raising kids. Says Susan, "I drove her to the hospital in Omaha when she gave birth. She baby-sat for my son. She calls and says, 'Hi, how are things going?' I haven't spoken to her in a while, but it doesn't matter. I could call today and we'd talk like yesterday. We also have lots of mutual friends. A lot of it is personality. Her husband was always the 'bad boy' in the family, but I like him and she appreciates that."

*Divorce* is a time of many shifts, when in-laws become ex-in-laws. In some cases, there's an ability to put kids' needs first and recognize that ties with grandparents are very important to child development. Other times, breaking with grandparents is part of the fight between the spouses. They may prevent access to the child, who is the one who loses.

*Remarriage* adds to the cast of characters. Fran, a thirty-one-year-old guidance counselor, has had a positive experience with her new mother-in-law. The latter has become a good friend—and a loving new grandma for her six-year-old son.

"She doesn't just tolerate the fact that I was married before. She goes crazy over my son at holidays and finds out exactly what he wants. She has three other grandchildren and treats them all as equals. She's always there for me, too." A case in point is the time Fran had to go for medical tests early one morning and was in a bind. Her husband wanted to accompany her, but someone had to take her son to school. "When I told my mother-in-law, she immediately volunteered, 'Why don't you bring him here and I'll drive him to school.' She always pitches in."

But it goes beyond that. They like the same books and authors, the same movies and food—and they talk every day. Fran's husband often teases, "Doesn't she want to talk to *me* anymore?"

*Midlife struggles* mean adults are changing. Some just change jobs or careers, others achieve personal growth—and some change their marriages. Spouses may form a more mature relationship with extended family—or they may break up the family unit. On the other hand, a compassion may emerge for your in-laws (and for your own parents) at this time as you realize that what they told you all along is true: "It ain't so easy to raise kids (or earn a living)."

*In-laws' retirement* can cause tension if they rely too heavily on your family to provide stimulation and focus for them, instead of filling their own lives with new activities and interests.

*Death of a grandparent* has impact, too. If a spouse survives, it's another time when boundaries are loosened and must be refigured. A widow or widower may turn more to her or his children for companionship, which can work well—or rekindle conflicts. A daughter-in-law often winds up a caretaker.

All of these changes have the potential to be weathered successfully and present opportunities to improve relationships—or to create a crisis. The outcome depends on factors such as the degree of goodwill on all sides and the quality of communication.

## COMMON PROBLEMS

Discord between family members is often fueled by issues of control, mistaken assumptions, competition, jealousy, and possessiveness. Though the nuances may vary, depending on the people and situation, tensions tend to be associated with:

### Amount of contact with in-laws

The most common in-law issue involves where people spend their time, according to William J. Doherty, Ph.D., professor and director, marriage and family therapy program, University of Minnesota, and author of *The Intentional Family*. Regular contact with family (face-to-face or by phone) is important for couples, but families differ in defining how much is optimal. "A controlling in-law makes it difficult," says Dr. Doherty.

Take Iris, twenty-eight, who finds her social life gobbled up by her husband's large family. There's little time for anyone else, since she and her husband are expected to go to every birthday and holiday celebration and weekly dinners—all at his parents' home. Though Iris's family is invited, they don't necessarily want to attend. Such situations raise loyalty issues for spouses—do you go to his family's turf or yours?

One of the adjustments when you marry involves setting appropriate boundaries around your new family, which allow contact with (and support from) both families of origin, but don't permit them to dominate your life. Lack of such limits sets up disagreement between the spouses, which can stir intense feelings of anger and hostility toward in-laws.

Sometimes a husband may feel a wife is putting her parents first and giving more consideration to their feelings than to his. Sometimes a partner is accused of never growing up and leaving mom and dad. In our culture, a man isn't supposed to remain close to his mother, though a daughter is; a wife often acts as a bridge back to his family.

On the other hand, some people want *more* contact with in-laws. One wife feels angry at her husband's parents because they don't invite her over when her husband is away on business trips. Another felt rejected because her mother-in-law called to speak only to her husband, never to her. When problems arise, they usually stem from the fact someone does not feel accepted. In a good situation, the spouse feels like a member of the family.

## Bias of in-laws

Some parents feel no one is good enough for their child—or, at any rate, *you* aren't. Your education or social status or your family's balance sheet doesn't make the grade. Intermarriage can intensify the problem. Dina, a thirty-eight-year-old department store buyer who is married for the second time, has lived out a nightmare with her old-world Romanian in-laws. Expecting their son to marry someone from their own culture, they threatened to boycott the wedding. They finally attended only after Dina signed a prenuptial agreement, protecting their son's assets from her.

Despite the inauspicious beginning, Dina tried hard to please. She and her husband visited her in-laws every Sunday, continuing to do so even though they refused to speak English (which left her out) and objected to any show of affection by her husband. "Don't hold her hand," his father would tell him. "Why does she get facials? Why did she buy those clothes?" both parents would demand.

Still trying to win them over, Dina (whose heritage is Scandinavian) tried to learn their language. She took cooking courses so that she could entertain the large crowds the family preferred. At the same time, behind her back, her in-laws were discouraging her husband from starting a family.

Eyes flashing, Dina recalls, "I wanted to have kids and my husband kept saying, 'Let's wait a year.' They wanted us to wait forever. They didn't want 'mixed' grandchildren."

Dina finally put her foot down when she and her husband, an architect, built a house. His parents didn't want her name on it. "I told him, 'I've given up my right to everything you had before the marriage, but this is where I take a stand.' I won on that issue, but everything was a battle."

Because she wanted the marriage to work so badly and couldn't bear the thought of a *second* divorce, it took eight years for Dina to finally say, "I can't live like this." She remembers, "It was awful. My husband and I went to two marriage therapists. Both said that what he felt for his parents was guilt, not love. They gave up their life to educate him—and that's a very tough tie to break. I was ready to leave when he finally changed."

She blames both her husband and herself for tolerating the interference. "Why were we listening to them? I should have sized them up from the beginning. Anytime parents have that much influence over their son, you're going to have to please three people—and it's hard enough to please one. I wasn't married to him—I was married to a family that didn't like me very much."

In a strange way, however, the years of turmoil have made the marriage stronger. Says Dina, "My husband is a wonderful person. He's honorable and devoted to me. He often says it's heart-breaking that this relationship he had with his parents all his life has changed so drastically in their old age."

## Unrealistic or different expectations

It's not uncommon for a new bride to expect instant closeness and love from her in-laws. One woman was distressed to find her brother's new wife expected her to be a soul mate. "Now I have a sister," she was told the first time they met, which made her uncomfortable and led her to withdraw. "I already *have* a sister," she says, "and I got that trapped feeling. I might eventually become a close friend of hers—I don't know—but you have to get to know and trust each other. I didn't choose her the way I'd choose a friend. She was dropped in my lap."

In-laws won't feel immediately like family or immediately like friends. It takes time for these relationships to grow and develop—and some will never be close. In-law relationships are the strangest ones we have because there's a sort of intimacy—you spend time together at holidays and parties—but you're also strangers.

The best idea is to try to be open to a range of relationships. If you expect supercloseness, you might be disappointed. If you expect little or nothing, you might wind up too close.

Some of us expect our in-laws to be like our parents (if we have a positive relationship), only to find they're quite different. One young mother remembers the time her husband's parents baby-sat with her eight-month-old son overnight. When she called to check in with them, they asked her to return home because the baby had a temperature. "I was shocked. My parents would have handled it themselves—it was routine," says the mom, who never asked her in-laws to baby-sit again. "I thought all grandparents are naturally good at this, but they obviously felt insecure about caring for a young child."

Or you may expect in-laws to know how much independence you want or need—and to respect that—without being told.

Expecting them to mind-read creates havoc. If you don't want people to visit unannounced—and if your in-laws are warm, gushy people who drop by—it doesn't work. They don't know your rituals or preferences. You have to communicate.

## Family of origin models

My mother *never* had a good word to say about my paternal grandmother, though I thought she was a hoot. In the days when anyone with grandchildren was considered really *old,* she met a man on the boardwalk in Brighton Beach and ran away with him to Argentina. When I saw the movie *Evita* I loved it because it brought back all those letters from Buenos Aires extolling the Perons. But the very same characteristics in her that intrigued me—her adventurousness and ability to have a good time—irked my mother. Grandmothers didn't *do* that; in fact, nobody, regardless of age, *did that.* My mother also disliked her (and my paternal aunt and uncle, too) because they never invited us to visit. They never invited *anybody* to visit, but she took it personally.

The message I got was: In-laws have no redeeming features. When I got married, it was therefore not surprising that I was prepared to dislike my mother-in-law. A new bride, feeling insecure and unsure of myself, I was out to prove that I was number one in my husband's life. But there was no one to compete with. My mother-in-law totally disarmed me. She was sweet and dear and welcomed me as a daughter. I love her to this day.

You're set up in a pattern by your family of origin—and unless you break out of the mold (or have such a fine in-law that she breaks it for you)—you're likely to follow it. If all you saw in your family was fights, you could easily adopt that model. But patterns can change.

## Criticism and interference

One woman remembers being called at work every day by her mother-in-law, who wanted to check out what she was cooking for her son for dinner. She kept her on the phone, telling her how to chop the carrots.

Someone else, now divorced, an artsy intellectual with a graduate degree, married into a working-class family. She remembers, "I wanted badly to be accepted, but they never cottoned to me. I always felt judged. If my husband wore a wrinkled shirt, my mother-in-law would blame me. She'd say, 'You let him go out of the house like that?' I thought to myself, 'Why are you telling me? He's an adult. His shirts are his responsibility, not mine.' "

Some families are volatile, don't hesitate to state strong opinions, and may focus on what's negative. Although Susan has a fine relationship with one sister-in-law, she feels constantly judged by others. Problems stem partly from her husband's birth order; he's the youngest of six children. "My two oldest sisters-in-law treat me like a little kid—and I hate it. One is always interfering and the other always criticizes. You can feel you're being talked about.

"I'm ten years younger than they are, but that doesn't make me less of a person. I hate to be given advice I didn't ask for, which happens in this family through a third party." When Susan had a miscarriage—and then got pregnant again with her second child—she received a call from the sister-in-law she's close to. "She told me my other sister-in-law said I should have an abortion because I can't afford more kids. I'll never forgive her for suggesting such a thing."

Instead of dealing directly with a person and problem, some families have a style of indirect communication. Backstabbing and feuds where people don't talk to each other for years are indirect ways to handle strong emotions and anxiety. Conflicts don't get talked out or worked out.

Relaying messages, as Susan's sister-in-law did, complicates matters. Communication involving three or more people tends to get tangled and opens possibilities for misunderstanding. The more people involved, the more complex it gets.

## THE PRICE OF CUTOFFS

Sometimes spouses who don't like their in-laws feel glad when a partner disconnects from his or her family. Let's say you both find his parents troublesome and your husband declares, "I don't want anything to do with them anymore." As an in-law, you might heave a sigh of relief and feel your life is now easier. But a cutoff is apt to be a serious mistake, destructive for everyone. When people refuse to see their family of origin (except in cases of extreme abuse), they usually pay a psychological toll that affects their own family.

Says Dr. Doherty, "Most people are more preoccupied and angry when *not* seeing their family than when they see them on at least state occasions. What happens is, your family looms larger in your life. If a card comes in the mail, it really bothers you. If you live in the same town, you can see them in the street. What if a call comes and your mother's in the hospital? It takes a tremendous amount of work not to see them at all. And that's psychological work drained away from your own family. What you've learned—and teach your kids—is: When things are hard in relationships, you walk away."

Kids can get hurt in other ways, too. My own children recently told me how upset they felt when cutoffs occurred in our family years ago. They wanted to admire and love these adults—who had become persona non grata in our household. It was a shock to see the pain on their faces as they remembered these times. Until then, I'd never realized the damage done to the next generation.

Cutoffs are bad for you as a spouse, too. If all of a person's emotional eggs are in one basket and you're "it" in terms of adult family relationships, that's a lot of pressure on the marriage. Whatever unresolved issues your mate has with his family are also going to surface in your marriage. Does he say, "Every time I'm around my family they put me down"? There are times in any marriage when you're put down by a spouse. If he walks out on his family when he feels put down, what will he do with you?

At times, conflicts with in-laws persist because they seem to "solve" (or allow spouses to avoid dealing with) other problems, according to Israela Meyerstein. For example, fights with others may actually be a distraction from the couples' own issues with each other. Or, if both spouses fight the family, it can superficially increase the couple's closeness. If a wife stands up to in-laws for her husband, it also allows him to remain a dutiful son. Ironically, when in-law fights cool down, trouble between spouses often increases temporarily until they deal with their own problems.

## KEEPING THE PEACE

It's a challenge to form a new household while balancing loyalties to your families—and hard work to maintain positive relationships throughout the life cycle. But family values and keeping families strong include working relationships with in-laws. That doesn't mean we'll necessarily love each other all the time, but we can find ways to get along—and send healthy messages to our children about relationships and conflict resolution.

Susan sums it up, "I think my kids should know their family. I think back to memories like Fourth of July when I was growing up. We'd light sparklers and my cousin's whole backyard would be lit up. I remember going to my grandmother's house, where all the cousins—ten of us—stood on the bed so my grandmother could take pictures. We still look at those pictures from when we were little and say, 'Remember when we used to _____.' I want that for my kids." So do I. Don't you?

## EIGHT WAYS TO GET ALONG

We all think everybody else's family is in perfect harmony. That's rarely true. Certainly mine never was—and isn't now. But there are ways to help keep relations steady:

1. *Set boundaries.*

In a healthy family relationship there is a boundary between the couple and both sets of parents. The primary loyalty and commitment has to be to your partner or the marriage won't last. That doesn't mean breaking up the relationship with parents, however. It means you and your mate must manage the problem together and commit to each having enough time and contact with his or her own family without somebody getting too much or too little. How much is right? Says Dr. Doherty, "A good barometer is how the two of you feel about the level of contact with both families. If it's not a source of struggle for either of you, it's a balance."

What if your in-laws want to hog all the holidays? Negotiate. The first person to talk to is your husband. Often wives deal with their husbands' parents, but it is the blood relative who is primarily responsible for conducting the relationship with his or her parents through life. (The spouse is a kind of partner in the journey.) The blood relative must take the lead in discussions about family contact, particularly if the conversation has conflict built in, as in "Mom and Dad, we are going to spend Christmas this year with Mary Sue's parents." If parents are going to be ticked off, it's better that they're annoyed at their own child for making that boundary than at the awful daughter-in-law who makes the nasty rules.

One approach is Israela Meyerstein's "good sandwich" technique: "Mom and Dad, we love that you care about us and like to visit—and we like to have you visit." That's the bread. Then the meat of the sandwich is: "But our lives are so hectic, it's important to us that you call before you come over. Since our schedule is really busy, we'd also appreciate it if you'd let us do the arranging because it works better for us that way." The other piece of bread, in closing: "We appreciate your thinking about it and we hope it won't be too hard to cooperate with our request." Yes, in-laws may be miffed—and get over it.

If there is hostility between your husband and *your* parents, ask yourself: Am I encouraging it without realizing it? If he feels you put them before him, agree to consult with him first when your mother invites the two of you over. Then he feels he's in on the decision. If your mother says something derogatory about him, stand up for him and tell her, "Please don't say that."

### 2. *Be realistic about socializing.*

If you have a hard time tolerating your sister's husband's bragging or your brother's wife's envy, carve out as much one-to-one time with your sibling as possible. Get together as couples only on major holidays.

I always remember the advice of a friend who had a very large fight-free family. When I asked for her recipe for peace, she told me: "Saturday night is for friends; don't go out socially with your relatives." It's not a rule for everybody because it depends; some families get along great together, regardless of the circumstances. But basically, if family absorbs all of your free time, then you don't develop the kind of supportive relationships with friends that are also good for the family.

### 3. *Avoid hot-button issues.*

Do you regularly talk religion with your in-laws when you know they disagree with you and the topic always leads to heated arguments? Do you extol the virtues of public school to your sister-in-law when you know she sends her kids to (and is a staunch advocate of) parochial school? Know when to keep your opinions to yourself.

One woman, whose father was a sergeant in Vietnam, will never forget the Thanksgiving her husband's family discussed the war. She told me, "They talked about the atrocities and how we were wrong to be there. I got madder and madder because I strongly believe my parents were divorced because of Vietnam. My dad's head got messed up because he had such bad experiences there.

"My face was bright red and I got up and said, 'This is nonsense,' and walked out. I heard someone whisper, 'Her father was in Vietnam. What did you bring it up for?' That subject was never mentioned again."

4. *Beware of making your spouse's fight your own.*

If your sister-in-law instigates a fight between your husband and his brother, the offense is to your husband, not you. If your husband is willing to forgive, then you should be, too. If you're angrier than he is, you're overidentifying. That's not to say you shouldn't have feelings about it. But if you hang on to them longer than your husband does, something is amiss. It's easier to nurse such anger and carry a grudge when you're an in-law because you don't have those powerful childhood connections that make rifts painful for family members. That's why we want to make up.

Such grudges are generally a mistake for two reasons: (1) They're inappropriate, and (2) you can put your spouse in a loyalty bind. If he forgives and you don't, then every time he says something positive about the person, you respond negatively, which can create problems in your own marriage.

5. *Pick your battles carefully.*

Not everything has to be a cause for war. If it is, it's a sign that an issue from the past probably hasn't been worked out. Some of us have issues with adult authority figures, for example. Let's say you feel people always bossed you when you were a child. When in-laws try to establish plans, you may have a built-in sensitivity and overreact. Maybe your in-laws *are* controlling and something has to be said to them by your spouse—but maybe *you're* the issue.

Be accommodating. Sometimes you have to ignore certain personality traits, try to put up with them, and move on, just as in a marriage. Says one wife, "I might not like what my in-laws do, but I try to set my differences aside. My husband and my sister don't mix well, but they make an effort to tolerate each other."

If someone does or says something outrageous, stop and ask yourself, "What's the intent?" before you explode. Says Lorraine, whose child's test score was disparaged by her sister-in-law, "She likes my kids. I don't think she was really trying to put my daughter down. But she doesn't realize how she comes off. She's always doing things like telling me stories about the children of other people (who I neither know nor care about) who are doing so much better than mine. She does the same thing to her own kids, so it's not like she's playing favorites."

According to Israela Meyerstein, there can be a great deal of caring emotion behind such behavior. You can't assume the motivation is negative. Let's say a sister-in-law calls your accountant to yell at him for "allowing" you to buy a more expensive house that will stress your budget. Some people interfere in such cases because they really care about your welfare. That doesn't justify the intrusion, but it does put it in a different context.

When you want in-laws to change their behavior—or want to discuss your feelings—keep it civil, polite, and noninflammatory. Don't scream, shout, or blame. Try to make direct statements—"It's important to me that Johnny do his homework *before* turning on the TV"—instead of name calling, judging motives, and making assumptions. A safe way to start is: "[Description of behavior] upsets me [in this situation] because [state reason]. I would appreciate it if you would [describe behavior you wish to see]."

6. *Be selective about volunteering information.*

Mothers-in-law are often accused of meddling, but one woman has found a way to get around it. She says, "If I call my mother-in-law and say, 'Hey, the kids went for a checkup' and I tell her what's going on, she's not intrusive because I volunteer information to her. Our relationship improved since I started doing that and she appreciates it. She does care and does want to know or she wouldn't pry to find out more information."

Where her sisters- and brothers-in-law are concerned, however, she's found less is better. "I don't volunteer information to them because then they may assume I'm asking for advice—and sometimes I'm just telling my story."

Use your own judgment about the people involved. Do you really want to tell your mother-in-law you're considering having your tubes tied? Is she likely to pressure you one way or the other?

7. *Do your part, depending on your role.*

Sisters-in-law face the same issues siblings do. They can bicker, compete, vie for position—or cooperate and sometimes even become good friends. Daughters-in-law can look for trouble— or hope and strive for harmony.

Mothers-in-law can respect their child's choice and welcome him or her—or push the person away. Did your son marry someone of another religion? Telling her "Well, I suppose he *could* have done worse" (as one mother-in-law did) will not endear you to her. Instead, know how to let go. Don't put her in a situation where she has to compete with you for her husband's attention.

A high school teacher tries hard to have a relationship with her son's wife. If her daughter-in-law mentions a sweater she liked or a book that interests her, she often goes out and buys it for her. She never criticizes. "You have to overlook things. My daughter-in-law makes my son happy and she's a good mother. *That's* what's important. I don't care if her house isn't spotless. She spends her time on her son, who reads at four years old. I have the smartest grandson in Wisconsin. So I'll sit on a couch full of dog hair. My grandson is what's important."

Don't take sides if your child confides in you about marital problems. Parents, being protective of their children, often begin to develop negative feelings about the spouse because the person is hurting their child. Realize instead that conflict between spouses is inevitable.

Don't make disparaging statements about a daughter- or son-in-law. Instead, help your child to look at alternatives as in "I wonder what you could do differently to make things better."

8. *Consider forgiveness.*

Forgiveness can heal family relationships. Even though it can be difficult to forgive, it's usually worth a try to stop family pain, hurt, and sometimes cutoffs. You don't have to be best buddies with the offender. You can do a minimal maintenance of family relations and be polite—send birthday cards and show up at your niece's wedding. Boycotting a child's wedding (or a family member's funeral) is usually considered a very hostile act.

Realize, too, that things *can* change. When Fran's brother got engaged, his fiancée tried to pull him away from his family. After the wedding, Fran saw the couple only on family occasions. When the sister-in-law suffered a series of miscarriages, however, Fran felt terrible.

"I sent her a sympathy card after the first one—and that was the turning point. After the second miscarriage, I helped out at her house. Then when they finally decided to adopt, they had a very hard time getting a baby. There were several disappointments—and despair. At one point, my brother called and cried. I tried to be there for them—and a wall came down."

When an adoption finally came through, her sister-in-law said, "You've done such a good job with your child. Will you be our baby's godmother?" Now they swap baby-sitting. Anytime her sister-in-law needs advice on parenting skills, she calls to ask, "How did you deal with this?"

Says Fran, "I never would have believed this was possible when they got married. We're still not best friends, but we've been through a war and there's a bond there. She's at a point where she knows it's not a competition. She's his wife, I'm his sister, and we can coexist."

## ADULT SIBLINGS: SUPPORTS OR SOURCES OF STRIFE?

Sibling warfare is covered graphically in the Bible and is obviously alive and well today. Yet Karen Gail Lewis, Ed.D., coeditor of *Siblings in Therapy,* believes the horror stories unjustifiably overshadow a positive picture.

"We don't hear enough about the many siblings who like each other and have vibrant relationships. Many adult siblings get along fine—and sisters are often best friends," she says.

Take Molly and her sister. "No one on this earth can lift me when I need it like her," says Molly. "My sister is an honest mirror and she always has my interests at heart. I remember when we were kids and wore school uniforms, if she tore hers at the playground, she would be upset—not only because of what my mother would say, but because that clothing was going to be handed down to me and I would not have a nice uniform like she did."

Lydia's sister has taken in Lydia's teenage daughter, a recovering drug addict. A single parent, Lydia says, "I feel like I failed so miserably. I bought the line that I could be both mom and dad. But my daughter needed a dad and didn't have one. Now, living in New Mexico with my sister and her husband, she has a father figure who is setting her straight. She always mouthed off to me, but never to him. She's even starting college in the fall."

Hearing stories like these, it's easy to wonder why other sisters and brothers are constantly locked in combat. When siblings have very intense anger at each other, according to Dr. Lewis, it's almost always triggered by unresolved jealousies or battles from childhood.

Here's how to keep sibling strife from contaminating *your* family life and how to grow better relationships:

1. *Find out what's bothering you.*

If you're not getting along, is it "You always got all the attention" or "You're always telling me what to do and you still do"? In fact, the oldest sibling's job was probably to be in charge. If you're younger, you may still feel as if you're being ordered around instead of realizing, "That's just the way she talks."

Did you feel abandoned when an older sibling entered adolescence, spending most of the time with friends and being no longer available to you? Feelings that she doesn't have time for you and isn't interested in you can continue to stir trouble throughout life if your sister didn't explain or a parent didn't help you understand by saying, "It isn't that your sister doesn't love you anymore. She's just got other friends."

2. *Talk together—or write a letter.*

Siblings get locked into life roles such as being an underachiever or a perfect kid. "You're the smart one and I'm the dumb one" gets repeated. Siblings can free us to break out of these roles by talking about how they experienced growing up. You can get in each other's shoes and it becomes "Oh, that's what it felt like for you." Tell your sister, "Mom and Dad always favored you," and she may respond, "I don't think that's true. When I went to college I bought my own bike. When you went, Dad gave you his Triumph."

An attorney was an angry child who verbally abused her sisters and sometimes hit them. She got lots of negative attention. After years of therapy, she recognized her responsibility for driving her sisters away. "I said to my youngest sister, 'You're right. We were all very mean to you. I can't apologize for anyone else but I can apologize for what I did.' " When her sister brought up favoritism in the family, saying, "Grandpa loved you best," this lawyer honestly replied, "Well, he did. I can't help that. He thought I was a queen and gave me things, but he gave you short shrift."

If you've fought with a sibling, you can open a discussion by saying "I miss you" or "We've got some rough spots I want to get past." In person (or on paper), let each side hear what the other is angry and hurt about.

Sometimes just airing feelings is enough, enabling you to say, "Now I understand. From now on, can you say that another way?" Simple reminders, as in "You're doing it again" can work. Or maybe you need to get more information about what really happened when you were kids—and go back to talk to Mom and Dad.

3. *Be alert to the parents' role.*

Parents play the biggest role in setting siblings against each other. Sometimes the seeds of lifelong resentment are planted when an older child is forced to take care of a younger one or when one child is treated as a favorite or another is labeled "the bad one." Familiar lines like "Don't be like your brother" can do lifelong damage to sibling relationships.

A parent may push one sibling against another in adulthood. If you call your mother and she asks why you don't phone as often as your brother, you're not going to feel warm toward him. If your parents tell your sisters how frequently you visit and how helpful you are, they are not going to be happy with you.

When parents get older and become infirm, the stress heightens tensions because the family as you know it is changing. Old unresolved issues and roles often play out, such as that of the ne'er-do-well who doesn't do as much as he or she should. If you realize you're being pitted against one another, you can say, "Okay, how can we handle this issue so it doesn't split us up again?" One set of siblings worked it out by never being in the house at the same time at the tensest period of their parents' illness. Instead, they rotated visits.

4. *Build a new history together.*

Get together without spouses and kids, so you can concentrate on conducting your relationship. One brother and sister have breakfast or lunch together regularly. If you live far away from each other (or don't have such a close relationship), consider spending one weekend a year together so you can build a present instead of only sharing the past. You won't necessarily wind up best friends. But she's your sister (or he's your brother) and you can have a relationship if both of you want one.

Learn how to sidestep certain issues, too. If a touchy topic comes up, say, "That's an area we'll never talk about." Or, "Let's change the subject."

One younger sister has a great system with her brother. "We don't talk politics, religion, or parents. Anytime we come near any of these, we lose any possibility of a good relationship and can't get back on track."

5. *Show that you care.*

You can love your family without giving up who you are— and the beliefs, dreams, and energy necessary for your personal growth. Says one sister, "Support each other. We are human. We will fall. In large families you learn to balance teamwork, competition, and independence if you have the right teachers. Think about all the time you spend looking at the TV set and how many good times you could be having with a real live person." She and her sister go out of their way to do something special together and to communicate.

The attorney mentioned earlier frequently initiates activities with her sisters and makes an effort to be a caring aunt to her nieces and nephews.

Of course it does take two—and sometimes peace isn't possible. When Maria was the first to marry, her sister didn't want to be maid of honor. She wouldn't attend rehearsals and ridiculed Maria's small engagement ring. "I was a goat for her jealousy," says Maria, now fifty-five. "Later, she put down my children. When my daughter lived with her fiancé before they got married, my sister called and moralized. I pointed out that she'd been living with a man herself for five years—and she hung up. I flew to California twice to apologize to her—to please my mom. But she couldn't accept it. So that was it."

Fortunately, such breaches are the exception. Over 60 percent of siblings over the age of sixty are in touch at least once a week, according to Dr. Lewis. Close relationships with siblings add to your psychological well-being as you get older—they're the longest-lasting relationships you will have. Good ones between sisters are especially important.

# Friends On-line:
# Opportunity or Narcotic?

A GROUP OF NINE men and women has met daily on-line for four years. Although it's their shared interest in fiction writing that brought them together, they've developed a concern for each other that transcends the original purpose of the group. They're a cyberspace family—and they act like one. When a member lost her job, the others rallied with emotional support and offers of help. When one member died, another wrote a moving eulogy. "I never met him. He lived in Texas and I'm in Ohio," she says. "But I knew him on-line and respected him."

She talks to the group four or five times a day, logging on to her computer in much the same way you or I check our answering machine for phone messages. "My other friends don't understand it. If I go away for a few days, I've got a hundred notes waiting for me on E-mail when I get back," she says.

Someone else found a friend on-line while attempting to adopt a child. She told me, "We met in an adoption forum on America Online. We were both trying to adopt older children out of state—and there aren't many people around in that situation. We really supported each other. We were constantly back and forth about which social worker we were talking to and what was going on. It meant so much. We're still in touch, though we've never met or even spoken on the phone. But I know we'd get along. We're two outspoken, pushy broads."

A single accountant has met on-line buddies face-to-face— lots of them. She joined an on-line "community" that scheduled regular get-togethers and outside events locally. Members met every other Tuesday night at a bar. They'd also go bowling and have picnics in the park.

These are just some of the ways friendship is being conducted on-line these days. It's easy to make new friends through chat rooms, discussion groups, even interactive games—and nurture established relationships via E-mail. Such options are expanding opportunities for communication and enhancing lives. And more and more women are using them. In 1993, the ratio of men to women on-line was twenty to one; it's three to one today.

Yet the explosion of interest (and possibilities) also raises disturbing questions. Although this kind of communication brings people together, can it also make some feel more alone and isolated? Does it encourage asocial behavior, fake relationships, a life indoors—even break up families? Because the medium is so new and is changing so rapidly, the full extent of its impact continues to unfold, and clear-cut answers can be elusive.

## THE BACKGROUND

The Internet enables you to reach out around the world while you're sitting at your computer at home. There will be over 108 million users of E-mail by the turn of the century, according to the Electronic Messaging Association (EMA). Although the Internet started as an American-educated white male university-based phenomenon, its reach has extended far beyond that scope. It has opened an exciting new world for millions of us, full of opportunities to meet a diverse group of people here and abroad. In the year 2000, the EMA estimates that we'll E-mail a total of over 6.8 trillion messages. As one user told me, "My phone hardly rings anymore." Says another, "E-mail has changed my life. I spend up to two hours a day responding to personal and professional messages."

According to Barry Wellman, Ph.D., professor of sociology at the University of Toronto, the big fear originally was that E-mail and the Internet would only be able to support narrow communication, such as requests for information. Supposedly there wasn't enough "social presence" to allow people to relate as friends on-line. "That's turned out to be generally untrue," says Dr. Wellman. "If people know each other, their relationships carry over quite nicely. Even if they relate exclusively on-line, as in my BMW car group, feelings of friendship can develop quite nicely over time," he says.

For women particularly, the benefits have become readily apparent. We thrive on conversation and connection—and E-mail is a lot cheaper than the telephone. It's time-flexible, as well, particularly useful for busy lives and for those who live in different time zones. It can be tough for two people to get on the phone together at an hour that's convenient for both. How many times have you played telephone tag with a friend? But you can write an E-mail message whenever you want. You probably wouldn't call someone at midnight, yet you can send an E-mail then if that's when you find the time. The message is there until the recipient signs on and reads it.

On-line capability allows you to:

*Keep up (or supplement) existing contact.*

For Nora, forty-five, a San Francisco fund-raiser for a nonprofit group, E-mail combines the unique values of letter writing with speed and practicality. Eight years ago, Nora, who is single, launched a correspondence with a man she met at a professional conference. He lived in Vermont, but frequent letters cross-country deepened their platonic friendship. When a job opportunity eventually led him to move to San Francisco, phone and face-to-face contact became more frequent and easier. E-mail is a bonus opportunity for in-depth communication across town.

"He gave me E-mail, over my mild protests, and installed the software. I wailed, 'We talk to each other on the phone. We really don't need this.' He said: 'We will. You will.' " He was right. E-mail offers Nora the same ability to reflect aloud that she enjoyed with letter writing. She explains, "He's my best friend and soul mate. We're both creative, both level-ten articulators, and that's been a bridge between us. My letters were always long. There was a real conversation going on—responses to the last thing being said. He'd say, 'So how are you really?' and I'd tell him what I was thinking, the feelings that were sitting on me at the time—when it was a puzzle to me and when it made sense. So instead of just writing news or information, it was writing to discover."

In writing to him, Nora was also writing for herself. The letters actually became her journal. She missed that when he moved close by. Phone conversation was not the same. E-mail, on the other hand, offered more. "There's the gradual unfolding, an amazing process which I capture on E-mail. Each of us stores what we write and then we can review—and see a pattern. I might say, 'You know, you told me such and such a long time ago—here I'll show you.' It maps the progression of our friendship."

Less poetic, though equally enthusiastic, is another woman who communicates by E-mail with her sister, seven blocks away. "Now when I think of something funny, I share it with her on-line. If she wants to remind me of my mother's birthday, she E-mails. We connect a lot more often."

*Keep contact with a friend far away.*

Women are more likely than men to use E-mail to maintain ties. I stay in touch with a colleague in Atlanta, a pal in Houston, and another friend two hours away in upstate New York. We don't get to see each other anywhere near as often as we'd like. E-mail increases our contact and brings us closer. It's so easy to share little details of life (such as how you spent New Year's Eve) that increase intimacy and bind you together, but that get lost when you don't speak regularly.

It astonishes me to be able to correspond by E-mail with an English couple my husband and I met on vacation in France three years ago. They sat at the next table at lunch one day and asked us to snap their picture. There was instant chemistry. Four hours later, we were still laughing and talking together until the waiter finally shooed us out. They live a few hours from London; we live in New York. Yet we recently met for a long weekend in Paris. We arranged the whole trip, complete with discussions of which museums to visit and restaurants to try, via E-mail. Now we're planning another rendezvous next year.

International on-line groups arrange meetings, too. In one case, twenty people (mostly women) from the United States and abroad met in an on-line chat room and communicated for months. A member finally suggested, "Hey, we've been talking so long, why don't we get together in person?" People from all over the country convened in Miami to meet the people they'd been in touch with and spend the weekend together. One woman from Australia couldn't make it. But she plans to visit the United States soon to see a good friend in the group.

*Put down a "marker" when you're pressed for time.*

Sometimes you hesitate to call a friend if you haven't spoken for a while because it will take hours to catch up and you're rushed. But you can send an in-between hello via E-mail. E-mail is also handy as a buffer. There are some friends with whom you can't have a short phone call. They like to talk—and you're interested. But you don't always have the time to listen. With E-mail, you control the time. You can say what you have to say, period—and read the reply at your leisure.

If people send you E-mail all the time, you may feel an obligation to respond. But you can say something like "I can't type another word. I'm bushed. I'll call you tomorrow"—and you're through. Or "The date was great. Details in the morning." You've made contact but it's quick and short.

What used to be a cute card saying, "Thinking of you," can also be converted to E-mail. It's an easy, fast way to keep in touch. One woman receives greeting cards on-line that probably wouldn't have arrived if the sender had to go to the trouble to buy them in a store. "A Halloween card had witches and goblins marching across the screen, with music in the background. It was fun. It adds a little joy to your life," she says.

E-mail is also great for quick support when someone is experiencing a difficult time. Let's say a friend is experiencing scary heart disease symptoms and must go for a series of tests. Although you want to be there for her, you can't talk every night for an hour. You *can*, however, check in every day by E-mail. She feels supported and you don't feel overburdened.

*Expand your network and connect with others who share an interest.*

You can meet people with common interests in chat rooms and forums available on virtually every subject—parenting, fitness, divorce, retirement, gardening, addiction, you name it.

One woman who has battled a weight problem since childhood values the medium as a place to air very difficult feelings. "I go to a general forum, but many women there also have weight problems and I've gotten a lot of support from complete strangers. One person talked about all the attention she suddenly got once she became thin. She said, 'I never got attention before and it's demeaning in a way'—which was exactly how I felt. I've lost a lot of weight, too. It's the sense that 'I'm the same person, but you didn't want to talk to me when I was very heavy. As soon as I got thinner, you noticed me.' Friends also started treating me differently. I found out from the forum that this is very common. It validated the way I was feeling and allowed me to get out the anger, rather than let it fester."

Friendship can be deepened through E-mail. The ease of transmittal brings people together in a way that might not have happened before. An administrator feels that E-mail enables her to reach out. She feels freer to E-mail someone she doesn't know very well. "If I had to write or call, I might not have such frequent contact, especially if it involved a long-distance phone bill. I notice I've become friendlier with people I've started E-mailing on a professional basis."

*Get real help.*

One way the Internet is useful is as a source of information. The woman mentioned earlier who was trying to adopt a child received crucial advice and information from her on-line friend—and was able to reciprocate. "She had a series of harrowing experiences and never knew from one day to the next whether she was getting the child or not. Because my husband and I are very knowledgeable about the child-care system, I could tell her, 'They're jerking you around. Don't take no for an answer.' In turn, she knew a lot about the laws in Pennsylvania and also gave me the name of a social worker who found kids for out-of-state couples."

A graduate student joined a group of international academics and journalists on-line who helped her professionally. One member aided her research for her Ph.D. dissertation. Another connected her with a book publisher for her thesis. Someone else helped publicize her book.

A receptionist whose sister had been molested found she could relate to members of an on-line group on sexual abuse. Over 10,000 Internet sites cover health and medical topics. You can find information on—and connect with others concerned about—anything from heart disease to retinopathy of prematurity, a condition which strikes some premature babies.

An Internet discussion group called the Breast Cancer List* offers women with breast cancer, their friends and relatives, clinicians, and interested others a new type of virtual community. Accessible to subscribers, it offers information, psychological support, conversation, announcements, analysis of news items, and a sounding board for opinions. Because it's available twenty-four hours a day, if you're anxious about something at 2 A.M., you don't have to wait till morning to log on and talk with someone. It's also a boon to the homebound and to people who lack transportation or who live in rural areas and don't have in-person support groups nearby. You don't have to leave the house to connect with helpful people.

On-line communication may encourage more uninhibited social connections, according to Barbara Sharf, Ph.D., professor of medical education and health communication at the University of Illinois College of Medicine in Chicago. "It probably frees people up to say what they want to say without worrying about being identified. With something like breast cancer, where there can be some appearance changes, such as surgery scars or baldness, no one can see you," she says.

*Search for people when you've lost touch.*

Wonder whatever happened to your best friend in junior high—or to your old flame? If you have the time and inclination, you can search for people you want to locate through the member directories of on-line services like CompuServe or America Online. Or you can check phone/address directories (http://www.four11.com is one such directory). Or type in the person's name on a search engine like Yahoo; if he or she has a Web site, you'll locate it.

One woman got an E-mail from someone she went to camp with twenty years ago. "She wrote, 'I noticed your last name

*E-mail: listserv@morgan.ucs.mun.ca. Type "subscribe breast-cancer" in the message field.

in the directory. Is it you? It has to be you!' I answered her, of course, and we're trying to get together."

## ON-LINE DATING

The Internet increases opportunities to meet eligible people. "It's a great place for women because it's 70 percent men. The odds are in your favor," says Lisa Skriloff, coauthor of *Men Are from Cyberspace: The Single Woman's Guide to Flirting, Dating and Finding Love on Line.* "When you run a personal ad [on-line], you're more likely to get a response than from a magazine. People get a ton of mail. Guys usually answer right away because they're already on-line."

There are also so many singles sites that you can specifically target your likeliest prospects—guys who share your religion, interests, and geography.

Faye, a thirty-year-old Los Angeles stockbroker, has met more than fifty men on-line. People have told her, "How can you do that? It's dangerous," but her attitude is: You can meet a psycho in a bar, too. "On-line you have more time to scope them out. If what they say doesn't ring true, you get out."

Up-front about the fact that she wants to get married and have kids, she's exuberant about what she views as an extraordinary resource of eligible men. "I'm new here and it's not so easy to meet men in this town. When I heard about a singles area on America Online, I tried it. I felt the population of men would be pretty upscale—and it has been. They're mostly professionals. You have to have a certain level of education, sophistication, and affluence to be there in the first place. High school dropouts don't have computers. I've met a bunch of good people," she says.

The crop includes a film producer she's now dating. (She answered his ad.) In some other cases, although romance didn't develop, men she's met (including a graphics designer and a tax consultant) have become good friends.

E-mail is also a good way to ask a man out. He has time to

think about it. If he isn't interested, you might as well find out early and in a gentle way. It softens the blow to read, "I don't know if you knew I have a girlfriend," rather than to hear it on the phone.

## THE DOWNSIDE

On-line relationships can be healthy, helpful, and supportive for women, but the medium itself also facilitates certain problems. Because it's so new, there isn't necessarily a well-established shared set of expectations about how it will be used. You can be exposed to toxic people and situations—and get hurt. Here's why:

*You don't know who you're talking to.*
    The Internet is a great leveler because basically all you get is the text of the message itself. There's not much information about the gender, class, or appearance of the person on the other end other than what he or she chooses to reveal. That anonymity leaves you vulnerable. Lacking visual cues or other sensory information, you can't tell that someone belches in public, wears white socks with a blue suit, has bad breath—or has a crazy look in his eyes.
    People can lie and assume other identities on-line. They may pretend to be the opposite sex (it's a rare phenomenon, but it happens). You may be talking to a woman on-line (you think)—and discover it's some man impersonating a woman. There's no way to know. If it happens to you, it's natural to feel angry and exploited; the person has violated your trust.
    Men aren't the only ones who change gender, incidentally. Women have said, "The only time I get to be heard is when I pretend I'm a man."

*Quick bonding is risky.*
    Because this is a much more confessional medium, you're

more apt to reveal important and serious information sooner than you would in person. "You're anonymous and writing is qualitatively different than speaking face-to-face. You think, 'I'm not going to meet this person. Why not?' And you start talking. You tell about your life—and two hours later you're communicating intimate thoughts and feelings and dumping your soul at a complete stranger. It often takes years to form a close friendship, but it only takes days or weeks on-line," says Kimberly S. Young, Psy.D., author of *Caught in the Net: How to Recognize Internet Addiction and a Winning Strategy for Recovery.*

People are more likely to open up about their sex lives immediately. In revealing such information, however, you're placing trust in someone you don't know. Disinhibition can be dangerous.

*Misinterpretation can occur.*

Because you don't have face-to-face contact on-line, you miss body language and you don't get feedback. You don't see smiles, grimaces, or raised eyebrows—or see someone shrug or nod or look away. You miss verbal cues like eloquent pauses or a sarcastic tone of voice. As a result, you can be misled. If you send an interesting man an E-mail—and he responds with a short reply—it's hard to tell whether he's being abrupt or not. In a phone conversation, you know right away that he's not interested—or that he's glad to hear from you.

Misunderstandings can arise even with people you know. Suppose you become reacquainted with an old roommate and start communicating with her via E-mail. Because you're busy and don't check your mail regularly, you don't respond to messages immediately. One day you could receive an irritated ultimatum: "Answer me on a more regular basis or I'll have to cancel you off my list." It happens. Some people consider it rude not to reply to E-mail within twenty-four hours. Others wonder what the fuss is all about, viewing E-mail response as something to take care of when you get around to it.

*There's the potential for abusive messages.*

People have received annoying E-mails and sent nasty ones back before they've had time to stop and think about it. It's so easy to respond fast, without reflection and sober second thoughts.

The lack of intimidation on-line has led to a practice called "flaming"—sending abusive messages. If you're the target, it can be very upsetting. Flame wars (back and forth attacks) have developed even between colleagues. Although people who work together wouldn't usually scream at one another and slam doors, they can yell at the screen and express anger much more strongly on-line than face-to-face. Other people may feel freer to join in, too.

One on-line expert comments, "If I say something stupid on the phone, I doubt that you'd tell me I'm 'a dumb asshole.' The fact that the other person isn't there seems to lead people to do it."

Expressing an unpopular opinion on an on-line bulletin board can elicit abuse. One woman received hate mail on-line after posting her ambivalence about abortion. "I was personally attacked by proabortion people. A lot of people are afraid to express opinions on controversial subjects because they know what happens to others," she says.

### On-line addiction has arrived

For some people, on-line connections with others can become a narcotic. An estimated 2 to 3 percent of users are addicted to being on-line—and women are much more at risk than men, according to Dr. Young. Addicts seek social support, sexual fulfillment (without the risks), and the creation of an identity on-line (a persona)—not simply an exchange of information, she says.

A lot of women are depressed, lonely, bored in their lives, and they want some excitement. They may get it by playing roles and meeting somebody on the Net. A wallflower type is able to flirt.

In her on-line survey of 396 Internet-dependent users, Dr. Young found that 20 percent more women than men responded. Almost half were homemakers or students; only 8 percent were employed in technology. Twenty-eight percent of respondents reported participating in "Multi-User Dragons" or MUDs (interactive on-line fantasy games), where a role is assigned (or the person chooses to play a role), while only 10 percent reported surfing the Web.

Thirty-five percent used chat rooms. Women tend to frequent chat rooms because the exchange is faster than E-mail and interactive dialogue is much more appealing. Says Dr. Young, "Women make friendships that are very sincere and important to them. Two homemakers are home alone. They have a couple of kids. Maybe they talk about their pregnancies. They pass the time. It's not necessarily harmful, unless it takes over. When used in moderation, these relationships can be healthy and helpful and offer support groups for women." Sometimes, however, women go into a chat room and start flirting with men. They get involved in the romance of it and become so enmeshed that they forget about their families.

Imagine spending fifteen hours a day on-line. You stop shopping for groceries and forget to pick up the kids at school. The computer becomes the focal point of arguments with your husband. Such cases have become increasingly common—and can lead to divorce. Sometimes these relationships are downright dangerous. In one case, a twenty-seven-year-old restaurant manager was impressed by an accountant she met in a chat room. She tried to be careful, calling his firm to check him out and make sure he was legitimate. She flirted with him on-line for months, then finally agreed to meet him in person in the lobby of a Dallas hotel. They'd go out for dinner from there.

When she arrived, she called his room. He said, "I'm not quite ready. Why don't you come up for a few minutes?" She did. Finding the door ajar, she walked in—to find him hiding behind it, stark naked. He was also obese, bald, and nothing like the fantasy prince she expected. Although he had been honest about his occupation, he had deceived her about everything else through role playing. She ran out and, fortunately, got away. Yet she went right back on-line, looking for her next connection.

Says Maressa Hecht Orzack, Ph.D., a psychologist who heads the computer addiction clinic at McLean Hospital in Belmont, Massachusetts, "[Computer addiction] is very much like gambling. There are hits—or rewards—and losses. People think, 'The next time it's going to work out.' "

Many suffer from clinical depression or bipolar disorders. They're dissatisfied with their lives and turn to the Internet as an escape mechanism, much as some people use food to cope with bad feelings. Some literally have cravings for on-line interaction—and it feels good. Some probably use chat rooms as nonthreatening ways to get approval.

Says Dr. Orzack, "Everybody has certain needs and people who are depressed or shy need to belong, to have respect, and they need sex. All of these needs can be met on-line. They're respected for their ideas; somebody thinks they're important and listens to their advice. Nobody knows they have a big nose.

"As they stay on the Net longer and longer, they obviously sacrifice something. Ask their families and they'll say they're neglecting husbands or not spending time with the kids or in danger of flunking out (if the addict is a student). There are a few documented cases where people were granted custody of their children because the spouse was on the Net all the time and neglecting the kids."

## The Cybersex Phenomenon

One of the many side effects of meeting people on-line is the emergence of cybersex, the playing out of erotic fantasies and sexual acts via computer. Two people type fantasies back and forth to arouse each other. There's flirting and mutual stimulation without actual physical contact with the other person. In *On-line Friendship, Chat-Room Romance and Cybersex,* authors Michael Adamse, Ph.D., and Sheree Motta, Psy.D., describe virtual sex as more spontaneous and adventurous than real-life sex. You don't have to worry about how physically attractive you are (or wear lacy lingerie) or be concerned about AIDS or other sexually transmitted diseases.

Says anthropologist Cleo Odzer, who chronicles her own experiences in her book *Virtual Spaces: Sex and the Cyber Citizen,* "It's fun, it's compelling, it's emotionally arousing. You learn a lot about yourself if you look."

There are major emotional risks, however. Your on-line partner may not be who he says he is. He may be married—who knows? "He" may even be a "she." The partner can disappear at any time, never to be heard from again. There are jealousies and rejections. It's addictive. Burnout is always a possibility. An Internet affair may explode with passion, then fizzle after a few weeks because it's too much too fast. The frequency and intensity of highly charged emotional exchanges may lead to overload. In real life, a romance usually unfolds over time.

Meeting in person is a mistake, according to Odzer, because you can never match your fantasies. "Don't go to cyberspace for a boyfriend," she warns. "Take it for what it is—a really nice relationship, but one that probably won't work out in real life. It's an additional experience, not an 'instead of.'"

She's even made a close woman friend on-line. They started out as rivals, sharing the same cyberboyfriend. At first they were intimidated by each other. Then they started comparing notes on men and found they had lots in common. When the woman became ill, Odzer checked in with her every day on-line, although they have never met in person.

## WHAT WE KNOW SO FAR

The Internet is an extraordinary tool that broadens horizons and enhances lives. It's made to order for our busy lifestyles today. But is on-line communication more susceptible to misunderstandings and abuse than face-to-face situations? It depends on who you ask. Supporters say the negatives are overemphasized— that people get burned in real life, too, and are no more or less lonely than they used to be. They view the Internet simply as a new medium to which we are just becoming accustomed.

Others voice mounting concern that although computers may not create asocial behavior, if tendencies lie in that direction, computers reinforce them. People used to go out and socialize because entertainment was available only outside the home. Now we have so much going on inside—TV, videos, CDs, and the computer. Still, a machine is not the same as reality.

Who's right? Maybe both camps. As on-line communication continues to expand, we're still discovering applications—and sorting out implications. On-line relationships can be fulfilling, but you have to be careful how you use this medium. Enjoy the benefits, but to protect yourself, understand the risks.

## SMART WAYS TO CONDUCT A FRIENDSHIP ON-LINE

Don't believe everything you see and read on the Net. Remember the computer is only a machine.

1. *Use safeguards.*

To meet people on-line safely, watch what you say. Don't give out your last name, address, or phone number—so you can disappear if you decide that you don't like someone. In other relationships, you don't reveal how much money you make and other personal details unless you have a certain level of trust. Don't reveal personal information on-line either until you have that trust.

If you're interested in getting together with a guy, get his phone number and *you* make the call when you feel comfortable. To protect your identity, use caller ID block—dial * 67, wait until you hear the dial tone again, then dial.

Faye's routine runs like this: If someone seems appealing, she progresses to a phone conversation (she calls him). If she likes what she hears, coffee in a public place follows. She takes her own car.

A cybercafe is especially appropriate and has the right theme. Or go to a restaurant for a drink. The important thing is it's public and you've limited the amount of time spent; you're not stuck for a two-hour dinner. If you like the person and feel comfortable, only then give your number—or continue to call him. What if you don't make music together? Say, "It was nice meeting you. Good-bye."

At SmartDate (http://www.smartdate.com), each time you go out with someone, you can enter information on his identity, when and where you're going, and when you expect to return. If you should disappear (and a missing persons report is filed), the information goes to the appropriate authorities.

If you feel bad vibes from E-mail, ignore the message. People *have* been harassed and stalked by individuals they met on-line.

2. *Be prepared for disappointment.*

A cosmetics executive met another woman on-line who was very lively and articulate. They got along famously, were roughly the same age, and shared a love for Japanese culture and gourmet dining. When their on-line subgroup scheduled an in-person get-together at a member's house for tea, the pair finally met face-to-face. Says the executive, "What a dud! She was so animated on-line and so boring in person. I've since learned that it's pretty common. On-line communication lends itself well to people who don't have a lot of social skills because they're sitting at a computer—they don't have to go out of their way to connect with people."

She has mixed emotions about on-line relationships. "When you meet someone on-line, you can attach your own preconceived notions about the person that have nothing to do with reality. It has to do with how you're feeling at the time you see the words on the screen."

Faye has met some losers. "I'm originally from Des Moines and one guy was so dumb he didn't know where that was. He asked if it had beaches. I'm something of an intellectual snob and I never saw him again." Some respondents to *her* ads have ignored her stated preference for someone of her own religion who hasn't already had children. "Don't answer my ad if you don't fit the description. But some guys do. One wrote me a long E-mail telling me how love can overcome all obstacles. I thought he was bright but disturbed. He didn't even know me. It was inappropriate. But people don't like being rejected."

3. *Be aware of signs of addiction.*

Red-flag signs include: sneaking on-line and lying about how long you're staying there, loss of interest in other activities (including TV viewing), and inability to disconnect despite the trouble it's causing in your life. One typical pattern is people meeting on-line earlier and earlier each day—they have to be there because it's the only way they can feel good.

How much is too much? If you're on-line longer than you've intended—or if you're spending as much as thirty-eight hours a week or more at it—you may be in trouble.

Addiction is a symptom and treatment depends on what's causing the underlying problem. Someone whose problem is caused by depression is treated with medication or therapy to deal with low self-esteem, fear of rejection by others, or the need for approval. The goal is not abstinence, but less reliance on being on-line. Since we're expected to use computers today, people must learn to deal with using them in moderation. Part of the answer is self-monitoring and alternatives to being on the Net. When you're bored, can you call up a friend or exercise instead of going on-line?

The computer is a productive tool. It has useful functions. People aren't getting addicted to Internet banking. You can still stay in touch with your friend far away. But you might stay away from chat rooms if you can't use them in moderation. Removing yourself from a specific application may be your key to control.

4. *Watch your marriage.*

You can join a chat room innocently and before you know it, find yourself flirting. "Women fall in love on-line and want to leave their husbands. Husbands say, 'I can't control her,' and the wives say, 'I can't stop.' It's an obsession that is changing family life and the stability of marriages," says Dr. Young. Yes, you can fall in love with someone at the office, too, but cyberspace is a new arena for potential problems—especially since the anonymity factor can be seductive.

As for cybersex, if you're married, you're probably playing with fire. Although some users claim it adds spice to a marriage, experts warn it can destroy it. How many husbands would tolerate wives who engaged in cybersex? It's easier than you think to get sucked into an affair.

Realize that you can also get bad advice on-line. People can make recommendations, such as 'You should leave your husband,' when they don't know what they're talking about. Heeding on-line advice can get you into trouble and can even be dangerous.

5. *Realize you can't control who sees your message.*

Let's say you join an international on-line discussion group.

You meet a man you like and begin an E-mail correspondence—then discover everyone else in the group is reading your messages to him. It happened to Claudia Odzer. "I was attracted to him and we E-mailed each other until I found out he was sending my messages to everyone else, too. I thought, 'Wait a minute! Everyone is reading this!' It was a shock. They don't have the same etiquette rules in some parts of the world as in the United States. You really have to be careful because anything you say can wind up in weird places."

Of course, your E-mail can also be easily forwarded without your consent or knowledge in other situations. If you make a nasty comment about a client or your supervisor in an E-mail, the recipient can forward it to the person mentioned. The safest course: Don't say anything you wouldn't want featured on the six o'clock news.

6. *Educate yourself.*

Learn the technology and know what is possible to take advantage of the benefits, make new friends, protect yourself, and police your kids. Computer courses are available at colleges and in the community. I attended one sponsored by my college alumni association. Or hire the kid who's the neighborhood computer whiz to help you.

Over 120 SeniorNet Learning Centers are available throughout the country to promote computer literacy for people fifty-five and up. (Web site address: http://www.seniornet.org.) On-line safety tips are offered at http://www.cyberangels.org, which is associated with the Guardian Angels.

## 9

# Live Longer, Thanks to Friends (But Beware of Those Who Aren't Therapeutic)

YOU'VE GONE THROUGH half a box of tissues in a morning. Your nose is red and sore from blowing, your sinus passages congested, and your body feels tired and achy. The cold that's been coming on for two days is now in full bloom and you just want to crawl into bed. What do friends have to do with your misery? More than you know. Having a wide variety of social relationships can reduce your risk of *developing* a cold in the first place, according to research at Carnegie Mellon University in Pittsburgh.

When Sheldon Cohen, Ph.D., and colleagues exposed 276 men and women (ages eighteen to fifty-five) to cold viruses, they found that those with varied social ties were far less susceptible to infection. Subjects with few types of relationships had over four times the risk of developing upper respiratory illness of those reporting six or more kinds.* What counted most was the *diversity*

---

*Relationships included those with a spouse, family members, neighbors, friends, coworkers, schoolmates, fellow volunteers, or members of organizations and religious groups.

of relationships rather than sheer numbers. It's having many roles in your life that seems to be protective.

But the common cold is just the beginning. Evidence strongly suggests that social ties defend us against illness in general—and, when we do get sick, they boost our odds of survival. The more friends you have—and the more socially well-rounded you are— the longer you're likely to live. Friends are good for your health in other ways, as well.

## PHYSIOLOGICAL EFFECTS

There's a correlation between health and longevity—and the degree to which you feel loved and respected, feel you belong, and can turn to others for information and assistance. It's not clear why or how social support enhances health, but it seems to have a direct physiological impact. It is associated with faster recoveries, better outcomes from surgery, and a positive effect on the cardiovascular, endocrine, and immune systems.

In contrast, isolation can kill you. It boosts the risk of heart disease, death after heart attack, and other negative health outcomes. The research repeatedly cited is the nine-year study, reported in 1979, conducted in Alameda County, California. It found that people with the fewest close relationships with friends, family, and fellow church or organization members were twice as likely to die as those with the most social contact. Research elsewhere has reported similar results.

Having someone with whom you can freely discuss what's on your mind seems to be particularly important. In a much discussed study, Redford B. Williams, M.D., and colleagues at Duke University Medical Center found that a confidant can be truly lifesaving for people undergoing cardiac catheterization. Patients who were single and had nobody to confide in had three times the chance of dying within five years of those who were married or who had a confidant.

What is it about a confidant that's protective? Says Dr. Williams, "When something is stressing you, you're able to share what you're experiencing with another person you trust. Apparently just getting it off your chest and talking about your concerns with another caring human being reduces the impact of that situation on your stress levels."

And stress is key. The more of it you experience, the likelier you are to get sick. Stress increases your body's production of epinephrine and other hormones that can suppress the immune system, contribute to depression and anxiety, and may increase cholesterol. Research suggests that stress even slows down the healing of wounds.

Friends may protect us by reducing our physical response to stress. A study by Thomas W. Kamarck, Ph.D., and colleagues at the University of Pittsburgh found that when women engaged in stressful laboratory tasks, those who took a supportive friend along had lower heart rates and lower blood pressure than those who were alone.

Stress-related changes in heart rate and blood pressure may injure arteries and, potentially, trigger heart attack and stroke. If the same results found inside the lab occur outside, as well, it's possible that the presence of people you're close to (or the knowledge that they're available and can help you) may calm your response to stress in daily life. It might even be a lifesaver.

## OTHER HEALTH BENEFITS
## OF FRIENDSHIP

When illness strikes, supportive friends help you to cope with what's going on. They can boost your self-esteem and feelings of control over your life. If you're single and living alone, like Lynn, a forty-year-old Minneapolis corporate consultant, friends mean safety and security. Two years after undergoing a lumpectomy for breast cancer, Lynn was diagnosed with stage 3 (advanced) ovarian cancer. Friends not only made her feel loved, they also pitched in with material assistance.

Lynn's treatment ordeal began with a total hysterectomy and other surgery. She then endured marathon sessions of chemotherapy—twenty-nine hours of it at a time, every weekend for nine weeks. Although nurses tended her from Friday morning to Saturday afternoon, Lynn worried about what might happen when they left. If she fainted or suffered other reactions to the chemo, who would be there to know she was in trouble? To calm her fears, three friends alternated with her sister staying over on Saturday nights and Sundays. One friend, who had a child and a husband, drove four hours to take her turn. The effort meant everything to Lynn. "Just having someone there made me feel safer."

Although most weekends went well, Lynn recalls one unforgettable Saturday night. She stepped into the shower and began sudsing up, when she looked around and suddenly realized that hair was everywhere—a side effect of chemotherapy. "Hair was on the tiles; hair was on the ceiling, on the shower door, on the floor. It was all falling out and I started screaming hysterically. I had so many losses. I would never bear a child. I would never feel invulnerable again. I had a scar from my belly button to the pubic bone—and now I was going to be bald. It was just too much."

Her friend, who was sitting in the next room, came running. Says Lynn, "She immediately took charge. She told me, 'You get out of here right now. I'll take care of it.' She calmed me down—and then she got down on her hands and knees and cleaned up every last strand of hair."

Other friends' contributions were less dramatic, but they were no less appreciated. Some of them sat with Lynn while she was undergoing chemotherapy. "We'd order in Chinese food and talk and eat," she remembers.

Despite such remarkable support, however, Lynn also needed something else that her existing friends could not provide. She found it in a support group for gynecological cancer patients. She explains, "When you have cancer, you feel you're very different from your friends. It's wonderful to be with other women who are experiencing the same thing, who know what it's like to feel really scared and have options taken away from you—who have the same questions, such as 'What do you disclose to a new man you've met?' "

Research suggests that social support groups actually prolong survival. In a study by David Spiegel, M.D., and colleagues at Stanford University School of Medicine, women with advanced breast cancer who participated in psychosocial support groups lived almost twice as long (34.8 months) as patients who did not (18.9 months).

Social support groups also had major advantages for patients suffering from lung and other cancers (and who were depressed) in a study by social worker Ron L. Evans, A.C.S.W., at the Veterans Affairs Medical Center in Seattle. Depression, anxiety, and discomfort declined in participants after six months. Patients benefited from the encouragement in such groups and the chance to openly express anger and other strong feelings.

When you become chronically ill and have a family to take care of, friends can literally keep your household together. A group of eight devoted friends has stood behind Monique for years. Monique was first hospitalized with Crohn's disease when her children were four and six. She subsequently returned to the hospital ten times and had several operations involving major complications.

During long stretches when she could not care for her own kids, her friends took over. They took turns picking up the children after school and cooking family meals. It happened so often that Monique's husband started writing funny notes to them. "I'm tired of chicken," he'd say. "How about fish?"

Monique's best friend even shopped for her clothes. One size larger than Monique, she could try on a pair of slacks or a blouse and judge whether it would fit Monique. When she guessed wrong occasionally, she'd return the item.

Says Monique, "This went on for years. Yet when I talk to them about it today, they don't even remember. They don't think it's special. It's what one does for a friend."

## POSITIVE PEER PRESSURE

The people around you may also positively influence your behavior. You're stuck with your genes, for example, but you can make positive changes in your lifestyle. Friends may lead you to take better care of yourself and adopt healthier habits, such as regular exercise. Research in England found that women's friendships tend to promote health and fitness. One woman, devoted to a high-fat diet of beef and French fries, told me it was a lifelong friend who persuaded her to become a nutrition-conscious vegetarian. "She didn't lay any guilt trips on me or argue. She simply showed me that vegetarian food can be delicious and varied, something that I would never have believed. I am now more strict than she is—I don't even eat fish."

In research by Clifford L. Broman, Ph.D., at Michigan State University, social relationships were associated with taking preventive-health measures. People who belonged to organizations and were friendly with members were likelier than others to avoid damaging behavior. They were more apt to buckle up their seat belts. They smoked less and drank less alcohol.

Friends can also persuade you to get help when you're in danger—and denial. Take Barbara, who spent her nineteenth year adjusting to a new paralegal job at a San Francisco law firm— and to her parents' divorce. Remembering that painful time in her life, she told me, "Since sixth grade, I was the only one of my friends to grow up in a two-parent household. I had more security and stability than anyone I knew—and suddenly it was gone. It really hit me hard. I felt so shaky and uncertain—and rejected by my father. I had always been 'daddy's little girl.' How could he leave?" Her parents' split was traumatic enough to trigger a depression that evolved into anorexia nervosa, the eating disorder that involves self-starvation and affects 1 percent of women.

Barbara quietly began skipping meals. When she *did* eat, she reduced the portion sizes. Although her mother and her friends voiced concern about how drawn and thin she looked, she laughed off their worry. It was her pal since kindergarten who finally confronted her one night as they were having dinner together. Says Barbara, "I was only eating a small salad and I wouldn't even finish that. She's a very tough person and she came right out and said to me, 'Are you anorexic?' I got really mad and yelled back, 'No, get out of my face!' I couldn't admit to myself what was happening. But after she said it out loud, I began to realize that maybe I did have a problem.

"It took a while before I did anything about it, but finally I took the first step and went to my mom. She encouraged me to see a doctor and then wound up taking me to an anorexia expert." Barbara had therapy every week and attended a support group. Through it all, close friends provided support. "Part of anorexia is isolating yourself and not being social. They knew it was important for me to have a good time. They took me out a lot and tried to keep me occupied," Barbara explains.

She considers herself very lucky. "It took about two years to get past it—if you can ever totally get past something like that. I think there's always a part of it that's with you."

## NOT ALL FRIENDS ARE THERAPEUTIC

There's healthy support that empowers and energizes you—and the kind of support that can compromise your well-being. Some relationships and people (well-intentioned or not) make a negative contribution.

For example, we're affected by those around us—and any relationship in which health-compromising behaviors occur can be toxic. If you spend your time with someone who engages in risky actions (such as using drugs, drinking and driving, or speeding on highways), your own life can be at stake. Friends who make you feel insecure are downers. If someone makes you feel unacceptable or not good enough—if you always feel criticized or put down—that's a toxic relationship. Watch out for friends who depress you. They're not much fun and they can make you sick. Anxiety and depression affect immune function and boost your susceptibility to infection.

Friends who give unwanted advice can upset you and those who overdo assistance can reinforce helplessness instead of building on your strengths. Warns Lynn, "People who constantly moan 'Oh, it's so terrible' are not helpful. You don't want to feel that you have to take care of *them* when you're sick."

People who make demands can sap you. "One of the things the social support field is beginning to recognize is it's possible to have ties that are draining. It's one thing to have a lot of friends, but if the main exchange with them is they're always asking you to pick up their kids from school because they're too busy—and they're also too busy to pick up yours—that's not a very supportive tie. So it is possible for social ties to cost. Clingy friends are people who always make demands on you and don't reciprocate. I try to avoid them," says Dr. Williams.

The point is that healthy friends protect us from stress. They don't add it to our lives.

Then there are friends who disappoint us. Illness can be the test of true friendship. Some people pull closer; others fail to deliver support when it's needed most. Just the *belief* that you're not getting enough assistance can be a killer. In a study of heart attack survivors in Manitoba, Canada, perceived lack of help with daily tasks from friends and family reduced chances of long-term survival. Patients reporting that they needed a lot more help had a 6.5 times greater risk of dying than those who felt supported.

Peripheral friends often disappear when illness strikes. I remember one experience years ago when catastrophe struck my family. Out of nowhere, my husband suffered a stroke. He was hospitalized in a major medical center renowned for stroke care, but located in an older urban area that had seen better days. At one point, a casual friend volunteered the information that she couldn't possibly visit my husband because she "wouldn't go to such a neighborhood." The fact that *I* went to that neighborhood every day apparently slipped her mind. I'd never expected her to visit; we didn't have that kind of close relationship. But her insensitivity to the life-threatening crisis my husband and I were facing was enough to end the relationship. I never discussed it with her. I just stopped calling.

The supply of friends shrinks when a great deal of effort is required, according to social worker Wendy Lustbader, M.S.W., in her book *Counting on Kindness*. It's easy to have good times together, but inconvenience requires dedication in people.

The dedicated people in my crisis turned out to be my husband's best friend and his wife, who dropped everything and drove two and a half hours to be with us—and my friends Harriet and Martha. They'd listen, soothe me at a time when I felt I was falling apart, and allow me to be totally honest. I could talk about the unspeakable: my fear that my husband wouldn't survive—or worse, that he would live, but as a "vegetable." The fact was, I'd rather have him dead. Feelings raw, I needed total acceptance at that point—and I got it.

Fortunately, we were very lucky: My husband had a full recovery. But I'll never forget the friends who came through for us.

Wendy Lustbader told me, "If you get sick in midlife, you learn what kind of friends are the real keepers, which ones to invest in—who will be there for you. It's often the people who are humble and who have had their own share of trouble. When you're younger, you collect interesting people, but later, you're interested in traits that matter like loyalty and generosity. One true blue is worth a thousand others."

Monique had a friend whose self-indulgence destroyed the relationship. "She was always unavailable, except for what she wanted. One day when I was very sick, she was coming over with a few friends who were bringing a pizza for our lunch. She didn't want pizza and insisted on bringing something else that required me to get involved in preparations like setting the table since we could no longer use paper plates—and I was in no condition to do it. I felt so angry, I refused to come downstairs.

"When I was well enough to go out and we went somewhere, I always drove and picked her up. The one time she picked *me* up, I asked her to let me run into the post office for a minute and she refused. 'It's out of the way,' she told me. I lived through several painful experiences with her. Everything had to be her way."

Nobody's perfect, however. One of Lynn's friends had difficulty talking about cancer—and listening to how frightened Lynn felt. She was the only one who didn't want to see Lynn without her wig. "I was able not to blame her because many people close to her had died. I knew that illness was so painful for her. And she didn't abandon me. She did other things. Once, a few months after surgery, when I had no money and was really down, she took me on an all-expenses-paid vacation to Maine for a week. It was heaven." Time has passed and Lynn has been cancer-free for four years. Just recently, her friend was able to talk about her behavior in the early days. "She apologized for not being there for me as fully as she felt she should have been."

## HOW IT ADDS UP

Your network of friends, neighbors, coworkers, and other supportive people not only makes life easier, it boosts the odds you'll live longer, healthier, and happier. Social ties protect us from the stresses of life and from stress-related killers like heart disease, high blood pressure, and alcohol abuse. In the 1980s, the California Department of Mental Health ran the public service campaign "Friends Can Be Good Medicine." As the evidence mounts, that's truer than ever today.

## HOW TO TAKE CARE OF YOUR HEALTH

1. *Strengthen your support system.*

Figure out who provides what in your life—and what's missing. Then you can target specific areas for improvement. As mentioned, research shows that inadequate social support can hurt your health and raise death rates. Look around, think of the people you know, and evaluate the type and quality of each relationship. Is there someone with whom you can talk over concerns with complete honesty? In a Yale University School of Medicine study, lack of emotional support for hospitalized elderly heart failure patients (mostly women) increased the risk of additional heart problems in the next year. Discussing what bothers you with someone can be good for your immune system, reducing the need for medical care.

Says Kristine Jacquin, Ph.D., professor of psychology at Union Institute, Los Angeles, "When you confide, you're no longer the only one who knows, and there's a kind of release in that. You also may gain acceptance, empathy, understanding—and it's likelier you'll get some help." Friends and family also can increase compliance with doctors' orders, according to the Yale study. Having someone with whom to discuss problems may lead you to follow medical and lifestyle advice.

Is there someone who gives you a hug when you need it? Emotional support is caring that makes you feel loved, liked, or respected. Who can you go to for good advice or help in an emergency? A next-door neighbor helped provide Lynn with a sense of security while she was being treated. The woman told Lynn to ring her doorbell anytime she needed help, including the middle of the night. What a stress reliever!

Conversely, are you tolerating friendships that sap, rather than nourish, you? Monique finally dropped her self-centered friend, deciding, "I don't have to put up with this anymore. Who needs it?" The balance of the relationship had tipped way over to the negative side.

2. *Try to increase intimate interactions.*

Intimacy—the feeling that someone is connected to you, understands you, and that you in turn understand them—may protect your health. Heart disease expert Dean Ornish, M.D., goes even further. He has spoken of "emotional heart disease"—and a *Newsweek* magazine article quotes his statement: "Love and intimacy are at the root of what makes us sick and what makes us well."

Try to increase intimate interaction with people. Physical and verbal affection, simple things like shaking hands, a simple touch on the arm or shoulder in greeting, and eye contact, increase the sense of intimacy.

"Other things you can do that are intimate but disconnected at the same time include having someone wash or brush your hair. Or you can do that for a friend. There's something soothing and healing about these experiences, especially in our high-tech society where many people feel isolated. There's a lot of research recently on the importance of touch," says Dr. Jacquin.

Physical contact is a need basic to all of us. Yet because touch is viewed in so many different ways, many people are afraid of others touching them (understandably) or of touching others. Some people are more naturally touchers. But friends can easily give each other a literal pat on the back. A hug and a good cry together is emotional support, too.

3. *Provide social support to others.*

Providing support to others increases social support for yourself because it expands the contact you have with others, including those you help. Even if they don't give much back (or don't give back the same things), there's intrinsic importance in giving. It's also part of increasing your intimate interactions. There's something about helping people that builds your self-esteem and confidence even if the other person's response is lukewarm.

A good example is volunteer work with children or the elderly. For years I was a volunteer phone counselor at the Covenant House Nineline, a crisis hot line for teenagers and their families. After receiving intensive training, I was able to connect many desperate young people (such as runaways and/or abused and neglected children) with real help. Once a week for four hours, I had the satisfaction of knowing I made a difference in somebody's life. It was a feeling money can't buy. I also met other volunteers and staff members—an altogether enriching experience for *me*.

4. *Specifically ask for what you need.*

It's possible to have a number of friends, but still feel your needs aren't being met. Sometimes it's simply a matter of asking. Dr. Jacquin observes, "I think that's particularly true of women who are very independent. They may get stuck in 'I'll do it myself,' but they could ask others to help them out or give them something." Even asking someone to walk the dog or feed the cat or water the plants can improve the nature of the relationship and the sense of social support.

5. *Put yourself in places where you're apt to meet compatible people.*

You can have people around you, yet still feel lonely, which may or may not indicate a toxic relationship. Some people move to a new place and don't meet (or become friends with) new people. An estimated one in four Americans has experienced loneliness in the past few weeks and as many as 10 percent of Americans suffer from severe and persistent loneliness, according to the National Institute of Mental Health.

If you feel you need more people in your life, frequent places where you're likely to find those with similar interests. Intrigued with writing or art? Take a class. Join a social club, civic or professional organization, a church or other place of worship. Then be patient—recognize that friendships don't grow overnight. Sometimes you may go to a group over and over and fail to meet great friends; it takes time. But it's worth the effort. There's a link between loneliness and physical illness. Having multiple social ties has been associated with reductions in anxiety and depression.

6. *Try religion.*

The social support of a religious community can help you deal with a medical crisis. Fellow church members may baby-sit the kids, bring cooked meals, assist with rides to the doctor and other services. Regular attendance at a house of worship brings you in contact with others and helps build that support.

7. *Consider a support group.*

Today there are support groups not only for cancer patients and survivors but for those who must deal with AIDS, arthritis, heart disease, infertility, diabetes, stroke, depression, epilepsy— you name it. A group can be helpful in raising self-esteem and empowering you—as well as offering the opportunity to connect with others in the same situation you are in. Many participants wind up becoming close friends. Lynn laughs that she and a friend from her group know the intimate details of each other's sex lives. They do know that—and more.

There are a half million self-help groups of all kinds today. For information on one that might interest you, contact the American Self-Help Clearinghouse, Northwest Covenant Medical Center, 25 Pocono Road, Denville, NJ 07834 or call 1-800-367-6274 (out of state) or 973-625-9565 (New Jersey residents). You can also contact your local chapter of a national organization like the American Cancer Society or the American Heart Association.

## HOW TO BE A FRIEND TO SOMEONE DEALING WITH CANCER

Virtually all of us know someone who is being (or has been) treated for breast or other cancer. What we often *don't* know is what to say to express caring and concern to the person and what to do (or not do) to be truly helpful. As a result (and because of our own fears about cancer), we may feel awkward and uncomfortable. Cancer puts a strain on any relationship. But you can be

the best friend possible to someone who needs your support.
Here's how:

1. *Know the dos and don'ts.*

Do ask "How are you?" or "How is it going?" The person
needs to know that others care. But realize that she may not want
to discuss it. Each individual has her own way of coping. Don't
take it personally if she changes the subject or responds in a
brusque, abrupt, or angry manner. If you're the fifteenth person
to ask the same question today, it can be grating. Patients can't
always respond politely and thoughtfully.

You might add, "If you don't want to talk about it, let me
know. You tell me," suggests Robin Zarel, M.S.W., a New York
psychotherapist (and cancer survivor herself) who works with
people facing serious illness.

Do ask "How can I help?" (But only if you want to. Understand how involved you really want to be.) The response may
be, "It would be great if you could make some meals I can put
in the freezer. Then while I'm at treatment, my husband can pull
them out and heat them in the microwave." Or, "If you really
want to help when I'm going to radiation, could you pick up
Suzy at ballet class?"

*Do not,* on the other hand, say "I know how you feel," because
you *don't* know how someone else feels. The emotional experience of cancer is different for everyone.

2. *Accept the person's feelings.*

Do so even if they're unpleasant ones, such as anger, despair,
and feelings of "Why me?" (at least initially). The best thing a
friend can do is hear those negative feelings out, rather than tell
the cancer patient how she should feel. Instead, well-meaning
people often respond, "Don't worry about it. You'll get through
it," or "Don't be upset. You're still the same person," or "It
could be worse. You'll be fine" when the friend doesn't feel that
way at all. Such statements only deny her feelings and increase
her sense of loss.

One patient told me, "My own sister would say, 'You have to think positive' and 'You're okay.' Finally I said to her, 'I probably am, but that's not what I need to hear from you right now. What I need is for you to let me be as upset as I am.' " Everybody likes to be around someone upbeat. But if the person isn't, expecting her to be a hero simply adds guilt to an already heavy emotional burden.

3. *Be patient—and understand what's going on.*

When women are diagnosed with breast cancer, for the first time in their lives many truly have to be self-absorbed. To move ahead, they need to concentrate on themselves, understand what's happening to them, and take control of their lives because cancer often stirs feelings of being out of control. Sometimes this change can erode support. It's very hard for others who are used to depending on the person to understand that the roles totally change. Family and friends can feel neglected. Focusing on ourselves is also totally at odds with what society has taught us as women. We're supposed to take care of others. Thinking of ourselves is often considered self-indulgent.

In the short term, the self-absorption is tolerated by friends and family, but many expect patients to snap out of it quickly. If it continues too long, understanding *can* turn into resentment. Friends often withdraw. That puts a great burden on someone who's struggling with survival. Realize that everybody's different; everyone has a unique experience. The kind of cancer it is counts, too. Some people may need a lot more time to heal than others.

Robin Zarel suggests, "If self-absorption persists, then you have to say to a friend, 'Look, I know it's horrible, but hopefully you will get better.' The word 'hopefully' is important because you don't know the ultimate outcome. Giving false reassurance makes people feel angry—and isolated."

Almost all cancer patients experience feelings of loneliness and isolation, even though they're getting a lot of support. Existentially, they're alone with it.

4. *Recognize your own feelings.*

Friends or family members experience some of the same feelings as patients (such as loss and anxiety)—but in a little different way, according to Karrie Zampini, C.S.W., director of the post-treatment resource program at Memorial Sloan-Kettering Cancer Center. It might take the form of "This could happen to me," or "I'm going to lose the person," or "She will be sick all the time, have a lot of pain, and I'll have to take care of her." You may feel guilty because this person is upsetting your life also. "But these feelings are normal. You're not a selfish person if you have them," says Zampini.

Sometimes you need help to enable you to help someone else. Says Zampini, "A social worker, psychologist, or other helping professional can help you understand feelings of anxiety and guilt and deal with them. We have open-house meetings for caregivers, which includes friends as well as family members." The American Cancer Society or the social services department of your local hospital can help you find counseling services, as well.

# How Friends Can Make or Break Retirement—and Life Beyond

LISTEN TO THIS poem," says the older woman, who proceeds to read the verse from a poetry newsletter to her friend seated in the next chair in the beauty salon. Woman number two listens, then observes, "I like this one better." As she reads her own selection, she reassures her listener, "You're going to love it."

I'm eavesdropping on a conversation between two women having hair-coloring touch-ups. What strikes me most is not only the topic of conversation (poetry isn't the usual beauty-parlor fare), but how firmly they present their opinions, how patiently each listens to what the other has to say, and how honestly they sometimes differ. Bess, the tall redhead is eighty-two, though she looks years younger. Never married, she explains, "I'm an unclaimed treasure," attributing her barely lined skin to "Crisco on my face every night." Helen, the petite blond divorcée in Ferragamo shoes and fashionable gold jewelry, is seventy-two. Both are retired, and as I open a conversation with them, they gleefully tell me the story of how they met on a golf course thirty years ago. They've shared the links, poetry, vacations, joys, and trials ever since.

Bess observes, "She's more attractive—and younger. But our relationship works because she doesn't look upon me as older. I introduce her to interesting new areas—and we don't compete. She always gets the men, but she includes me in her social life. I've already had a thousand lovers. We're both independent and we respect each other."

Think about retirement and positive aging—and chances are your health and the state of your finances come to mind as the secrets of success. Although their benefits can hardly be denied, they do not eclipse another type of capital—the human kind. As the bond between Bess and Helen illustrates, friends are also essential to the later years. In fact, research suggests they are even more important than family to psychological well-being in later life. Friends not only help fill leisure hours, they're sources of assistance and emotional support. "Even having just one person to confide in—someone to talk to about your concerns, who will understand you and provide affirmation—is really important. It matters if someone thinks you're worthwhile. Socializing also supplies mental stimulation—and the motivation to get out of bed every day," says Rosemary Blieszner, Ph.D., professor of gerontology and family studies at Virginia Polytechnic Institute and State University.

Which is why one of the best ways to take care of yourself at this stage of life is to value your positive friendships, enhance them, and be open to new ones.

## WHY FRIENDSHIP MEANS
## SO MUCH NOW

When you retire (or your partner does), everything changes. There are shifts in lifestyle, relationships, and activities—whether you decide to play golf every day, pursue important hobbies or further education, travel, get a part-time job, or become involved in church or civic activities. Change is stressful—and friends help ease the transition. People with more friends and acquaintances experience a smoother adjustment to retirement, according to research at Penn State University that analyzed the impact of men's retirement on marriage.

Friends serve as a buffer to the stresses of this major life change, boosting self-esteem and morale, and offering opportunities to participate in activities like sports and clubs. They validate your abilities (now that feedback isn't coming from the workplace) and reassure you that you aren't the only one who can't remember where you put the keys. They're resources for advice and information on everything from services and discounts for seniors to job and volunteer opportunities.

If you're married, friends are good for your relationship with your spouse in retirement and are associated with marital satisfaction. Says Alan Booth, Ph.D., coauthor of the Penn State study, "Part of the benefit of friends is having a rich interpersonal environment that can be extended after retirement. But friends also provide ideas on how to deal with problems. Friends were especially helpful for those who had left very attractive jobs—or who were dealing with division of labor in the household."

Who does the vacuuming, who makes the beds, and who cooks dinner become thorny issues for some couples once men are home. Although some retired husbands slip right into sharing chores, others resist. It helps to be able to ask friends, "How did you deal with it?" More and more wives also continue their employment after husbands retire, either because they enjoy their jobs or wish to move to a lower family income at a more gradual pace. Friends can tell you how other husbands filled their time while wives went to work. "The more extensive your networks, the more opportunities you have for getting both practical and emotional help," says Dr. Booth.

## TYPES OF FRIENDS

Both old and new relationships serve important needs. Long-term friends help us adjust to aging and the limitations gradually imposed on us. They provide continuity, telling us who we are—and how we were. They share a lifetime of memories—of raising children together and surviving trials and tribulations. No need to explain the cast of characters or fill in the blanks; old friends know the history and the people important to you. The chance to reminisce with those who can relive your youth and other enjoyable experiences with you validates you and your life.

A pattern of lifelong friends (both mutual and individual, often from childhood) is vital to the well-being of marriages of fifty years or more, suggests research by Finnegan Alford-Cooper, Ph.D., associate professor of sociology at Stetson University, DeLand, Florida, and author of *For Keeps: Marriages That Last a Lifetime*. Dr. Alford-Cooper told me that both husbands and wives have enduring friendships that provide strong social supports.

If you're a widow, old friends provide sociability in the face of tremendous loss. Take Vera, who was widowed at sixty-nine. Shortly after her retirement as a jewelry craftsperson, Vera's husband of fifty years died in a tragic automobile accident. Having worked at home for decades, managing household and family, Vera hadn't spent much time developing her own outside friendships. Her husband was her best friend, confidant, mentor, and lover.

Since his death, however, she has made an effort to revive relationships with two other women who frequently exhibited with her at crafts fairs. These friendships, which began thirty years ago, have deepened and grown. She told me, "One friend is married; the other lost her husband but now lives with a man. We're all amateur artists and meet regularly once a week in one another's houses to paint, talk, and have coffee together in a relaxed and peaceful atmosphere. In the summer we paint outdoors, taking a picnic lunch along. We know each other so well that we can spend long periods quietly working, without the need for constant chatter."

To help cushion the loneliness, Vera has also reached out to new friends. She's made many acquaintances by joining a mystery book club and participates in folk dancing. "I try to have some activity where I meet people every day of the week," she says.

Vera has also connected on-line. She started her own on-line group and corresponds daily with four other women (including two in Australia and one in Canada) in what she calls "my own little fun forum." As she describes it, "We enjoy wordplay and what one member calls 'delightful idiocy.' We've developed quite a deep bond between us—and have our more serious moments, too." They even send photos of themselves, pets, and grandchildren to each other via E-mail. She participates in a chat room, too, that includes two retired men.

New friends like these have their own special roles to play. They expand our horizons and introduce us to options and possibilities we hadn't considered before. My mother seems to have grown into her own skin since my father died two years ago. Virtually paralyzed by being alone at first, she gradually began tiptoeing into the world, not as somebody's wife or mother, but as a person in her own right. She has blossomed, adding several new friends and broadening her activities.

It was a friend who literally took her by the hand to enroll in classes for senior citizens at a local college. She's now a regular there, taking bridge lessons each week and attending lectures on everything from health to history. She sees movies and vacations with a woman she met at the beauty parlor. Another new friend has introduced her to transportation services for the elderly and has also initiated a mutual security check: They alternate calling each other every morning to make sure they are safe and well. Such support has brought my mother a new level of confidence and pleasure.

Her experience is fairly common. In research by sociologist Rebecca Adams, Ph.D., of the University of North Carolina at Greensboro, some widows felt that their friendships flourished more after their husbands died. Some said their spouses had directly interfered with their friendships and discouraged their involvement, both out of jealousy and fear that they might be stuck with the check for an unattached woman.

Dr. Adams found other shifts in later-life friendship patterns. As we age, we don't sever our ties, but develop a new style once we are relieved from the concerns of middle age. "Women who used to be involved in children and the PTA became more cosmopolitan—traveling and establishing broader friendships with other kinds of people. Corporate wives tended to gradually withdraw and focus on a few close friends. Working women who hadn't much time for relationships while on the job tended to move toward senior centers and bridge clubs—places where people congregate—and added many friends," says Dr. Adams.

A Purdue University study of people eighty-five and older found that the key to adapting well to aging may be talking daily with friends and rolling with life's changes. Many of the subjects interviewed remained socially active, despite health problems and losses of children and spouses in many cases; 54 percent of them talked with non–family members every day.

Many felt they could count on neighbors when they needed help—an important plus. Although family is usually the first social-support network called into action, not all older adults have family (or relatives nearby); 20 percent have no children. There may be no one else to turn to except friends and neighbors, who help with tasks like picking up a prescription at the mall or driving you to medical treatment. Friends also provide solace when there's a death in your family and support if you're a caregiver.

## OBSTACLES IN LATER LIFE

Although later-life friendship has great rewards—intimacy, dependability, support, and shared interests—tensions and restrictions in the retirement years can strain ties and reduce or eliminate contact between friends. Distance is a major issue because as you get older, close friends often live elsewhere. You (or they) may have relocated for a job years ago or after retirement. According to the U.S. Census Bureau, 26 percent of people sixty-five or

older who move relocate to another state. Sally, sixty-five, a retired social worker now living in Phoenix, found the miles can
stress the most committed relationship. When she decided to
move from her home in Michigan, her best friend of forty-five
years felt abandoned. "How could you *do* this?" she responded
angrily on hearing the news.

Sally, who is divorced, recalls, "I told her, 'I'm not going to
the moon. You'll come to visit.' But she and her husband came
the first year and she was sick the whole time. That was the end
of it. She never came again. It was really tough. Now we've made
an arrangement where we take turns calling every other weekend
so we can keep up. It's a phone friendship, and I do miss her,
but what can I do?

"I always said I'd never move. My children and friends are
back there, but I've always been the adventurous one, and it was
too depressing to stay. I saw so many people my age having a
good time in Arizona. I've made new friends who share my interests in golf and the arts. I also met a man there and felt it was
time to have a relationship. Everything fit.

"I know she's hurt and I do what I can. I'm going to spend
next weekend with her when I go back to see my children. She's
like a sister to me. But she's got to do her share."

Women who stay connected, who correspond with and call
old friends despite the inconvenience are happier than those who
lose touch, according to Dorothy Clarke, M.P.S., director of the
National Center for Women and Retirement Research, Long
Island University, Southampton, New York. "If you've worked
on friendship throughout your life, you have more support and
comfort available from people who care and know you very
well," she says.

Yet many friendships do fade. That happened to a Chicago
retiree who relocated to San Diego. She remembers, "Some
friends were so happy for me about the move. One even did
research and got information for me. But another became jealous
and threatened because I wanted a new kind of life. I was chang-

ing—and she wasn't. The friendship was stronger on her part than mine; it had no influence on my plans. I've seen her only once since I moved," she says.

Changes in financial circumstances may come between you, as well. If one of you lives mainly on Social Security and can't afford to travel, go out to lunch regularly, or buy theater tickets, it can limit contact. If it's hard to stay in touch with coworkers after you retire, friends you used to work with may drift away.

Shifts in health status can make you less compatible. If circulation problems force one of you to stop playing tennis, it may create a conflict of interest. Does the active person find another partner and spend less time with the friend? Long-term illness that leaves one person housebound may strain close friendships.

Even if you're in relatively good shape, transportation can be an issue. Dr. Alford-Cooper found that for some older couples who had difficulty driving (due to hearing or vision problems), it was harder to keep up active friendships. "Though not everyone liked age-segregated communities, what they did like was the ease with which they could make friends in such settings. Social life was built in. They didn't need a car to visit," she says.

## PERSON-TO-PERSON DIFFICULTIES

Envy is a major source of anger between older friends. In a study of fifty-five male and female members of an urban senior center (ages sixty to seventy-nine), 29 percent of women reported conflicts with friends caused by one being more affluent or healthier than another—or one having a husband. The authors of the study speculate that declining resources may make women more sensitive to these differences. Another major cause of distress, especially for those in their sixties, was failure of a friend to live up to what is considered an appropriate role as an older person. Subjects felt that people have a responsibility to age successfully. They were miffed at friends who didn't behave like positive, productive senior citizens by, for example, not taking care of their health despite being advised to do so.

Issues that arose when you were in high school may still cause problems at this late date, too. A sixty-six-year-old Connecticut divorcée was virtually dropped by her friend when a man came along. Like many women, the pair did everything together. They depended on each other to go out to dinner, to concerts, to antique shows. When the friend found a sweetheart, however, she reduced the friendship to phone contact. The excluded woman felt abandoned and cut off. It took months for her to adjust. Eventually, the romance did level off and the friend began to make some time for her. But these hurts are not forgotten.

In contrast, Helen often invites Bess to join activities with her new male friend, explaining, "If you're sure about yourself, you include your friend."

The three of them often spend Sunday afternoons together and it's easy to see why. Bess is dynamic, fun to be with, and full of ideas. Knowledgeable about investments, she sometimes supplies Helen and her guy with stock tips. She always pays her own way and also invites *them* to the movies or to visit flea markets with *her*.

Bess comments, "She's not worried I'll steal her boyfriend and I never whine to her, 'Why can't I come along?' That's why I get involved in my own activities." She teaches poetry classes to senior citizens at two New Jersey community centers and rarely misses a museum exhibition.

Bess also comes through in tough times. Years ago, when Helen's significant other left her, it was Bess (a former sportswear buyer who traveled the world on business) who pushed her out of the doldrums by proposing a trip to Greece together. They had a ball. By the time they returned, Helen was ready to get on with her life.

Although these two mesh seamlessly, Bess had a grating experience with someone else. This friend continually bombarded her with "why don'ts." Bess shakes her head in resignation, recalling the woman's unsolicited advice. " 'Why don't you get call waiting? Why don't you take vitamins? Why don't you eat broccoli?' She was so anxious she couldn't tolerate friendship. She didn't understand human nature. I spent four weeks with her in Hilton Head playing golf. The days were okay, but she held me hostage at night. I wanted to go home, but she had the car."

Irritating personality characteristics stress friendship. In a study of adults fifty-five through eighty-four by Drs. Rosemary Blieszner and Rebecca G. Adams, women complained that certain friends were bossy, self-centered, pushy, nosy, gossipy, moody, jealous, belligerent, overly demanding, scatterbrained, or competitive. Easily angered people can be a challenge. They might misinterpret others' words and personalize what was said even though it didn't concern them. Dr. Blieszner observes, "Some people are touchier than others and see the negative side where something may be unintended. Generally it's how you interpret things that influences behavior. Imagine two thin-skinned people being friends. It would be difficult."

Other tensions are associated with taking advantage and asking for too much help—or giving too much. If you get more than you give, you feel guilty; if you give more than you get, you feel used. As Karen Rook, Ph.D., has observed, friendship is based on fun and social contact, not aid. It also involves equals; when one person becomes dependent, it can be difficult. Most friends provide assistance only for a short time.

Dr. Blieszner recalls one woman whose neighbor asked her for rides to a local doctor. The woman didn't mind doing it—the neighbor had serious vision problems—but the neighbor also had a daughter. Why didn't *she* drive her mother?

The neighbor's requests became more frequent, then escalated. She asked for longer rides, this time on an interstate highway, to another medical facility. Says Dr. Blieszner, "[The neighbor's friend] was afraid to drive on big highways and didn't do it for herself. Given her driving limitations, the friend felt the request was inappropriate. Though racked with guilt, she said no. It served two purposes: She didn't have to drive—and it cooled down the relationship."

Maureen, a sixty-seven-year-old retired personnel director, was asked to stay with a friend's husband during his recuperation from a hip replacement to give the wife a break. She was happy to come over to help, but quickly discovered that the wife (in a second marriage) had lined up a number of people to substitute for her—while she pursued her own activities. The friends were spending more time on the husband's care than the wife was. Maureen firmly told her, "People are talking. I'm not going to take care of him. He feels abandoned by you." Annoyed at first, the wife later called and said she appreciated Maureen's honesty. Says Maureen, "Her life was based on what she wanted other people to do."

Nobody likes public criticism, but it's especially irritating to older adults. Some people don't mind being teased about talking too much (or thinning hair); others are offended. Part of having social skills involves the ability to predict how people will react, to know what the sensitive buttons are and that certain things shouldn't be mentioned in public. If a friend brings up that subject, especially if she does it repeatedly, her behavior can end the relationship.

So can betrayal of trust—someone who doesn't stick up for a friend or reveals a friend's secrets. If a friend confides her worries about a daughter's alcoholism—or that a grandchild is gay—she's seeking support, but she doesn't intend that the world should know about it. The discovery that you gossiped about it can be a serious blow to the relationship.

Some people think financial discussions are very private. On the other hand, sometimes you *want* people to reveal things. If you had heart surgery and need help around the house, you might want a friend to call everyone else so they can organize and bring over dinner. If she *didn't* spread the word, it might be considered betrayal.

## THE BALANCE SHEET

Not all later-life friends are dependable or supportive; some can *add* stress to your life. Despite these realities, friends (along with money and health) form part of the mosaic of positive aging and successful retirement. And their importance is likely to grow. At the same time that we're living longer, adult children are working and juggling other commitments, leaving less time and energy for caretaking. Households have shrunk; in the future, fewer adult children will be available to pitch in. Friends helping each other can pick up the slack.

Fortunately, as women, we are at an advantage. We keep more lifelong friends than men do and develop new friendships more often in later years. Our adaptation and relationship skills are assets.

As Dorothy Clarke sums it up, "We're finding women who nurture their friendships feel better about themselves and approach the whole aging process with grace. They're not lonely."

## HOW TO BENEFIT FROM FRIENDSHIP IN LATER LIFE

Exercise, making friends, and participating in activities are three of the most important factors in health and functioning, according to the Center for the Advancement of Health.

1. *Develop and maintain existing friendships.*
The quality of your friendships is important to life satisfaction. Work on them. Evaluate how important your long-term friends are and appreciate what you have to offer each other. Make time to be together and try not to lose contact. Fortunately, technology can help. Nowadays you can get E-mail and keep in touch without worrying about long-distance phone bills, even if you live a continent apart or illness gets in the way. Don't underes-

timate the power of short letters and cards to keep you updated and connected with friends.

Don't take friends for granted. Remember to act like a friend. Be tolerant, accepting, and patient. "Everything can't always be just how you want it to be. You must be able to tolerate differences," advises Dr. Blieszner. Be trustworthy. Stick up for your friends and don't reveal their secrets. Don't fail to reciprocate. Reciprocity is related to satisfaction in friendship for older women.

Don't leave it up to others to show affection; give it. Let old friends know you approve of them and like them by saying, "I agree with your decision." Older adults consider it important to remember birthdays, have little celebrations for holidays, and rituals like Tuesday morning coffee. These are ways of interacting that are successful anywhere.

## 2. *Keep making new friends.*

To age well, you need friends who provide the emotional, social, and practical support you require—and do it effectively. Since it's common to lose friends in later life—they move, they die—it makes sense to try to expand your resources. Old friends are irreplaceable, but it may take new additions to help buffer losses and fill your life.

If you add friends, but also keep old ones, you benefit from both continuity and new experiences. Many people actively seek out new connections when they move into retirement communities or spend winters in warm climes. If friends have relocated while you've stayed in place, new relationships can revitalize your social schedule.

Think about what you want in a friend and seek those people out. Says Dr. Alford-Cooper, "Don't be too shy; other people feel just like you do. It's risky, but you have to reach out to people rather than stay home and get absorbed in everything that is wrong with you."

Options differ, of course, depending on factors like your

health, whether you're employed, finances, geography, and personal preferences—but you can act on whatever opportunities do exist. Vera found living alone very hard and made an effort to take up new interests that would move her out into the world. She volunteered for the ASPCA and taught an adult literacy class. When she moved to a smaller house, she found a next-door neighbor who shared her love of gardening and literature and joined her at fitness classes.

Only a small percentage of people take advantage of senior citizens centers. Yet centers offer opportunities to meet others and sponsor important activities ranging from exercise to bridge lessons to trips to places of cultural interest. Observes a grandmother of twelve, "The senior center has all sorts of things going on, including a drama club. I have always wanted to be a movie star and here is my chance. I think I will join."

She also loves the Internet. "I've been on it for three years and often wonder what my life would be without it," she says. "There is a whole new world out there to investigate. When I was still working, there was no time to get into it, but now I feel blessed. I've found friends with the same interests and, most of all, I have lots of fun writing and reading E-mail. I think it is important for retired people who cannot get out much or for caregivers who have to look after someone who shouldn't be left alone too long. The Internet is a connection to the outside world."

If you are not yet computer-literate, educate yourself. See Chapter 8 for information on computer classes, including those at SeniorNet Learning Centers, which are specifically for people fifty-five and over.

Some people grow weary of starting new friendships. The deaths of friends can sap your will to make new ones. But losses are less devastating if you can turn to other relationships.

3. *Cultivate retired friends.*

People who share your retirement interests and have the time to pursue them are important. Employed friends can't spend

Thursday afternoon at a museum or the mall. Says Bess, "It's important to find people who aren't working full-time. You can easily share and discuss your feelings, go places and do things together. I know one lady who works. Her husband just died and I'd like to comfort her. But she's at the office and she has other problems to take care of. It's difficult to maintain a relationship."

Many of her friends retired at the same time she did, enabling her to continue the relationships. She spends a lot of time with two of them, plus her golf buddies. "Everybody should play golf because you connect with a variety of people, both men and women, at a municipal course. I saw one man I met on a golf course for three years."

4. *Consider intergenerational friends.*

Many older people make younger friends in order to fill in for losses and to stay active and in contact with the rest of the world. We might not expect that friendship can cross generational boundaries, but friends who do so have a good understanding of the benefits—and they know that relationships don't have to be based on money or physical vigor. Older adults can contribute advice, wisdom, and support. Younger adults can offer energy, fresh ideas, and even instruction in technologies and trends.

For years my husband and I reveled in a friendship with an artist in his eighties and his wife, a retired school principal. The four of us shared a passionate interest in art in general—and a local arts organization in particular. They regaled us with stories of the old days and their circle of artist friends in the 1930s, some of whom are world-famous today. In turn, they wanted to hear about our lives and those of our children. We visited or went out to dinner with them two or three times a month and found them more interesting, more exciting to be with than many peers we knew. Their crusty personalities, outspokenness, sense of self, and lack of interest in what other people thought about them (or their opinions) put off some people but delighted us. Their authenticity seemed like a gust of fresh air in a world of doublespeak and political correctness. They died a few years ago. I miss them still.

5. *Don't be too picky.*

Bess remembers the time she attended a barbecue and stood talking to a man who was clearly interested in her. To her shock, a friend tried to steal him. "She walked over, wrote her phone number on a piece of paper right in front of me, and handed it to him, saying, 'Be sure to get in touch with me.' I was speechless. Later she apologized, 'I don't think I should have done that.' I told her, 'No, you shouldn't. Don't do it again.' Someone else would have scratched her eyes out."

Bess didn't for two reasons: She knew the man was interested in her and she had enough confidence to restrain her anger. She was also realistic. "I thought, 'What am I trying to prove? I'll just make her aware. Why should I hurt her? You have to be cool and logical. I don't entirely trust her, but I find she's valuable for what she is. We play golf and she's in touch. I'm alone. She calls and says, 'How are you?' "

As we grow older, we tend to drop superficial relationships and we may have stiff standards of what a person has to be in order to be our friend. You can't be friends with everyone. But isolation is negative, too, taking its toll both physically and psychologically. Very choosy people can wind up alone.

Be more open-minded and tolerant of someone who could potentially be your friend. Nobody is perfect, and if the pool of candidates narrows (and you've changed), you may no longer be looking for what you once would have expected in a long-term friend.

New friends are not going to relive your history with you, but they can be morale builders, confidants, and supporters. They may not have the same values, but they can participate in activities with you. People who are not necessarily like you can still be good companions. Occasionally a new friend may even be as supportive as an old one. Vera recalls, "At one point, I became very depressed and couldn't bear to be alone in the evenings. I'll always be grateful to my friend next door who invited me in to spend every evening until I could manage on my own again."

6. *Encourage your partner to develop and maintain friendships.*

Men are less likely to have close friends and to replace lost friends than women. Overall, they tend not to confide or exchange intimate information with friends. When they retire, they lose the context for interaction with coworkers, which causes problems.

Men's tendency to depend primarily on their wives for emotional support may put extra pressure on (and stir resentment in) you. You may not have the time or inclination to fill in for the work buddies he no longer has. You may still be working yourself and find your job exciting at the same time he's come to the end of his career. One woman in such a situation, whose husband has been ill, told me, "He's depressed and he's choking me."

If you're not employed, your husband's lack of friends can disrupt your own routine. One woman finds that her small apartment has become even smaller now that her husband is home. "I can't talk to my friends on the phone. He's always within earshot and he doesn't like it." When he was at the office, he neither knew nor cared about her conversations. Some women give up activities they enjoy—such as a women's book club—because they feel they must keep their husbands occupied.

Ideally, men should be encouraged in their forties and fifties to develop their own interests and friendships in preparation for the retirement years. If your husband is already retired and lacks friends, however, it's a difficult problem. Try to help him identify his interests and find ways to extend them socially. One man who always wanted a career in medicine (but went into business instead) loves volunteering at a hospital. Some enjoy computer clubs for senior citizens, available in certain communities. Colleges often offer courses specifically for older adults.

If your husband likes bowling, suggest a local bowling club. Did he once play golf but gave it up? Remind him of how much he enjoyed the game. Point out the expertise he has to offer from years of work experience—and how valuable it could be to a committee for the American Association of Retired Persons (AARP) or other organizations. Check out the section of your newspaper that lists local events, as well. One small-town paper featured notices for a ballroom dancing club—and for volunteers for positions on the planning board and the environmental commission.

You may have to participate in some activities with him at first. Say something like "I'm going to check out the chess club. Want to come along?" Then you can pull back after he becomes involved. Even if he refuses, he may eventually follow your lead when he sees how much you enjoy the activity.

7. *Think of your own friends as insurance.*

Half of women over sixty-five are widows, according to the National Center for Women and Retirement Research. Dorothy Clarke observes, "Some women are very dependent on their husbands, which is not a good idea. It's better to have togetherness along with independent interests that each of you pursue. That way you have outside as well as couples friends. If something happens to a spouse, the other has activities and friendships that continue."

It's not being disloyal or selfish to have your own interests and relationships. Friendships (yours or his) don't have to compete with your marriage. They can enrich your relationship with your spouse. It's just as important to develop and nurture friends on your own as to exercise and eat properly. Think of it as staying emotionally and socially fit.

## 11

# *Friendship Lessons*

**N**OW THAT YOU know the benefits and pitfalls of friendship, what remains is to sharpen your awareness and basic skills. Friendship is maintained by similar attitudes, values, sensibility, affection, and satisfying communication and interaction. There is much you can do to keep your relationships running smoothly, prevent trouble, and repair or control damage when it occurs.

## EXPECT CONFLICT AT TIMES— AND DEAL WITH IT

Hopefully your friends are honest and true, but that doesn't mean you won't ever disagree, argue, or challenge each other. Any meaningful relationship will have tensions and conflict. There are constraints in adult life that affect what we are able to do (and when we are available) and they may not be negotiable. Friends can love each other yet have different needs, may be out of sync at times, or may perceive situations differently. Because we are human, well-meaning friends may sometimes act insensitively, get impatient, feel vulnerable, jealous, and angry. Opportunities for mistaken assumptions and misunderstandings lurk all around us. Fortunately, conflict does not have to erode satisfaction. If differences are faced and worked through, the result can be a deeper, more fulfilling relationship.

To get past the rough spots that inevitably arise, we can keep each other aware of our obligations (such as those to work and family), so that they don't come as a surprise. We can manage change and feelings and try to be a little more tactful to (and understanding of) each other.

We can also learn how to communicate when differences surface. If we as women are to enjoy the full potential of our friendships, we *must* know how to talk to each other at the difficult times. Often, we do not, fearing that the friendship will shatter if we say no and acknowledge and discuss feelings of hurt and disappointment. In fact, it is when we guess and assume that friendship suffers.

We can learn from others. Sophie's best friend of thirty years is like a sister. Yet her friend's last visit, on the occasion of Sophie's fifteenth wedding anniversary celebration in Chicago, became a painful experience for both.

When the afternoon party ended, the two friends walked along the lake together. It was a beautiful day and Sophie was still flushed with the joy of the occasion. Her friend, however, was somewhere else. "She was talking real fast about her affair with a coworker at her law firm and was very upset about their ongoing struggles. I didn't know how to handle it because I just wanted to relax and have a good time. I felt happy and was just so glad to be outdoors. I remember the scene. She was going on and on, discharging. And I said, 'Look at the sun's rays on the water.' It was this really horrible moment because in a way I felt I was failing her. But I just couldn't listen anymore.

"We went back to the apartment and just sat and watched the sunset out the window together—and it was over. But it was very uncomfortable and we're not used to that."

The next day, both women were able to talk directly. Bursting into tears, the friend wept, "I haven't seen you for a whole year and I have all these things I want to talk to you about." Sophie replied, "I know. I felt I was letting you down, but it was too distressing. I just wanted to be out with my best friend, strolling along—and I guess I wanted silence."

Says Sophie, "I think it was resolved in the sense that we accepted that we can't always need the same things at the same moment. We have to give each other room to want other things. You can't romanticize that you're never going to have conflict. You don't want to consciously hurt the other person; it just happens sometimes."

## COMMUNICATE CONSTRUCTIVELY

Conversations like these keep relationships growing and help prevent discord from permanently gumming up the gears. It's sad that we can't *always* be on the same page, but no relationship (including marriage) can always be in tune. At difficult times, however, we *can* say "ouch!" appropriately, let a friend know about our needs, and make the language of communication part of our vocabulary. Tensions build. A heart-to-heart discussion once in a while helps prevent neglect and keep conflict from getting out of hand.

1. *Express feelings (without attack).*

As you can see in the interchange between Sophie and her friend, sticking to "I" works best. "I feel really hurt that you didn't recommend me for the job" comes across quite differently from "You're so selfish and thoughtless," which understandably puts the other person on the defensive. When that happens, nothing gets discussed. It isn't easy to get comfortable with terms like "I feel upset (or taken advantage of)." It takes practice. But we must be aware . . . and try.

This "I" approach can be especially helpful when a friend does something that doesn't directly affect you, but that you consider destructive, such as getting romantically involved with a loser. In general, no one can really know what's right for someone else. The person involved has to figure it out. But you can be an expert on how you feel and focus on that. You can say, "I'm really afraid that you're going to get hurt here." She might not listen, but it would be a different encounter from the one that would follow a statement like "Are you crazy? How can you do this to yourself?" In the latter case, she's likely to feel insulted and that you don't care about her.

Unasked-for advice, which tends to be experienced as criticism, frequently makes the other person angry. No matter how wonderful the advice is, people often don't take it. So "I" is effective on all counts: It communicates information in a way that could benefit your friend and makes *you* feel better, too.

### 2. *Be direct.*

To avoid conflict we're often not straight with each other. We think being nice will take care of everything. But the result can be misunderstandings or not getting your needs met.

Take Marian, a Seattle broadcasting executive, whose relationship with her lifelong friend virtually ended because she couldn't say no. From birth, they were set up for competition by their mothers, who were close friends, and they constantly vied against each other in a volatile relationship that continued into adulthood. Real trouble erupted when Marian invited her friend (who lived in another state) to spend two days at her country place. The friend responded, "Great! I can stay for the week." That was far too much togetherness for Marian. But instead of reiterating her boundaries with "Gee, I'm sorry, but that won't work for me. Two days is good," she reluctantly went along. By the third day, she and her friend were squabbling. By the fourth, they were at each other's throats. The friend left in a fury. Since then, they've communicated only via Christmas cards.

There are people we love but with whom we couldn't live or take a vacation. There are people we enjoy only in small doses. They're too intense or argumentative or they have habits we can't abide beyond certain limits. We all have different needs for personal space. We must be aware of what we can tolerate and respect that.

Directness also works when you're unhappy with a friend's behavior toward you. A key question, according to psychiatrist Redford Williams, M.D., in his book, *Lifeskills,* is "Can the situation be changed?" If so, say exactly *what* you want to change, as in "I need more statistics for this project." Or (as I've said to a tennis partner), "Please don't give me a tennis lesson in the middle of a doubles game. It makes me angry." If the person repeats the behavior, you can remind her with "You're doing it again."

You can also prevent some objectionable behavior by saying in advance what you *do* want, as in "I just want you to listen," or "I just want to brainstorm out loud. I don't want advice." Otherwise, people can be misled. They also can't read your mind. If you want something, state it, as in "I want this information kept confidential."

3. *Listen.*

You can't be a supportive friend unless you know how to listen. But listening can be hard. I had no idea *how* difficult it is until I became a volunteer at the Covenant House Nineline and participated in its rigorous training program for phone counselors. At one session we were asked to listen to the person next to us talk for a minute or two without interruption. It's a surprisingly long time and it was very difficult *not* to interject a comment or ask a question. But listening means you *don't* jump in and talk—and you allow time for silence rather than waiting to pounce with *your* contribution as soon as the other person finishes a sentence. Some people don't know how to listen; they think conversation is a monologue—theirs. A supportive friend also accepts the other person's feelings without saying "Don't be upset" or "It will be fine" or "You shouldn't feel that way."

4. *Empathize.*

Not everyone feels the same way about a situation. To understand why people do the crazy things they sometimes do, put yourself in their place and try to understand their point of view. For example, it's important to value and celebrate friends' milestones and family events. Sharing such important times binds us and builds our history together. But sometimes external issues get in the way. Take the case of the marketing manager who booked a vacation trip to Japan with her husband, then later learned her friend was throwing an engagement party for her daughter at the same time. The friend thought the couple should change their plans, but they already had the plane tickets and hotel reservations and had scheduled the vacation dates at work.

The marketing manager didn't want to hurt a dear friend. She appeared at her house with flowers and said, "Our friendship is too important to let this get in the way. We understand how important the party is to you and we wouldn't miss it under ordinary circumstances. If it was the wedding, we might cancel the trip. But we feel differently about an engagement party."

The friend was not happy, but she knew she was being treated with respect. That's part of what communication in friendship is all about. Try to tackle problems together by saying, "Is there a way we can resolve this?" But solutions that make everyone happy aren't always possible. If the manager had postponed her trip, she would have felt resentful.

A lot of issues can't be resolved so both of you feel good. The best you can do is recognize the significance of events and try to treat each other's needs as fairly as possible. In this case, the manager might also have invited her friend and the engaged couple over for dinner before or after the trip. Negotiation means nobody wins, but the pressure is relieved.

5. *Communicate early.*

Sometimes friends disagree; sometimes they do things that hurt. We have to expect and handle that. Many difficult situations can be avoided if we acknowledge problems when they appear rather than keep quiet, sizzle, and allow them to escalate. Two women I know, who have been best friends for fifteen years and tell each other everything, found this approach works for them. If one feels the other is giving her a hard time, she immediately says, "Are you having PMS? What's wrong?" Or, "Has someone licked the red off your apple?" That clears the air and relieves a lot of tension. It puts a marker down and forces the other person to focus on what's *really* going on. She might be snapping because she's upset about a battle with her boss.

Of course, you do have to act judiciously. You can't be picky and complain all the time. You have to put up with a certain amount of irritation and "stuff" in human relationships—and let some things go. Sometimes you need a thick skin.

Pick your shots by selecting issues that are truly damaging to the friendship. For something serious, such as feeling that a friend is disloyal or is not giving you the support you need, it's essential to talk early because it's possible there has been a misunderstanding or that the offense might be unintentional.

A flight attendant never told her friend when she was angry. Instead, she told the world. "I'd talk behind her back and tell Mary and Sally and Sue. And you'd never know anything was wrong until one day, I'd explode." Her friends behaved the same way. Since then she's changed friends—and herself. Now anger comes right out. She coaxes it out of others, too, before it does damage. She told me, "One of my friends has a hard time saying when she's annoyed, but I'm so attuned to her tone that I'll get on the phone and say, 'Something's up. You don't sound right. You've got to tell me what's bothering you.' "

6. *Be aware of sensitive issues.*

Part of being friends is being sensitive to each other's vulner-abilities, what hurts each of you, what makes you angry or self-conscious. Once you say something that stings a friend, you can't "unsay" it—and it can damage a relationship. Someone may be touchy about the fact that she didn't go to college. You don't want to make snide remarks about cats to someone who adores them or belittle someone's passionate hobby. I can tell *you* about my rotten kid, but don't *you* disparage my child. It's one thing if I tell *you* I'm an insecure hostess, quite another if you tell *me*. Healthy friends support each other. Hot-button issues have to be handled with care.

Friends who care about each other understand each other's sensitivities and need for privacy. Friendship is really not an "anything goes" relationship. It's rare that you can just fire from the hip; nobody likes to be hurt.

One evening, a designer and her husband went out for dinner with another couple. As her husband ate a large filling meal, she was told by the other woman, "You're going to be a young widow." She admits there was a grain of truth in the remark, but as she puts it, "It was none of her business. I didn't want anybody to point it out. I felt really angry."

In some cases, you have to observe and learn about a person's individual sensitivities; others are universal. Nobody wants to hear "I told you so," for example. If someone ignores your advice and gets involved in a losing proposition, it's hard not to feel resentful. If you care about the relationship, however, you'll hold your tongue when the deal goes bad.

Talking about money—how much I've got and how much you've got—is often off-limits. Money may be a place to set boundaries. If you're going to lend money to a friend, decide at the start how much you're willing and able to lose (in case the loan isn't repaid)—and don't lend more than that amount. But don't lend anything if you're going to obsess, "Why is she buying a new dress when she still owes *me* money?" If you borrow from a friend, pay it back as quickly as possible.


## THE ART OF APOLOGY

I remember the biggest upset my friend Harriet and I ever had. Four years ago, my son suddenly developed a runaway sinus infection. He needed emergency surgery to prevent it from spreading to his eye. Naturally, I told close friends what was going on, and for the next six days of my son's hospitalization, I received concerned calls from everyone—*except* Harriet. I grew madder and madder. She had been acting very self-absorbed in recent months, but this lack of support during a scary medical crisis was the last straw.

When she finally did phone, I told her, "I feel really hurt and angry. This was *serious*—and you knew it. How could you *not* call to see how he was?"

She offered an embarrassed, lukewarm apology, which made me even angrier. Then she called back the next day and made a *real* apology. "I don't know what's the matter with me," she said. "I've been so obsessed with the possibility of losing my job that I've shut out everyone else's needs lately—not just yours, but others', too. I don't know what I can say to make it up to you, except that I'm truly sorry." She meant it; I knew it. We went on to have one of the most honest and intimate conversations we've ever had. Her apology took courage—and it strengthened our friendship. It was a turning point that took our relationship to a deeper level.

Apology is a special repair tool in friendship. Unless you sleep with my husband or hurt my child, I can forgive just about anything—if you take responsibility and say, "I'm sorry." Genuine apology specifically states the offense (shutting out others' needs in the above case) and explains why it happened (worry over being downsized). It has enormous power to heal relationships.

Apology is wonderful, too, in cases where *you've* behaved in a less than exemplary manner. I admit I've done my share of apologizing.

Consider the time a relatively new but very important friend mentioned to me at lunch one day that she would undergo a breast biopsy in a few weeks—her fourth biopsy over the years. I made a mental note to call at the time of the procedure, then promptly forgot about it. I was preoccupied with a number of stresses in my life. I'm also the eternal optimist. Since previous biopsies had been benign, I was sure this one would be, too, but neglected to realized that *she* might not feel that way. When I called her a few days before the procedure to discuss another matter, I never mentioned the biopsy.

I got a call from her a few days later. "I have a bone to pick with you," she said calmly, "and some advice for your book. I told you a month ago I was having this procedure. It's important to pick up on information like that and put it on your calendar to call a friend the night before and say, 'Good luck.' I'm terrified of cancer and I would really have appreciated hearing that. My good friends called after it was over, not before." I, of course, called not at all.

I was mortified at my own behavior. "I truly messed up," I immediately told her. "I was so focused on my own life, I forgot about you. And I was insensitive about how scary this probably was for you. I feel terrible and I apologize." I also told her, "I really appreciate your telling me how you felt."

My friend was frank about being hurt, which gave me the chance to examine my behavior, figure out what happened, and try to avoid a repeat in the future. Other friendships may be more tacit and cloaked in politeness. The offended person might mope a bit and you have to tease it out of her that she's hurt you didn't call.

Apology is difficult for many of us who have been taught that it's a sin to make a mistake or to admit we're wrong. If it's hard for you, realize that it takes a change in thinking—and practice. But the rewards are major. It's a tremendously freeing experience—a relief—to say, "I'm sorry." It also opens the door to forgiveness, which is another valuable friendship tool. When we were kids, we were able to say, "I'm sorry. Want to make up?" And we did. We apologized *and* we forgave. We need to do both as adults.

## FOLLOW THE RULES

There are also rules of friendship that help avoid difficulties and minimize conflict. When you follow them, relationships are more likely to stay on course. When they're violated, friendships fade or fail. To be a good friend:

1. *Don't betray a confidence.*

You can't have a friendship without trust, as Michelle, a forty-two-year-old graphic artist, well knows. She kept her friend's secret for sixteen years. While in college, Michelle's friend, Wendy, had a baby out of wedlock, which her family forced her to give up for adoption. Years later, Wendy married the father, who had not known about the baby. The couple moved to Houston to start a new life. They subsequently had two children. Neither they nor any of the couple's friends and neighbors knew there had been another child—except Michelle. As Wendy often pined for the baby she had to give up, it was Michelle, her only confidante, who listened. Every year on the child's birthday the two women went out to celebrate. Michelle recalls, "We'd pick a special restaurant and make a toast to her daughter. Then we'd have a good cry."

Although Wendy never wanted anyone to know, she always hoped that someday her daughter might look for her. Two years ago, she *did*. Of course she not only found Wendy, but a whole family—her father and two brothers. And she got an extra bonus, as well—"aunt" Michelle.

2. *Don't fail to reciprocate.*

Pull your own weight. If there's severe imbalance in a friend-ship—one person always giving, the other always getting—it leads to lack of trust. One feels overbenefited; the other feels cheated. Friends don't keep ledgers on each other, but there's a sense of fairness that should be kept in mind over the long run. We need to do well by each other. We're expected to be there when help is needed in an emergency.

Reciprocate affection, too. Give compliments. They don't cost anything and they mean a lot to people. There are so many ways to affirm a friend. You can say: "You do this so well," or "What a great idea," or "You always know how to [make me feel better, deal with kid problems, or pull an outfit together]." Although relationships with old friends are less dependent on shows of affection than with new ones, it's important to nurture all your friendships and not take them for granted.

Remember birthdays, if they're important to a friend, and do the nice things that make people happy. Part of being a friend is knowing what matters to the other person. A food consultant writes friends' birthdays down on her calendar so she automatically sends a card or calls. "How long does it take?" she asks. "A few minutes."

3. *Make an effort to get together.*

Simply being with each other is a source of satisfaction for women. The frequency may change, depending on what's going on in your life, but be conscious of staying in touch. With life so hectic today, it's easy to let friendships slide. If someone feels neglected, it might affect the friendship.

The food consultant keeps a weekly calendar-diary and regularly records the highlights of her day—what she's done and with whom. At the end of the month, she tallies which friends she hasn't spoken to recently and calls them. She also identifies those she's seen and how often. At year-end, she evaluates. "When I list my New Year's goals, I include five to ten people I want to see or talk to more—and I'm one of the few who meets my goals."

One way to see each other more regularly is to start rituals. When I wanted to take my friend Martha out to celebrate a big birthday, she suggested tea at a hotel. We had the best time sampling delicate sandwiches, scones, and pastries while sitting in an elegant stress-free oasis far from the cares of the world. It was such a magical experience, we're planning to have a simple tea every month or two to relax and catch up.

If intimacy is what close friendship is about, the phone connection is very important, too. Some friends "steal" time to speak to each other in the midst of family time or work. You can also combine activities. When I'm frantic for time, I often meet a friend of mine at a large local supermarket that includes a cafe. We both do our shopping, then relax and catch up over a muffin and a cup of coffee. You can take a friend along and chat at your child's hockey practice.

4. *Beware of criticism or intrusion.*

"Nobody wants to be judged all the time. You get evaluated everywhere in your life—at work, at home, by your kids. You don't want to hear it from friends," says Dr. William K. Rawlins, Ph.D., author of *Friendship Matters.*

There's also a difference between constructive criticism and the other kind. The former involves compassion and stems from good intentions. It aims at helping—bringing someone's attention to something that may be damaging.

Let's say a friend is going to a job interview wearing an inappropriately short skirt. If she needs the job, you might feel you have to risk irritating her and say, "You look really good, but that skirt is too short. It's not professional." That might irk the person, but chances are, even if she's peeved for a while, she'll be grateful. A friend has to make this judgment call. Criticism creates tension because women tend to be more sensitive than men; they care about what friends think.

One friend told another, "I love you a lot—and you're gaining too much weight. Lose it." This might not be good news, but it's caring. Says Dr. Rawlins, "The thing that's so sweet about lots of friendships is we develop what I call an assumption of benevolence. It's 'I assume that you'll do what you think is for my best interests even if you hurt my feelings. I assume there's a reason.'"

Friendship can be crippling if you become an enabler who commiserates with a friend's destructive behavior all the time. You can keep someone from growing the way they need to or from getting help.

Unhelpful criticism springs from envy, insecurity, or insensitivity. I remember the time I was held up for a few minutes on my way to a PTA meeting and a casual friend made the mistake of yelling at me in front of everyone for being late. I dropped her. Public criticism is a friendship killer.

5. *Celebrate others' success.*

Some friends are great when things are going poorly, but can't or won't share the good times. It takes a strong ego to celebrate someone's happy events.

Let's say you've been having infertility treatments. Then you learn that a good friend has become pregnant with her second child. Says psychologist Constance Buxer, Ph.D., "It would take a saint not to be envious of that. You don't have to be malicious to feel that way. But that doesn't mean you can't share. It may take a while to get past the 'Why her and why not me?' But people do it."

It's a good thing to express that you are happy for the person and admit, "How I wish it would happen to me." It doesn't detract from the other's happiness—it's "I'd like to be there, too." Some friends are even able to derive vicarious pleasure in such situations. It's a case of "If it can't happen to me, at least I can get close to it."

Envy can also be motivating. It worked for me years ago when a friend sold an article (her first ever) to a magazine that had twice rejected my work. Adding insult to injury, she'd dashed it off in one morning, while I labored over my work, which required research, for weeks. I felt furious. It was "How dare it be so easy for her? She isn't even a professional writer."

I finally used my anger to challenge myself: "If *she* can do it, *I* can do it." I proposed a new idea to the magazine—and *this* time I received my first assignment.

It's important to share *your* good news, too. However, discretion, kindness, and good editing should govern when talking to someone who can't match your success. Says Dr. Buxer, "I wouldn't tell someone whose son is in drug rehab that your son became president of the company."

On the other hand, women often hold each other back by not wanting to stand out from each other. It's "I don't want to be a star because I don't want you to feel bad." There are women who stay depressed because a friend is depressed—who don't go back to school because a friend is stuck in her own life and it would amount to leaving her. I know someone who walked out in the middle of her law school entrance exam. If she'd stayed, she might have passed it. Then she might have gone to law school and become an attorney while her friends remained behind. She couldn't take the chance. It's wonderful to care about a friend, but when taken to this extreme, it becomes destructive. When you fulfill your own potential, you also give your friend permission (and sometimes a push) to move ahead and reach *her* potential, as well.

## *Where Trouble Starts*

Jeffrey E. Young, Ph.D., who has studied friendship, loneliness, and relationships for over twenty-five years, told me, "Patterns of thinking developed in childhood can affect friendship for a lifetime." They can interfere with the ability to conduct close friendships, affect your expectations, and lead to toxic relationships unless you deal with them. In his book *Reinventing Your Life: How to Break Free from Negative Life Patterns and Feel Good Again*, Dr. Young outlines underlying patterns that cause problems in starting or deepening relationships, including friendships.

If your parent was very critical, for example, you may feel unloved, incompetent, and expect rejection—and therefore be very sensitive to criticism or any behavior that you perceive as rejecting. There may be the sense that if people get to know you, they wouldn't like you, leading you to keep people at a distance. This can interfere with making friends.

Such thinking patterns can lead you (or a friend) to be mistrustful, smothering, too judgmental, controlling, overly demanding, and competitive, keeping score of who does what for whom. Or they can cause someone to be an excessive caretaker, to tolerate unsupportive friends, to be overly dependent.

These patterns affect the selection of friends because we're often drawn to people who treat us the way we expect. Someone sensitive to criticism may unconsciously pick critical people as friends. Someone mistrustful may choose selfish people who are likely to hurt her. A "doormat" often chases a controlling person. We're attracted to people who push our sensitive buttons because they're familiar—similar to our parents, siblings, or others of significance in our childhood.

Toxic friendship occurs where one or both friends' issues get in the way, creating imbalance. One person is (or feels she is) doing most of the giving (or taking). One or both are very unreliable, unpredictable, and unable to commit to things. One person may always be needy and the other may always be the caretaker or decision maker.

We can all see ourselves in some of these situations. The question is, whose issue is it? If it's the other person's, you have to figure out how to work around it—or perhaps stop being friends. If it's your issue, you have to try to avoid repeating the same pattern over and over again. Do you need to lighten up? Are you oversensitive? Patterns can be broken. One woman, betrayed by several friends, told me, "I always chose the bitches. They were strong women and I looked for that; they were like my mother and her friends, who weren't so nice. They were always gossiping. I've changed my friends. I've learned how to recognize lovely, wonderful people."

Someone else told me, "I've accommodated for 90 percent of my life and put everybody else's interests before my own. I thought that was the only way to be. But I don't want that role anymore. I'm not going to feel bad anymore. Life is too short not to get your needs met."

Another made a conscious decision to get out of her life people who are always involved in severely dysfunctional relationships. "I'm not a social worker," she says. "I've heard their stories over and over again and there's nothing I can do to help them. In fact, I was probably an enabler—sitting there in rapt attention. I don't want to be there anymore."

Therapy often helps to make such changes, but someone else changed on her own. She had surrounded herself with friends who constantly asked for (and received) favors, but were never there when she needed support. "A male friend finally said, 'If you don't pull yourself out of these friendships I'm going to come yank you out. You deserve better.' That term, 'I deserve,' made the difference. I don't want to give myself away anymore."

## FINE-TUNE THE FRIENDSHIPS YOU'VE GOT

Things change; we change. To keep your mix of relationships in line with your needs (and to nurture positive friendships), you need to do housekeeping and maintenance work—defining the boundaries of the relationship and every so often asking yourself, "How is this friendship doing?"

Do some of your friendships need improvement? Are they downright unsatisfying? The key to satisfaction is a good match between your expectations and preferences—and the friendships you have. If you see people as often as you'd like to (not too much, not too little), if there's the right amount of reciprocity of assistance and affection, if the right type of help is given, and if what you want is matched in other ways, then the friendship is a good fit. Some of us like to be out all the time and want activities and friends to do them with; others are happy with a few friends with whom to have good talks. Some of us need more affection or to be listened to more than others. What do you need in a friend?

What's missing (or wrong)? Are some of your friends shallow or boring? What changes would make you happy? I fine-tune my own friendships periodically. I realized I was seeing one friend more often than felt comfortable. We didn't have *that* much in common. I reduced the frequency to an appropriate level. *Now* the friendship is satisfying.

I wanted to see another friend more often and broaden our range of activities. We had fallen into a pattern of eating encounters— "Let's have lunch (or dinner)"—and we weren't having much fun. It turned out that she felt the same and we've become more creative, going to lectures, taking tours, and shopping.

Do you have friends for different needs? Are there gaps? Do you long for someone to share your interest in aquariums, antique dolls, or tai chi? Someone with whom to go hiking? How would you complete the statement "I wish I had a friend who _____"? Do you need a confidant and emotional support? Without truly intimate ties we feel isolated and often anxious. Do you want friends for pleasure and fun, good advice, intellectual stimulation, encouragement? We often need friends who recognize our potential and reflect it to us, helping us to take positive risks that are good for us.

I've added friends recently. Moves, divorces, and other changes had depleted my supply of satisfying couples friends. It's difficult enough to meet *one* new friend with whom you feel a connection; it seems like a miracle to find four people who mesh. Yet I did find them, including a pair with whom my husband and I have renewed a relationship. We all attended the same college together. At the time, we were too different to be close. But we've grown in certain similar directions and now, decades later, we have become close friends.

Another new pal shares my budding interest in spirituality. We met at the home of a mutual friend and instantly connected. I try to keep my antennae up, always open to chance meetings or opportunities—then follow them up when I find someone who seems congenial. My husband and I met our old college friends at a bar mitzvah, of all places. We played catch-up, talked about old times, and called a few days later to propose going out to dinner. Someone has to take the first step; often it has to be you.

Joining clubs, organizations that interest you, a church, synagogue, or other place of worship are also good ways to connect with both couples and singles. Or start your own group. A military wife made friends all over the world by launching her own woman's group every time she was transferred. She talked to everyone, asked around, and inevitably found five or six other interested women through word of mouth. They met once a week, focusing on setting professional or personal goals (which could range from meeting a great man to starting a business) to realize their dreams.

My new spiritual friend and I launched a women's Bible group; I got the idea—she researched how to set it up. Through the group, I've gotten to know other interesting women. We're all different—covering a span of ages, occupations, personalities—and each of us contributes something unique and valuable to our ensemble.

Although some people are content with a few friends, and although there are costs to friendship, such as time and obligations, a variety of connections means more opportunities to grow. The more friends you have, the more options and choices you have, and the better your chances are of getting your needs met. If one friend isn't available, someone else is.

## SHOULD THIS FRIENDSHIP BE SAVED?

Toxic friends stress you out, try to use and abuse you, are over-demanding, unreliable, lie, manipulate, don't give anything back, and may betray you. What you do about it depends on whether *you've* created or contributed to the situation (and need to work on yourself) and factors like how important the friendship is to you and whether changes are possible.

The big issue is: What's in it for you? Are you getting enough out of this relationship? Over the long haul, do the positives outweigh the negatives? If not, why bother? It takes five positive interactions to every negative one to have a healthy relationship, according to Dr. Williams.

Some people need a lot of your energy and constantly call with "Could you help me with this?" or "Could you get me through that?" But if you need help, they're not always there for you. You don't necessarily have to end a friendship that's soaking up your attention. You can say, "I really don't have the time to talk about this now," or "We covered this ground and I don't know what else I can tell you." Says one woman, "You get to a burnout stage. You have to learn which friends want advice and will take it and which just use your ear as a crutch. Some need advice and some just need."

Are you remaining in an abusive or otherwise unsatisfying re-lationship? Why? Therapists say that we're not using our best judgment when we do this, or that there's some need—some-thing we're getting out of it—that keeps this negative relationship going. If it's just someone's annoying habit that irks us, maybe loyalty will win out. Maybe honesty will change the irksome habit, or maybe the person gives us access to important business contacts and we decide to put up with some aggravation. Only you can decide when a friendship isn't working anymore.

Some friends' transgressions are unfixable and intolerable, however. If your platonic friend seduces your teenage daughter, there's nothing to discuss. There are a few people who do not wish you well, often because of money or status envy they can't get past. If a relationship has strength and a compassionate under-pinning, there are ways to get around one of you having a great deal more money than the other. You can compromise on restau-rants and fancy vacations. But out-of-control envy is deadly.

I ended a friendship of twenty-five years because the person (and the relationship) had changed in a way that became toxic to me. The first law of friendship is that it be supportive and caring. It was neither anymore—and all the fun was gone, too.

Most friendships break up because of external problems—someone moves or you drift apart or you get promoted, stirring envy in the friend. In my case, the relationship started shifting a few years ago. Helene was in financial straits, divorced, and had little social life. Feeling guilty that my life was better than hers, I tried to be supportive. I called often, listened to her tales of woe, invited her to my home for holidays. Unfortunately, when you try to give some of your "stuff" to someone else to equalize an imbalance and ward off envy, you may wind up feeding it instead. The person often resents your generosity.

Every time I called Helene, the voice on the other end of the phone did *not* sound happy to hear from me. (Toxic enviers often don't want to see or talk to people who have what they want. They can't tolerate their envy and withdraw rather than face their feelings.) When I wrote my first book, which meant so much to me (I was not an overnight wonder and it took years to get there), she was the only good friend who didn't buy a copy to show support. An unpublished writer herself, she (not I) always brought it up: Somehow the stores were always out of stock. It apparently never occurred to her to place an order. Through tone and selected silences (like not ever asking about my work—we only talked about hers) she let me know she was uninterested in my professional life or didn't consider it of importance. I did talk to her and tell her I felt she devalued my work—and she did not deny it. Envy was in full bloom.

The final blow was a phone call in which she told me in detail about a friend (someone I do not know) who was being madly pursued by publishers to write a book. She wasn't sharing shop talk. It wasn't a case of "You're a writer and you'll understand what is happening to her." It was: "Don't think *you're* so special."

She followed it up with a discussion of a movie that I liked and she didn't. She let me know that she attended with five other women—and all of them agreed with *her*. I got off the phone shaking with rage—and feeling that I had just experienced the longest put-down of my life. There was nothing left for me in the relationship. The laughs and understanding and acceptance that had made the relationship precious to me had disappeared long ago. She had changed. And so had I. She could not tolerate that I had achieved many of my goals. She had become a toxic friend. We all feel envious occasionally, but that doesn't mean we have to express it maliciously or inflict pain.

Sometimes toxic friendships can fade gracefully rather than end abruptly. Somebody moves away and there isn't enough in common to keep it going when so much effort is required. Simply letting it peter out may be best.

In my case, it was a fast fade. I stopped calling. When she finally called me six weeks later, I was cool. When she proposed getting together, I mentioned pressing assignments that would keep me very busy. Months later she sent me a birthday card on which she'd drawn a "smiley face" and wrote: "Thinking about our friendship."

"What friendship?" I thought. It was over.

Part of me is sorry I wasn't more forthright. I could have used another approach. When a friend's manipulations and dishonesty got to her, one woman said, "I can't be friends with you right now. It's too hurtful and infuriating."

I've let go of other friends in recent years less dramatically. Some casual ones have become immersed in golf, when I have no interest in the sport. Since golf takes up a lot of their leisure time, we don't see each other anymore. Some friends have moved elsewhere. Our relationships have faded not because the people are toxic but because it takes too much effort to keep in contact.

Most of us can also remember a time when we've dropped a relationship with a casual or new friend without explanation, perhaps because the truth was too embarrassing. Who wants to tell someone, "You're nice, but very boring"?

One woman I know doesn't hesitate to sever ties. "If someone over time proves to be less interesting because of life changes or whatever, I'll minimize my contact in as nice a way as I can. Time is precious and I don't want to spend it with people who don't enhance my life. I'm demanding of my friends in that way. A turn-off is people who can't figure out their lives and can't make anything happen for them. It's very wearing. I'm a loyal friend. But if someone after six times can't get over 'Why me?' it's enough."

## MOURNING THE LOSS OF A FRIEND

Over and over again, women have spoken to me of feeling devastated about a broken friendship. One party says, "I don't want to be friends anymore," or stops returning calls, or becomes cold—and the result is trauma, sometimes on both sides. When I wrote off my friend, Helene, *I* felt anguish and pain. If you share friends in common, it can be like a divorce. What is the best way to deal with it?

1. *Accept that it's a loss like any other loss.*
   One woman told me, "It's hard to really mourn the end of a friendship because you haven't lost a family member or spouse." It may be true that you haven't lost a mother or a husband, but you have lost something—a relationship has died. A mourning process is necessary to lay it to rest—and move on. No matter how angry and upset you are, you've still lost something, and loss hurts.

2. *Recognize the role of anger.*
   If you're furious, it's difficult to go through the mourning process. The rage keeps you connected and doesn't allow for the kind of separation you need. I was obsessed with the end of my friendship for several months, replaying it over and over in my mind. I felt betrayed and assaulted. I felt, "I've been such a good friend to you. I don't deserve this."

3. *Recognize your contribution.*
   If anger is an issue, both friends were usually involved in the breakup. You need to get to the stage where you recognize your part—so that you can feel sadness instead of just anger. Perhaps

you did something that precipitated the other person's toxic behavior. I did. I gave advice that Helene didn't ask for or want to hear. I also ignored the signals that she didn't want to talk to me. I was too busy trying to "make it up to her" that my life was happier than hers. Or your contribution might be something as simple as not talking about a problem early enough, so that it mushroomed out of control.

But don't get stuck in blaming yourself (or the other person). People think there are only two options—it's your fault or hers. This stops you from feeling sad that it didn't work out and moving through the loss.

When there's no closure and/or you have been flat-out rejected, it's more difficult to take. You can question what is it about you that created the problem (which could be something positive or negative). Still, you may never stop feeling hurt as to how the friendship ended. You have to get to the point of being able to say, "It's just as well."

## LOOKING AHEAD

In his book *Friendship Matters*, Dr. Rawlins notes that problems can arise in friendships throughout our lives and can hurt and get us into jams. But we *can* take steps to improve our relationships. I'm much better at getting my needs met—and a far better friend than I used to be. Just recently, my friend Martha observed, "You've finally accepted I am who I am. I'm different from you. You've accepted that I'm not going to change." It's called maturity. I've grown up. How about you?

# Notes

### What You Must Know Before You Read This Book

p. xv   Along with family: Roper Starch Worldwide survey for Condé Nast Publications, *American Demographics* (February 1996).

### Chapter 1: The Realities of Friendship

p. 3   Most people with normal friendship patterns: Jeffrey E. Young, "A Cognitive-Behavioral Approach to Friendship Disorders" in *Friendship and Social Interaction,* eds. Valerian J. Derlega and Barbara A. Winstead (New York: Springer-Verlag, 1986).

p. 6   Both external and internal tensions can stir trouble between friends: William K. Rawlins, *Friendship Matters* (New York: Aldine de Gruyter, Inc., 1992).

p. 11   In her book: Clarissa Pinkola Estés, *Women Who Run with the Wolves* (New York: Ballantine Books, 1992).

p. 13   Humorist Fran Lebowitz has written: Fran Lebowitz, "Fran Lebowitz on Money," *Vanity Fair,* July 1997.

p. 13   Because women find it so hard: Lillian B. Rubin, *Just*

*Friends: The Role of Friendship in Our Lives* (New York: Harper & Row, 1985).

p. 14   In her study of the friendships of professional men and women: Linda A. Sapadin, "Friendship and Gender: Perspectives of Professional Men and Women," *Journal of Social and Personal Relationships* 5 (1988).

p. 14   In their book: Luise Eichenbaum and Susie Ohrbach, *Between Women: Love, Envy, and Competition in Women's Friendships* (New York: Viking, 1988).

p. 15   In an article: Karin Schultz, "Women's Adult Development: The Importance of Friendship," *Journal of Independent Social Work* 5 (2) (1991):19–30.

## Chapter 2: Friends on the Job

p. 23   They make your work life infinitely more pleasurable: Louis J. Kruger, Garrett Bernstein, and Harvey Botman, "The Relationship Between Team Friendships and Burnout Among Residential Counselors," *Journal of Social Psychology* 135 (2) (April 1995): 191–201.

p. 24   American employees now spend: Families and Work Institute of New York, "1997 National Study of the Changing Workplace."

p. 25   Treating someone as a confidant: Barbara A. Winstead et al., "The Quality of Friendships at Work and Job Satisfaction," *Journal of Social and Personal Relationships* 12 (2) (1995): 199–215.

p. 25   The more formal the work setting: Kennan Bridge and Leslie A. Baxter, "Blended Relationships: Friends as Work Associates," *Western Journal of Communication* 56 (Summer 1992): 200–255.

p. 32   Research suggests that the support of others: Vivian K. G. Lim, "Job Insecurity and Its Outcomes: Moderating Effects of Work-Based and Nonwork-Based Social Support," *Human-Relations* 49 (2) (February 1996): 171–194.

p. 38   Psychologist Linda Sapadin found: Linda A. Sapadin, "Friendship and Gender: Perspectives of Professional

Men and Women," *Journal of Social and Personal Relationships* 5 (1988): 387–403.

## Chapter 3: Friends Who Boost Your Marriage

p. 48    Early in marriage, strong mutual friendships: Alan Booth, John N. Edwards, and David R. Johnson, "Social Integration and Divorce," *Social Forces* 70 (1) (September 1991): 207–224.

p. 49    For retired couples: Scott M. Myers and Alan Booth, "Men's Retirement and Marital Quality," *Journal of Family Issues* 17 (3) (May 1996): 336–357.

p. 49    Long-term mutual and individual friendships: Finnegan Alford-Cooper, "Commitment for a Lifetime: The Long Island Long-Term Marriage Survey," *Long Island Historical Journal* 7 (2) (Spring 1995): 220–234.

p. 52    Close women friends fill wives' needs: Stacey J. Oliker, *Best Friends and Marriage* (Berkeley and Los Angeles: University of California Press, 1989).

p. 52    Research suggests that only 30 percent: William K. Rawlins, *Friendship Matters* (New York: Aldine de Gruyter, Inc., 1992).

p. 53    Friends and family help army wives: Suzanne Wood, Jacquelyn Scarville, and Katherine S. Gravino, "Waiting Wives: Separation and Reunion Among Army Wives," *Armed Forces and Society* 21 (2) (Winter 1995): 217–236.

p. 63    There's nothing wrong with single friends: Scott J. South and Kim M. Lloyd, "Spousal Alternatives and Marital Dissolution," *American Sociological Review* 60 (February 1995): 21–35.

p. 64    Research shows that husbands report: Edith Burger and Robert M. Milardo, "Marital Interdependence and Social Networks," *Journal of Social and Personal Relationships* 12 (3) (August 1995): 403–415.

## Chapter 4: Separation/Divorce

p. 69    It is friends who are turned to: David A. Chiriboga et al.,

"Divorce, Stress and Social Supports: A Study in Help-seeking Behavior," *Journal of Divorce* 3 (2) (Winter 1979): 121–135.

p. 69 The most difficult emotional time: Constance Ahrons, *The Good Divorce: Keeping Your Family Together When Your Marriage Comes Apart* (New York: HarperPerennial, 1994).

p. 71 Health problems frequently show up: R. M. Countsa and A. Sacks, "The Need for Crisis Intervention During Marital Separation," *Social Work* 30 (2) (1985): 146–150.

p. 71 Friends are the most important source: M. Henderson and M. Argyle, "Source and Nature of Social Support Given to Women at Divorce/Separation," *British Journal of Social Work* 15 (1) (February 1985): 57–65.

p. 84 In her book: Rubin, Lillian B., *Just Friends: The Role of Friendship in Our Lives* (New York: Harper & Row, 1985).

p. 85 In his book: Graham Allan, *Friendship—Developing a Sociological Perspective* (London: Harvester Wheatsheaf, 1989).

## Chapter 5: Friends Can Make You a Better Mom

p. 93 Approximately 72 percent of mothers with children under eighteen: U.S. Bureau of Labor Statistics, "Employment Characteristics of Families in 1997" (May 21, 1998).

## Chapter 6: Friends and the Single Life

p. 116 They're number one (along with family): Karen Gail Lewis and Sidney Moon, "Always Single and Single Again Women: A Qualitative Study," *Journal of Marital and Family Therapy* 23 (2) (April 1997): 115–134.

p. 118 In their book: Natalie Schwartzberg, Kathy Berliner, and Demaris Jacob, *Single in a Married World* (New York: W. W. Norton & Company, 1995).

p. 125 Carol Anderson, Ph.D., coauthor of: Carol M. Anderson and Susan Stewart with Sona Dimidjian, *Flying Solo: Sin-

*gle Women in Midlife* (New York: W. W. Norton & Company, 1994).

p. 130 Research shows that life satisfaction: Sophie F. Loewenstein, "A Study of Satisfactions and Stresses of Single Women in Midlife," *Sex Roles* 7 (11) (November 1981): 1127–1141.

## Chapter 7: Making Family Your Friends, If You Can

p. 145 At times, conflicts with in-laws persist: Israela Meyerstein, "A Systemic Approach to In-Law Dilemmas," *Journal of Marital and Family Therapy* 22 (4) (October 1996): 469–480.

## Chapter 8: Friends On-line

p. 157 In 1993: Janet Morahan-Martin, "Gender Differences in Internet Use," paper presented at the annual convention of the American Psychological Association, Chicago, August 15, 1997.

p. 167 An estimated 2 to 3 percent of users: Kendall Hamilton and Claudia Kalb, "They Log On, But They Can't Log Off," *Newsweek*, December 18, 1995, p. 60–61.

p. 169 In *On-line Friendship*: Michael Adamse and Sheree Motta, *On-line Friendship, Chat-room Romance and Cybersex* (Deerfield Beach, Fla.: Health Communications, Inc., 1996).

p. 169 Says anthropologist Cleo Odzer: Cleo Odzer, *Virtual Spaces: Sex and the Cyber Citizen* (New York: Berkley Books, 1997).

## Chapter 9: Live Longer, Thanks to Friends

p. 176 Having a wide variety of social relationships: Sheldon Cohen et al., "Social Ties and Susceptibility to the Common Cold," *Journal of the American Medical Association* 277 (June 26, 1997): 1940–1945.

p. 177 Evidence strongly suggests that social ties: Center for the Advancement of Health, "Health: That's What Friends

& Family Are For," *Facts of Life* 2 (6) (November–December 1997).

p. 177 The research repeatedly cited: L. F. Berkman and S. L. Syme, "Social Networks, Host Resistance and Mortality: A Nine-Year Follow-Up Study of Alameda County Residents," *American Journal of Epidemiology* 109 (2) (February 1979): 186–204.

p. 177 In a much discussed study: R. B. Williams et al., "Prognostic Importance of Social and Economic Resources Among Medically Treated Patients with Angiographically Documented Coronary Artery Disease," *Journal of the American Medical Association* 267 (4) (January 22–29, 1992): 520–524.

p. 178 The more of it you experience: Kenneth R. Pelletier, "Between Mind and Body: Stress, Emotions and Health," in *Mind Body Medicine,* eds. Daniel Goleman and Joel Gurin (New York: Consumer Reports Books, 1993).

p. 178 Research suggests that stress: Janice K. Kiecolt-Glaser et al., "Slowing of Wound Healing by Psychological Stress," *Lancet* 346 (November 4, 1995): 1194–1196.

p. 178 A study by Thomas W. Kamarck, Ph.D.: Thomas W. Kamarck et al., "Social Support Reduces Cardiovascular Reactivity to Psychological Challenge: A Laboratory Model," *Psychosomatic Medicine* 52 (1990): 42–58.

p. 180 In a study by David Spiegel, M.D.: "Psychological Treatment Effects on Cancer Survivors," paper presented at the annual meeting of the American Psychiatric Association, San Francisco, May 10, 1989.

p. 180 Social support groups also had major advantages: "Support Eases Cancer's Mental Pain," *Science News* 148 (5) (July 29, 1995): 79.

p. 181 Research in England found: Dorothy Jerrome, "Frailty and Friendship," *Journal of Cross-Cultural Gerontology* 5 (1) (January 1990): 51–64.

p. 181 In research by Clifford L. Broman: Clifford L. Broman, "Social Relationships and Health-Related Behavior," *Journal of Behavioral Medicine* 16 (4) (August 1993): 335–350.

p. 183 Friends who give unwanted advice: Karen S. Rook, "Strains in Older Adults' Friendships," in *Older Adult Friendship,* eds. Rebecca G. Adams and Rosemary Blieszner (Newbury Park, Calif.: Sage Publications, 1989).

p. 183 In a study of heart attack survivors: Steven Woloshin et al., "Perceived Adequacy of Tangible Social Support and Health Outcomes in Patients with Coronary Artery Disease," *Journal of General Internal Medicine* 12 (October 1997): 613–618.

p. 184 The supply of friends shrinks: Wendy Lustbader, *Counting on Kindness* (New York: Free Press, 1991).

p. 186 In a Yale University School of Medicine study: Harlan Krumholz, "Circulation," *Journal of the American Heart Association* 97 (10) (March 17, 1998): 958–964.

p. 187 He has spoken of: Geoffrey Cowley, "Healer of Hearts," *Newsweek*, March 16, 1998, p. 54.

### Chapter 10: How Friends Can Make or Break Retirement

p. 194 People with more friends and acquaintances: Scott M. Myers and Alan Booth, "Men's Retirement and Marital Quality," *Journal of Family Issues* 17 (3) (May 1996): 336–357.

p. 196 A pattern of lifelong friends: Finnegan Alford-Cooper, "Commitment for a Lifetime: The Long Island Long-Term Marriage Survey," *Long Island Historical Journal* 7 (2) (Spring 1995): 220–234.

p. 198 A Purdue University study: Peg Krach et al., "Opening the Doors to Home Care Nursing," paper presented at an international nursing research conference, Padua, Italy, 1995.

p. 200 In a study of fifty-five male and female members: Celia B. Fisher, James D. Reid, and Marjorie Melendez, "Conflict in Families and Friendships of Later Life," *Family Relations* 38 (January 1989): 83–89.

p. 202  In a study of adults fifty-five through eighty-four: Rosemary Blieszner and Rebecca G. Adams, "Problems with Friends in Old Age," *Journal of Aging Studies* 12 (3) (1998): 223–238.

p. 202  As Karen Rook, Ph.D., has observed: Karen S. Rook, "Strains in Older Adults' Friendships," in *Older Adult Friendship,* eds. Rebecca G. Adams and Rosemary Blieszner (Newbury Park, Calif.: Sage Publications, 1989).

### Chapter 11: Friendship Lessons

p. 212  Fortunately, conflict does not have to erode: Celia B. Fisher, James D. Reid, and Marjorie Melendez, "Conflict in Families and Friendships of Later Life," *Family Relations* 38 (January 1989): 83–89.

p. 215  A key question: Virginia Williams and Redford Williams, *Lifeskills* (New York: Times Books, 1997).

p. 219  Genuine apology specifically states: M. D. Lazare, "Go Ahead Say You're Sorry," *Psychology Today*, January/February 1995, pp. 40–43, 76–78.

p. 225  Jeffrey E. Young, Ph.D., who has studied: Jeffrey E. Young, "A Cognitive-Behavioral Approach to Friendship Disorders," in *Friendship and Social Interaction*, eds. Valerian J. Derlega and Barbara A. Winstead (New York: Springer-Verlag, 1986).

p. 225  In his book: Jeffrey E. Young and Janet S. Klosko, *Reinventing Your Life: How to Break Free from Negative Life Patterns and Feel Good Again* (New York: Plume/Penguin, 1994).

# Resources

Adams, Rebecca G., and Rosemary Blieszner, eds. *Older Adult Friendship*. Newbury Park, Calif.: Sage Publications, 1987.

Allan, Graham. *Friendship—Developing a Sociological Perspective*. London: Harvester Wheatsheaf, 1989.

Blieszner, Rosemary, and Rebecca G. Adams. *Adult Friendship*. Newbury Park, Calif.: Sage Publications, 1992.

Derlega, Valerian J., and Barbara A. Winstead. *Friendship and Social Interaction*. New York: Springer-Verlag, 1986.

Eichenbaum, Luise, and Susie Ohrbach. *Between Women: Love, Envy, and Competition in Women's Friendships*. New York: Viking, 1988.

O'Connor, Pat. *Friendships Between Women*. New York: The Guilford Press, 1992.

Oliker, Stacey J. *Best Friends and Marriage*. Berkeley and Los Angeles: University of California Press, 1989.

Pogrebin, Letty Cottin. *Among Friends: Who We Like, Why We Like Them, and What We Do with Them*. New York: McGraw-Hill, 1987.

Rawlins, William K. *Friendship Matters*. New York: Aldine de Gruyter, Inc., 1992.

Rubin, Lillian B. *Just Friends: The Role of Friendship in Our Lives.* New York: Harper & Row, 1985.

Yager, Jan, Ph.D. *Friendshifts: The Power of Friendship and How it Can Shape Our Lives.* Stamford, Conn.: Hannacroix Creek Books, Inc., 1997.

# Index

245